Student Workbook

Student Workbook
for Ronald J. Comer's

Abnormal
Psychology

EIGHTH EDITION

Ronald J. Comer
Princeton University

Gregory P. Comer
Princeton Academic Resources

WORTH PUBLISHERS

Student Workbook
by Ronald J. Comer and Gregory P. Comer
to accompany
Ronald J. Comer: *Abnormal Psychology*, Eighth Edition

Copyright © 2013, 2010, 2007, 2004 by Worth Publishers

Printed in the United States of America

ISBN 10: 1-4641-1066-2
ISBN 13: 978-1-4641-1066-5

First Printing 2012

Worth Publishers

41 Madison Avenue

New York, NY 10010

www.worthpublishers.com

Contents

Preface

To the Student

This *Workbook* has been designed to help you excel in the study of abnormal psychology. While abnormal psychology is a fascinating course that should become one of the most memorable classes of your college experience, it is also one that is filled with detailed topics and numerous terms and concepts—so much so that you may find it a little intimidating at times. A key purpose of this workbook is to help you organize your study in this course so that you will have the time and the knowledge to delve more deeply into the disorders and the ideas presented.

The utility of the *Workbook* goes beyond simply being a concise way to organize the raw topic coverage of the textbook. A great deal of effort was put into designing review exercises that call upon you to apply rote information in a way that gets you thinking about the underlying meaning of the ideas. In addition to fill-in-the-blank and short-answer questions, many exercises present a hypothetical set of facts relating to a patient or a psychological disorder. Applying your knowledge to hypothetical situations helps to bring the information to life. We have tried to "mix up" exercise types wherever possible, in order to keep things more engaging for you.

Ways to Use the Workbook

There are at least a couple of ways that you can use this *Workbook*. We recommend that students first read the textbook a section at a time, and then attempt the corresponding section of review exercises in the *Workbook*. Exercises explicitly follow the textbook's order of coverage, and each section and subsection is clearly delineated in the *Workbook*. The topic headings within the chapter review exercises provide the page numbers of the coverage in the textbook. Many of the exercises call for a detailed knowledge of the material in the textbook—perhaps in far more detail than may be required on your exams. This is intentional, as one of our goals is to prepare you for anything you might see on an exam. If you take a week, or even a day, between reading the textbook and attempting the review exercises, you may be surprised at how difficult it can be to recall all the details.

There is an additional benefit to completing the exercises in the manner we have suggested. It provides you with an excellent set of study notes that can be used in conjunction with your lecture notes.

An alternative way to use the *Workbook* is to try to complete the review exercises after you have read the book and attended your instructor's lectures. This is a way to identify areas where you need to concentrate your remaining study time before a test. The risk is that you may discover that you don't understand the material as well as you believed, and that you haven't left yourself enough time to learn it.

We hope that your studies with the *Workbook* will be a rewarding experience that truly helps you to understand, appreciate, and profit from the study of abnormal psychology.

To the Instructor

During a class term, time is a valuable commodity—especially with a topic-filled course like abnormal psychology. As an instructor, you already know that there never seems to be sufficient time to cover everything you would like in a term. Just imparting the strictly factual information can take so much time that you are left with little time to go into greater depth. If your students are using this *Workbook,* it can mean that you will have more time to devote to the conceptual and applied aspects of the factual material of abnormal psychology.

The *Workbook* is structured to enable you to assign it to your students in sections that correspond to the topic headings in the textbook. Each *Workbook* chapter begins with an outline of the chapter presentation, which facilitates assigning parts to students, and also helps your students keep their studies better organized.

Our experience has been that the students who apply themselves to the kinds of review exercises you will find in this *Workbook* are usually the ones who are the most prepared and the most engaged. They are also the ones who tend to perform better on exams.

We have recommended ideas, but please use the *Workbook* in the manner that will serve you best. It could easily be used for homework to check that your students have completed and understood their reading assignments, especially in smaller classes. Also, if you have the opportunity for class involvement in your lectures, the *Workbook* can help your students come to class better prepared to discuss specific issues.

Acknowledgments

We are deeply indebted to Carmen R. Wilson VanVoorhis and Katherine M. Nicolai, who authored previous editions of this *Workbook*. We would also like to thank Peter Twickler, Nadina Persaud, and Julio Espin of Worth Publishers for their editorial input, as well as Stacey Alexander for her production expertise.

Ronald J. Comer
Gregory P. Comer

Student Workbook

1 ABNORMAL PSYCHOLOGY: PAST AND PRESENT

REVIEW EXERCISES

I. and II.   What Is Psychological Abnormality? What Is Treatment?, 2–7

Although no single definition of abnormal mental functioning is universally accepted, most definitions share four common features: the notions of deviance, distress, dysfunction, and danger. You can think of these as the "four D's" of defining abnormal functioning. All four are covered in this part of the workbook.

1.   Complete this table by first identifying the feature (or the "D") associated with each definition listed, then giving a hypothetical example of a behavior that illustrates the defining feature.

Feature	Definition	Example
a. danger	Patterns of behavior, thoughts, and emotions that pose a risk to one's well-being and safety are considered abnormal.	A young woman abuses cocaine and alcohol on a daily basis, drives recklessly when high, endangering herself and others.
b.	For patterns of behaviors, thoughts, and emotions to be labeled abnormal, the individual must experience them as unpleasant and adverse.	
c.	Behaviors, thoughts, and emotions that violate cultural norms are considered abnormal.	
d.	Patterns of behavior, thoughts, and emotions that interfere with an individual's ability to maintain important aspects of life are considered abnormal.	

2.   The major difficulty in defining abnormality is that the concept of "abnormality" is relative. Write a paragraph explaining what this means.

_____

_____

_____

_____

3.   **Treatment** or therapy is defined as a procedure to help change _____ behavior into more _____ behavior.

4.   Jerome Frank, a clinical theorist, has written that all forms of therapy have three essential features or ingredients. Complete the following list of these key features.

   a. A _____ seeks help or relief from

   b. a trained, socially sanctioned _____ , in

   c. a structured series of contacts between the two that is designed to produce changes in the help-seeker's _____ state, attitudes, and _____ .

5. Clinicians differ on whether to use the term "patient" or "client" to describe those who seek help through counseling or psychotherapy. Identify which term *you* would prefer if you were to seek therapy services, and briefly describe why.

_____

_____

_____

PsychWatch: Marching to a Different Drummer: Eccentrics, 6

1. Researcher David Weeks suggested that eccentrics do not typically suffer from mental disorders, because their unusual behavior patterns are chosen _____ and provide _____.

2. David Weeks found that eccentrics that he studied had _____ emotional problems than individuals in the general population.

III. How Was Abnormality Viewed and Treated in the Past?, 7–13

1. Given that as many as 30 percent of adults in the United States display psychological dysfunction serious enough to warrant treatment, some speculate that certain aspects of our modern world foster emotional maladjustment. List two recent societal developments that may contribute to psychological dysfunctioning.

   a. _____

   b. _____

PsychWatch: Modern Pressures: Modern Problems, 8

1. In the wake of the September 11, 2001 terrorist attacks, some individuals have been afflicted with _____ , or the obsessive concern that they will soon be the victim of a terrorist attack.

2. Despite the fact that actual crime rates are falling, the number of people suffering from _____ _____ continues to rise, a fact many theorists blame on disproportionate media coverage of violent crimes.

3. The general term _____ _____ refers to a number of fears people suffer, including the fear of computer crashes, viruses, server overloads, computer hoaxes, and computer scams.

A. Ancient Views and Treatments, 9

1. It is believed that people in prehistoric societies viewed the human body and mind as sites of battle by _____ forces, and they viewed both normal and abnormal behavior as the outcome of battles between good and evil spirits.

2. List and briefly describe two treatments for abnormality that may have occurred in prehistoric societies.

   a. trephination; _____

   _____

   b. _____ ; _____

   _____

B. **Greek and Roman Views and Treatments, 9**

1. Define each of the following mental disorders that were identified by early Greek and Roman physicians.

   a. Melancholia: _____

   b. Mania: _____

2. Complete the following statements regarding **Hippocrates,** called the father of modern medicine.

   a. He saw abnormal behavior as a disease caused by internal medical problems; specifically, he thought that _____ pathology was the culprit.

   b. Hippocrates believed that like all forms of disease, abnormal behavior resulted from an imbalance of the four fluids, or _____ , that flowed through the body.

C. **Europe in the Middle Ages: Demonology Returns, 10**

1. What was the primary reason for the return of demonological views of psychological abnormality in the Middle Ages?

   _____

   _____

2. Large outbreaks of _____ _____ , in which large numbers of people shared similar delusions or hallucinations, are an example of abnormal behavior present during the Middle Ages, a time of great societal stress and unrest.

3. List and briefly describe two prevalent forms of these shared delusions.

   a. _____ ; _____

   _____

   b. _____ ; people thought they were possessed by wolves or other wild animals, and acted as though they were these animals.

4. If you could go back in time to the Middle Ages and witness clergymen performing exorcisms on people who behaved abnormally, what do you think you might see?

   _____

   _____

   _____

D. **The Renaissance and the Rise of Asylums, 11**

1. The German physician Johann _____ , thought to be the first medical practitioner to specialize in mental illness, rejected the demonological explanation of abnormality.

2. What was the purpose of the Gheel Shrine?

   _____

   _____

3. In the sixteenth century, the idea of asylums grew. Though usually founded with excellent intentions, such institutions as London's Bethlehem Hospital degenerated into sites of degrading conditions where treatments of unspeakable cruelty flourished.

List some of these horrible conditions.

_____

_____

E. The Nineteenth Century: Reform and Moral Treatment, 12

1. What was the initial site of asylum reform (around 1793), and who was the man most responsible for the reform?

_____ ; _____

2. Describe an overall theme of the reforms in the treatment of patients during this period.

_____

_____

3. In England, William _____ founded a "retreat" where rest, talk, prayer, and manual work replaced mechanical restraints and unfounded medical interventions as treatments for mental patients.

4. The methods of Pinel and Tuke were called _____ treatment.

5. Benjamin Rush was the person who is credited with bringing moral treatment to the United States. List two of his major innovations.

_____

_____

6. In 1841, a Boston schoolteacher named Dorothea Dix was shocked by the conditions she witnessed at asylums throughout the United States. Dix began a 40-year campaign of reform that addressed the plight of the mentally ill. Write a paragraph describing her remarkable effort.

_____

_____

_____

7. Complete these statements describing how each of the following three factors contributed to the decline of moral treatment.

   a. Moral treatment had advanced so quickly that many hospitals were built in a short period of time, leading to shortages of funding and _____ .

   b. The basic assumptions of moral treatment—that patients would begin to function normally if they were treated with _____—proved too optimistic.

   c. Many people reacted to the trend of patients being removed to large, distant mental hospitals with a new wave of _____ against the mentally ill.

F. The Early Twentieth Century: The Somatogenic and Psychogenic Perspectives, 13–15

1. In the late nineteenth century, the **somatogenic perspective**—the idea that abnormal psychological functioning has physical causes—once again gained acceptance and support. Explain how (a) the work of Emil Kraepelin and (b) the discovery that general paresis is caused by syphilis were important to the resurgence of the somatogenic perspective.

   a. _____

   4 _____

b. _____

_____

2. The **psychogenic perspective** has the view that the primary causes of abnormal behavior are
    _____ in nature.

3. Some scientists believed that the successes of the treatment called *mesmerism* (later called *hypnotism*)
    in treating patients with _____ disorders resulted from patients being induced into a
    trancelike state.

4. Briefly describe the disorders you identified above.

    _____

5. Two French physicians, Bernheim and Liébault, settled the debate over the cause of hysterical disor-
    ders by showing that they could be induced and then removed in otherwise normal subjects by
    means of _____ ; thus, these disorders were largely _____ in origin.

6. _____ , a Viennese doctor who later worked with Freud, discovered that his hypnotized
    patients sometimes awoke free of hysterical symptoms after speaking freely about past traumas un-
    der hypnosis.

7. Freud's theory of _____ posits that _____ psychological processes are at the
    root of both normal and abnormal functioning.

8. Freud's form of therapy was designed to help people gain _____ into their problems
    and was conducted usually in the therapist's office—a format now known as _____
    therapy.

IV. Current Trends, 15–21

A. How Are People with Severe Disturbances Cared For?, 16

1. The discovery and use of **psychotropic drugs** resulted in the nearly immediate discharge of many
    severely disturbed patients from public mental hospitals. This policy is now known as_____

    _____ .

2. _____ care has become the primary mode of treatment for people with severe psycho-
    logical disturbances as well as for those with more moderate problems.

3. Although the community mental health approach has admirable goals and has been effective in
    helping many people with mental disorders, it has not been entirely successful. Briefly, describe how
    the community mental health approach has failed in some respects.

    _____

    _____

B. How Are People with Less Severe Disturbances Treated?, 17

1. Over the last several decades, more people than ever have had access to treatment for psychological
    problems. Briefly describe the reasons for this trend that are associated with the key words provided.

    a. Cost: _____

    _____

    b. Settings: _____

    _____

2. Recent studies have suggested that one out of every _____ Americans receives treatment for psychological problems each year.

3. Almost 50 percent of people in therapy suffer from _____ or depression, and at least 20 percent seek help for problems with _____ , family, job, _____ , or community relationships.

C. A Growing Emphasis on Preventing Disorders and Promoting Mental Health, 17

1. Ms. Jenkins, a school social worker, has developed an educational group on proper nutrition and exercise for sixth-grade girls. She hopes to teach the girls skills to use to avoid problematic eating and exercising behaviors and ultimately eating disorders. Ms. Jenkins's approach is a form of _____ .

2. Write a short paragraph explaining how Ms. Jenkins might use **positive psychology** in her work with the sixth-grade girls.

    _____
    _____
    _____
    _____

D. Multicultural Psychology, 19

1. What do multicultural psychologists study?

E. The Growing Influence of Insurance Coverage, 19

1. Most insurance programs today require clients to choose from a list of approved therapists and dictate the cost and number of sessions for which the client will be reimbursed. These types of programs are known as _____ _____ programs.

2. List three reasons clients and therapists dislike managed care programs.

    a. _____
    b. _____
    c. _____

F. What Are Today's Leading Theories and Professions?, 20

1. At present no single theoretical perspective dominates the clinical field. Many theories have influenced the current understanding and treatment of abnormal functioning. Complete the following statements about some of the perspectives.

    a. Before the 1950s, the _____ perspective, with its emphasis on _____ conflicts as the cause of psychopathology, was dominant.

    b. The somatogenic or _____ view of abnormality grew in stature in the 1950s with the discovery of effective _____ drugs.

    c. Some of the influential perspectives that have emerged since the 1950s include the behavioral, cognitive, humanistic-existential, and sociocultural schools. They explain and treat abnormality in very different ways.

2. Complete the following statements regarding professional careers in psychology.

    a. Psychotherapy was the exclusive province of _____ before the 1950s. These people are physicians who have completed _____ to _____ years of training after medical school in the treatment of abnormal mental functioning.

    b. Clinical psychologists are professionals who earn a doctorate by completing four years of graduate training in abnormal functioning and its treatment and also complete a one-year _____ at a mental hospital or mental health agency.

    c. Counseling psychologists, educational psychologists, psychiatric nurses, marriage therapists, family therapists, and—the largest group—_____ _____ _____ fall into a category of professionals who have completed a graduate training program in their specialty area.

V. Putting It Together: A Work in Progress, 21–22

1. In your own words, describe some reasons why students of abnormal psychology can benefit from learning about historical perspectives on abnormal behavior and its treatment.

    _____

    _____

    _____

    _____

    _____

MULTIPLE CHOICE

1. Mary dresses exclusively in men's clothes (including the underwear). This is an example of the feature of the definition of abnormality called
   a. distress.
   b. deviance.
   c. dysfunction.
   d. danger to self or others.

2. Rae, who is running for public office, seems to be developing a fear of crowds. To which aspect of the definition of abnormality is this example most relevant?
   a. distress
   b. deviance
   c. dysfunction
   d. danger to self or others

3. An eccentric person is likely to display all of the following except
   a. intelligence.
   b. nonconformity.
   c. noncompetitiveness.
   d. disordered thinking.

4. Some ancient societies practiced trephination, which consisted of
   a. bloodletting.
   b. removing part of a patient's skull.
   c. imposing social isolation on a sufferer.
   d. a kind of exorcism practiced by a shaman.

5. During the Middle Ages, the dominant model of explanation for abnormal behavior was
   a. scientific.
   b. humanistic.
   c. philosophical.
   d. demonological.

6. The person now believed to be the founder of the modern study of psychopathology was
   a. Hippocrates.
   b. Johann Weyer.
   c. Philippe Pinel.
   d. Sigmund Freud.

7. The real beginning of the humane treatment of people with mental disorders began in
   a. Spain.
   b. France.
   c. England.
   d. the United States.

8. Which of the following is most consistent with the somatogenic view of mental illness?
   a. hypnosis
   b. physical ailments can cause psychological disturbances
   c. the symptoms of mental illness can be described and classified
   d. hysterical symptoms such as partial paralysis can be induced with hypnosis

9. The original developer of psychoanalysis was
   a. Josef Breuer.
   b. Emil Kraepelin.
   c. Sigmund Freud.
   d. Ambroise-Auguste Liébault.

10. Since the beginning of the deinstitutionalization movement in the 1950s
    a. the prescription of psychotropic drugs has significantly decreased.
    b. the daily patient population in American mental hospitals has increased.
    c. the number of violent crimes committed by mentally ill persons has doubled.
    d. outpatient care has become the primary treatment for persons with psychological problems.

2 RESEARCH IN ABNORMAL PSYCHOLOGY

REVIEW EXERCISES

I. What Do Clinical Researchers Do?, 26–27

The scientific method is the process of systematically acquiring and evaluating information by observation to gain an understanding of the phenomena being studied. It is a key concept of modern science. This section's exercises relate to this important basis for research.

1. Clinical research looks for a general, or a _____ _____ of abnormal behavior, such as truths about the nature, causes, and treatments of abnormalities, whereas clinical practitioners search for truths regarding the abnormalities in individuals, which are called idiographic truths.

2. To formulate a nomothetic explanation of abnormal psychology, scientists try to identify and explain relationships between **variables.** Any characteristic or event that can vary, whether from time to time, place to place, or person to person, is a variable. List some of the variables that are of particular interest to clinical researchers.

   _____

3. Clinical researchers seek to determine whether two or more variables change together and whether

   _____ .

4. The three primary methods of investigation—the case study, the correlational method, and the experimental method—enable clinical researchers to formulate and test **hypotheses.** Define the term *hypothesis.*

   _____

   _____

II. The Case Study, 27–30

1. What are the characteristics and goals of the case study method of research?

   _____

   _____

A. How Are Case Studies Helpful?, 29

1. Fill in the missing words in the following list of nomothetic roles case studies serve.

   a. They are a source of ideas about _____ and can provide tentative support for a

      _____ .

   b. They may serve to challenge theoretical _____ .

   c. They serve as a source of ideas for new therapeutic _____ .

   d. They offer opportunities to study unusual problems that _____

      _____ .

B. What Are the Limitations of Case Studies?, 30

1. Case studies are reported by **biased observers.** Why does this limit the usefulness of the research method?

   _____

   _____

2. A study is said to have internal accuracy, or **internal validity,** when an investigator can show that

    _____

    _____

3. Why do case studies have limited internal validity?

    _____

    _____

4. A study is said to have **external validity** when _____

    _____

    _____

5. Why do case studies have limited external validity?

    _____

    _____

6. Although case studies provide rich detail about single individuals, they do not provide nomothetic insights, or information about large groups of people. Only **correlational** and **experimental** methods can accomplish this. Below, summarize the three important characteristics of correlational and experimental research methods that allow investigators to gain nomothetic insights.

    a. _____

        _____

    b. _____

        _____

    c. _____

        _____

III. The Correlational Method, 30–36

1. Define **correlation.**

    _____

2. Formulate a question that might be asked by a researcher using the correlational method that includes the variables "procrastination" and "test anxiety." (*Hint:* Be sure the word "cause" is not used in your question—you'll discover why later.)

    _____

    _____

3. Why must a **sample** be representative of the larger population of interest?

    _____

    _____

A. Describing a Correlation, 31

1. Imagine that you are a researcher interested in studying the relationship between marital satisfaction and number of pre-marriage sexual partners. On the following graphs, draw in the "lines of best fit" that illustrate the labeled relationships between marital satisfaction and the number of pre-marriage sexual partners.

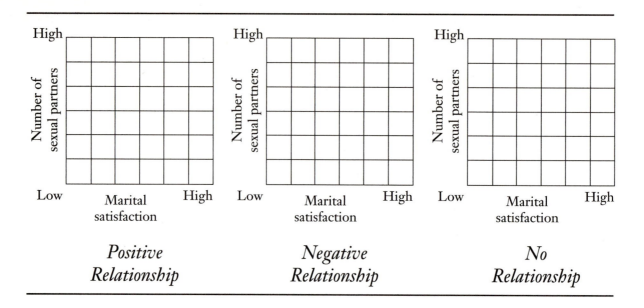

Positive Relationship   *Negative Relationship*   *No Relationship*

2.   Other than knowing whether a correlation is positive or negative, it is important to know the magnitude, or _____ , of the relationship between variables.

3.   The statistical term known as the _____ _____ , symbolized by the letter *r*, expresses the direction and the magnitude of the relationship between two variables.

4.   Put the following list of coefficients in order of their strength of correlation:

.61   −.01   .50   −.58   −.82

Strongest correlation _____ _____ _____ _____ _____ *Weakest correlation*

MediaSpeak: On Facebook, Scholars Link Up with Data, 31

1.   Identify one drawback of the kind of research on Facebook users described in this section.

_____

_____

B.   When Can Correlations Be Trusted?, 33

1.   Statistical analyses of data are performed in order to discover how likely it is that a given correlation has been found by mere _____ .

2.   What does the statistical notation $p < .05$ mean?

_____

_____

C.   What Are the Merits of the Correlational Method?, 34

1.   Correlational studies typically exhibit more _____ validity than case studies because findings can be _____ to people beyond those in the study.

2.   However, correlational studies lack _____ validity because they do not explain the _____ between variables.

3.   Let's say that in your study of marital satisfaction you also discover that couples who are satisfied with their marriages exhibit better communication skills than those who are less satisfied. (You find

a correlation of .65, which is significant at the $p < .05$ level.) What are the three possible reasons for this relationship?

a. _____

b. _____

c. Both marital satisfaction and good communication skills are caused by a third variable, such as a nondefensive personality style.

D. Special Forms of Correlational Research, 35

1. An **epidemiological study** determines the incidence and prevalence of disorders. Define:

    Incidence:

    _____

    Prevalence:

    _____

2. List two findings of the epidemiological studies reported in your text.

    _____

    _____

3. Longitudinal research methods provide information about the _____ of events, so they are more likely than conventional correlation studies to help identify which events may be _____ and which may be consequences. However, they still do not pinpoint _____.

IV. The Experimental Method, 36–39

1. Circle the term that best describes each variable in the experimental method.

    In the experimental method, researchers:

    a. manipulate the (independent / dependent) variable that is thought to cause some effect.

    b. observe the effect of the manipulated variable on the (independent / dependent) variable of interest.

2. Complete the following exercise by identifying the independent and the dependent variables of each fictional "study."

Hypothesis	Independent Variable	Dependent Variable
Drinking warm, as opposed to cold, milk causes people to be sleepy		sleepiness
Using shampoo X causes hair loss		
Group therapy is more effective than individual therapy in the treatment of depression	type of therapy	

3. Give a thorough definition of the term **confound.**

_____

_____

4.   Why does the presence of confounds make it difficult to establish cause-and-effect relationships in experimental studies?

_____

_____

_____

A–C.   The Control Group, Random Assignment, and Blind Design, 37

*The three features that researchers incorporate into their experiments in order to control potential confounds are (1) **control groups**, (2) **random assignment**, and (3) **blind design**. After completing the following set of questions that relate to these procedures, you will be asked to critique and redesign a study that contains numerous confounds.*

1.   Experimental methods require at least two groups of subjects: a control group and an experimental group. Ideally, what is the *only* difference between the control group and the experimental group?

_____

Read this! Students are often confused about how the control group and the experimental group can be exactly "the same" except for the independent variable, when, after all, the two groups consist of *completely different people.* How can researchers say that the independent variable *caused* a change in the dependent variable, when perhaps the difference between the two groups on the dependent variable was simply a result of the fact that one group was different to begin with (more outgoing, happier, more aggressive, etc.)?

When researchers **randomly assign** subjects to either the control or the experimental group, they assume that *preexisting differences between the groups are reduced* (or "evened out") so that the *average* level of outgoingness, happiness, aggression, and so on, is approximately equal for both the control and the experimental group.

2.   How might researchers randomly assign subjects to groups?

_____

3.   Subjects may bias the results of an experiment because they have attempted to please or _____ the experimenter to get the results he or she wants; if this occurs, changes in the dependent variable could be a result of _____ , rather than the independent variable.

4.   How might experimenter bias, also known as the **Rosenthal effect,** occur in an experiment?

_____

_____

5.   Provide a thorough definition for the following terms.

a. blind design: _____

_____

b. double-blind design: _____

_____

c. triple-blind design: _____

Here is your chance to improve a study that is full of confounds. Read through the following description of a study on classical music therapy and respond to the questions that follow it.

Case Study

Study:	Classical Music Therapy
Hypothesis:	People experience mood elevation after listening to classical music (i.e., listening to classical music causes people to feel happier).
Subjects:	Subjects were identified and recruited at a "Mozart by Moonlight" concert. Researchers told potential subjects, "We think listening to classical music will make you feel better. Will you help us?"
Method:	Subjects filled out a questionnaire designed to assess mood prior to engaging in experiment. They were then asked to sit in comfortable recliners in the research lab. Subjects were given headphones and told by an attractive, pleasant research assistant to relax and listen to 30 minutes of classical music. After listening to the music, subjects removed their headphones and filled out the same mood questionnaires in order to assess pre- and postmusic differences. Sandwiches and soft drinks were provided to the subjects as they filled out the postmusic questionnaire.
Results:	Pre- and postmusic scores were significantly different in the hypothesized direction. The experimenter concluded that classical music therapy results in people feeling happier.

6. There are numerous confounds present in the classical music therapy case study that could easily explain the results. List three of them.

   a. _____

   b. _____

   c. _____

7. Now, rewrite the Subjects and Method sections of this study (making sure that you address the confounds you identified in question 6) so that the experimenter's conclusion is justified.

Case Study

Study:	Classical Music Therapy
Hypothesis:	People experience mood elevation after listening to classical music (i.e., listening to classical music causes people to feel happier).
Subjects:	
Method:	
Results:	Pre- and postmusic scores were significantly different in the hypothesized direction. The experimenter concluded that classical music therapy results in people feeling happier.

8.   Explain the distinction between statistical significance and clinical significance in clinical treatment experiments.

_____

_____

V.   Alternative Experimental Designs, 39–43

Workbook coverage of subsection V is divided into four parts—one for each of the variations of experimental design discussed in the textbook. They are: "Quasi-Experimental Design," "Natural Experiment," "Analogue Experiment," and "Single-Subject Experiment."

A.   Quasi-Experimental Design, 39

1.   Quasi-experimental designs make use of groups that already exist in the real world as opposed to "true" experiments in which subjects are _____ assigned to _____ and _____ groups.

2.   Why must researchers who study the psychological effects of rape on women use a quasi-experimental (rather than a "true" experimental) design?

_____

_____

_____

3.   What is the benefit of using the quasi-experimental design of **matched control subjects?**

_____

_____

_____

B.   Natural Experiment, 39

1.   Natural experiments are those in which nature rather than the experimenter manipulates a(n) _____ variable, and the experimenter _____ the effects.

2.   The natural experiment conducted by research teams on the psychological effects of the December 26, 2004, Indian Ocean earthquake and resulting tsunamis showed that survivors were significantly more depressed and anxious than control subjects. List some other results of the experiment.

   a.   _____

   b.   _____

   c.   _____

3.   Limitations of the natural experimental method include the facts that natural experiments cannot be _____ , and broad _____ drawn from a single study could be incorrect.

C. Analogue Experiment, 40

1. A major strength of analogue designs is that researchers can manipulate the _____ vari-ables, while avoiding some of the _____ and practical limitations of other research de-signs.

2. How do analogue studies provide information about real-life abnormal behavior?

_____

_____

_____

3. **Martin Seligman**'s hypothesis about the cause of human depression says that people become de-pressed when they believe that they no longer have any _____ over the good and bad events that occur in their lives—that they are helpless.

4. Describe (a) the method and (b) the findings of Seligman's analogue research with humans.

a. _____

_____

b. _____

_____

5. What is the primary limitation of analogue designs?

_____

_____

D. Single-Subject Experiment, 41

1. Explain how experimentation is possible with only a single subject.

_____

_____

2. In single-subject experiments, **baseline data** are pieces of information gathered during an observa-tion period before any _____ or interventions, which establish a standard with which to compare later change.

3. Why is it so important to collect baseline data in single-subject designs?

_____

_____

4. Subjects serve as their own _____ in ABAB, or reversal, designs.

5. When are researchers most likely to use a single-subject experiment design?

_____

_____

_____

The information in the following case study will be used in exercises covering one of the most commonly used single-subject experimental designs: the ABAB design.

Case Study

Nathan is an 8-year-old boy who is in a classroom for severely disturbed children. He has been diagnosed with autism, a pervasive developmental disorder whose central features are a profound unresponsiveness to others, poor or absent communication, and a range of unusual— even bizarre—responses to the environment. Recently, Nathan's teachers have grown very concerned about his safety in the classroom. He has begun to repeatedly bang his head on his desktop, resulting in bruises and abrasions on his forehead. Autistic children who demonstrate this behavior are frequently equipped with helmets to prevent serious injury. However, Nathan became extremely upset when his teachers attempted to use this form of intervention. In fact, he became almost uncontrollable when the helmet was placed on his head.

Because Nathan has responded favorably to being rewarded with fruit juice for positive behavior in the classroom, his teachers would like to find out if this method of reinforcement would be effective in reducing or eliminating his head-banging behavior. They would like you, a clinical researcher, to design a single-subject experiment to test their hypothesis.

---

6.   Use the preceding information to complete the following chart of an ABAB design for this sample case.

Reinforcement Program (The Independent Variable)
Nathan will be rewarded with fruit juice for every 10-minute period of time that he does not bang his head on the desk.

A   The frequency of Nathan's head-banging is measured before the introduction of the independent variable (in the baseline period).

(Think of each of the following steps as the test of a separate hypothesis.)

B   *Step Taken:* Nathan is given a reward of juice for not banging his head.

Expectation:

A   *Step Taken:*

Expectation: Head-banging behavior will increase.

B   *Step Taken:*

Expectation:

---

7.   If your predictions are supported in this ABAB design, what conclusion can be drawn about the re-introduction of the independent variable?

---

8.   What is the primary difference between single-subject experiments and case studies?

_____

PsychWatch: Humans Have Rights, Too, 42

1.   Name four types of drug studies that have been cited in recent years as having placed sufferers of severe mental disorders at risk during the 1980s and 1990s.

a.   _____

b.   _____

c.   _____

d.   _____

2.   In recent years, the National Institute of Mental Health (NIMH) suspended some of its _____-_____ studies, as the clinical community has grown more aware of the risks associated with these studies.

VI. Putting It Together: The Use of Multiple Research Methods, 43–44

1.   Describe the factors that complicate or limit what we can learn about abnormal behavior and its treatment through clinical research. Try using your own words. That is, see how well you can explain these five scientific ideas without using the textbook's exact wording.

a.   _____

_____

b.   _____

_____

c.   _____

_____

d.   _____

_____

e.   _____

_____

MULTIPLE CHOICE

1. A psychologist doing research on anxiety studies a large and diversified group of anxious individuals in the hopes of understanding the phenomenon and developing a treatment. He is doing research.
   a. case study
   b. nomothetic
   c. idiographic
   d. experimental

2. The data that Freud used to develop psychoanalysis came from the use of
   a. correlational studies.
   b. experimental studies.
   c. the case study method.
   d. the nomothetic approach.

3. Dr. Vue gave a group of general psychology students a survey that measured their level of depression and substance use. Dr. Vue wanted to know if any relationship existed between the two. Which research method is Dr. Vue using?
   a. experiment
   b. quasi-experiment
   c. natural experiment
   d. correlation

4. If a difference is judged statistically significant, that means that the
   a. result has external validity.
   b. probability of a chance result is small.
   c. difference was experimentally determined.
   d. probability of the result being due to change is zero.

5. Which of the following is a characteristic of longitudinal studies in general?
   a. There is repeated measurement of the participants.
   b. There is manipulation of a variable by the researcher.
   c. There is the use of blind or double-blind control procedures.
   d. There is the ability of repeated observations to allow the conclusion of causality.

6. Research has demonstrated a **positive correlation** between children's behavior disorders and marital stress. Children with the worst behavior disorders tend to come from families in which the parents have the most marital problems. What can be said about this relationship?
   a. Children's behavior disorders are a result of the marital distress.
   b. Children's behavior disorders cause an increase in marital distress.
   c. Some outside factor, such as poverty, causes both the children's behavior disorders and the marital distress.
   d. Nothing can be said about the causation of behavior disorders or marital distress.

7. Dr. Ramirez required half of a group of healthy volunteers to study a passage for 1 hour. The other half of the group read the passage once (5 minutes). When both groups were finished, she administered a memory test to the participants who had studied for an hour and then to the participants who had just read the passage. She found that the participants who studied more remembered more. Which of the following was true?
   a. The results of the memory test were confounded.
   b. Study time and recall interval were confounded.
   c. She found that increased studying increased memory.
   d. The independent and dependent variables were confounded.

8. The principle behind random assignment is that
   a. placebo effects are eliminated from the study results.

b. every person in the population is equally likely to be selected.

c. it guarantees that the two groups will contain the same kinds of participants.

d. a participant is as likely to be in the control group as in the experimental group.

9. Kira conducted an experiment under two conditions in which she dropped a pile of books while another person approached her on a sidewalk. In the first, she dressed like a typical college student, wore make-up, had her hair neatly fixed, etc. In the second, she wore ragged clothing and no make-up, had messy hair, and muttered to herself. She then recorded whether the other person helped her pick up her books. The independent variable in Kira's experiment is

a. the dropped books.

b. the passerby's helping behavior.

c. Kira's appearance.

d. there was no independent variable in this study.

10. Which of the following is true of quasi-experiments?

a. They allow a clear conclusion of causality.

b. They employ random selection of subjects.

c. They employ random assignment of subjects.

d. The experimenters do not use random assignment.

11. One limitation of analogue studies is a potential lack of

a. control.

b. external validity.

c. the placebo effect.

d. the ability to rule out alternative explanations (by design).

3

MODELS OF ABNORMALITY

*In Chapter 1, you explored various modes, or **paradigms,** that were used to explain abnormal behavior from ancient times through the early twentieth century. You saw that treatment strategies (exorcism, moral treatment, hypnotism, etc.) followed directly from the assumptions of the particular model of abnormality that was popular at the time. Chapter 2 examined some of the research in abnormal psychology and the methods used by clinical researchers to discover the features of abnormal behavior.*

Contemporary researchers and clinicians adhere to one or more of several models discussed in Chapter 3. You will discover that each of the contemporary models articulates a unique set of assumptions related to how abnormal behavior develops and how it should be treated. Furthermore, each model has unique strengths and limitations. Students are often frustrated by the fact that there is no one "right" model that can explain all aspects of abnormal behavior. As you study Chapter 3, keep in mind that each model sheds light on a different aspect of human functioning, and that a solid understanding of the basic tenets of all the models will foster a greater appreciation for the complexities of human behavior—including abnormal behavior.

*This chapter of the workbook parallels the structure of the textbook, covering six central models of abnormality: the **biological model** (focusing on physical processes), the **psychodynamic model** (emphasizing unconscious processes), the **behavioral model** (concentrating on learning and overt behavior), the **cognitive model** (emphasizing thought processes), the **humanistic-existential model** (concentrating on issues of identity, values, meaning, and responsibility), and the **sociocultural model** (focusing on family-social and cultural influences).*

REVIEW EXERCISES

I.   The Biological Model, 49–53

A.   How Do Biological Theorists Explain Abnormal Behavior?, 49

1.   Biological theorists believe that mental disorders are linked to problems in _____ functioning.

2.   _____ are the nerve cells in the brain, and _____ are the supporting brain cells.

Be sure you have studied and can identify the various regions of the brain described and illustrated on page 49 of the textbook.

3.   In this exercise, give the names of the six terms relating to a typical neuron that are being described.

a. Found at the axon's terminus: _____

b. Neuronal chemicals: _____

c. Extensions located at the end of the neuron that receive impulses: _____

d. Sites located on the dendrite that receive neurotransmitter: _____

e. A long fiber on which electrical impulses travel: _____

f. A tiny space separating one neuron from the next: _____

Study the following diagram, which depicts how messages get from the nerve endings of one neuron to the dendrites of another neuron.

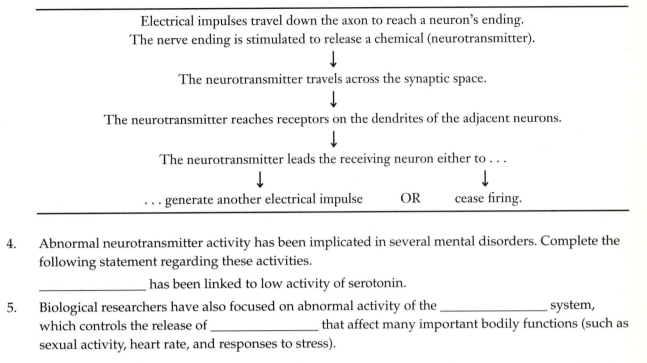

Electrical impulses travel down the axon to reach a neuron's ending.
The nerve ending is stimulated to release a chemical (neurotransmitter).

↓

The neurotransmitter travels across the synaptic space.

↓

The neurotransmitter reaches receptors on the dendrites of the adjacent neurons.

↓

The neurotransmitter leads the receiving neuron either to . . .

↓   ↓

. . . generate another electrical impulse   OR   cease firing.

4. Abnormal neurotransmitter activity has been implicated in several mental disorders. Complete the following statement regarding these activities.

   _____ has been linked to low activity of serotonin.

5. Biological researchers have also focused on abnormal activity of the _____ system, which controls the release of _____ that affect many important bodily functions (such as sexual activity, heart rate, and responses to stress).

6. Anxiety and mood disorders have been tied to abnormal secretions of _____ , which is released by the adrenal glands.

7. A person's genetic makeup can influence brain anatomy and neurotransmitter and endocrine abnormalities. _____ are segments within the chromosomes of each cell that control the traits each person inherits from his or her parents.

8. Although specific genes that cause abnormal behavior have not yet been identified, genetic factors have been linked to the development of certain mental disorders. List two of these below.

   _____

   _____

9. Evolutionary theorists believe that human behavior and the genes that guide human behavior survive because they have helped individuals to _____ and _____ .

10. Explain how behavior considered abnormal in current times could have been adaptive for our ancestors.

    _____

    _____

11. Research suggests that schizophrenia may be related to exposure to certain _____ during childhood or *in utero*.

12. Recent research has linked _____ infections to _____ , mood, and _____ disorders.

B. **Biological Treatments, 51**

   1. Complete the following tables of characteristics of drug therapies. *Organizing information from the textbook in this manner should help with studying.*

Antianxiety drugs

Purpose

Antidepressant drugs

Purpose

Antibipolar drugs

Purpose   help stabilize mood of person diagnosed with bipolar disorder (manic-depression)

Antipsychotic drugs or neuroleptic drugs

Purpose

2. A second form of biological therapy is **electroconvulsive therapy,** or ECT. Complete the following statements related to ECT procedure and effectiveness.

   a. ECT is used to treat patients suffering from _____ .

   b. Electrodes pass _____ to _____ volts of electrical current through the brain, causing a _____ (or convulsion) that lasts a few minutes.

   c. ECT treatment usually consists of _____ to _____ sessions, spaced two or three days apart.

3. In a lobotomy procedure, the connections between the brain's _____ _____ and its lower centers are severed.

4. Although neurosurgery, or psychosurgery, is still considered an experimental procedure, it is used in the treatment of very severe disorders that have _____ _____ to years of other forms of treatment.

C. Assessing the Biological Model, 52

1. The textbook lists two major criticisms of the biological model. Complete the summary of the first criticism, then give a summary of the second.

   a. Although biological processes certainly do affect our behavior, thoughts, and emotions, they are just as certainly affected *by* our behavior, thoughts, and emotions. Our mental life is a(n) _____ of biological and nonbiological factors.

   b. _____

   _____

II. The Psychodynamic Model, 53–58

1. One belief of psychodynamic theorists is that our behavior is determined by interacting, dynamic psychological forces outside of our awareness. Complete the following list of additional assumptions of the psychodynamic model of abnormal behavior.

   a. Abnormal behaviors are the result of _____ between internal forces.

b. Psychological conflicts are related to early _____ and _____ experiences in childhood.

c. Psychodynamic theories rest on the _____ assumption that no symptom or behavior is "accidental."

A. How Did Freud Explain Normal and Abnormal Functioning?, 53

Exercises covering this portion of the text are broken down in the same manner as the textbook's discussions. Coverage of the id, the ego, and the superego are followed by coverage of the Freudian developmental stages.

Freud believed that the "personality" is comprised of three unconscious forces: the id (instinctual needs), the ego (rational thinking), and the superego (moral standards). Complete the following list of characteristics that define each of these forces.

1. The Id, 53

1. The id operates according to the _____ principle, which means that it always seeks _____ .

2. Id instincts are primarily _____ in nature. _____ is the term that describes the person's dynamic, intrapsychic sexual energy, which fuels the id.

2. The Ego, 54

1. The ego operates according to the **reality principle.** What does this mean?

_____

_____

2. The ego develops strategies designed to control unacceptable id impulses that may create anxiety if they are "allowed" into conscious awareness. After reading Table 3-1 on textbook page 54, complete the following table by matching each ego defense mechanism with the appropriate illustration from the list of examples below. Then write a brief definition for each in your own words.

Ego defense mechanism	Example	Definition
Repression	d.	primary Freudian defense mechanism: dangerous or painful thoughts aren't allowed into consciousness
Rationalization		
Denial		
Projection		
Displacement		
Intellectualization		

Examples:

a. Eric is extremely upset when he sees his girlfriend, Donna, talking and laughing with her ex-boyfriend. Later Eric accuses Donna of being excessively jealous of any woman who happens to glance at him.

b. After Nancy's supervisor comments that her work is less than satisfactory, Nancy responds by telling the supervisor she will try harder, then goes home and yells at her children to clean up their rooms.

c. When the police arrested him on a domestic violence charge, 48-year-old Steven stated that his wife deserved the beating because she had burned dinner again.

d. At the age of 8, Anne witnessed her father severely abusing her mother, an event that Anne quickly "forgot" and still has no memory of at the age of 42.

e. Even after her third arrest for drunken driving, 30-year-old Loretta claims that she "doesn't have a problem" with alcohol.

f. When Shawna breaks up with her boyfriend, Anthony, after a two-year relationship, Anthony responds by calmly identifying the main reasons why they are, in fact, incompatible.

3. The Superego, 54

1. The superego is developed when we realize that many of our id impulses are unacceptable. This realization comes as we unconsciously adopt our _____ moral values and standards.

2. Another name for the superego is the _____ .

4. Developmental Stages, 55

1. Certain demands or pressures are so threatening to a growing child that the id, ego, and superego do not mature properly and result in the child becoming _____ (or entrapped) at a particular developmental stage.

2. Freud suggested that individuals move through five distinct stages in their development. Each stage corresponds to a particular area of the body that Freud believed was most important to the developing person at a given point in time. In the table to the right, list the five stages and the age range encompassed by each stage.

Stage	Age Range
Oral	–
	–
	–
	–
	–

3. Freud believed that at each stage, people face certain conflicts that must be resolved if they are to develop into psychologically healthy adults. Read through the text material on the oral stage. Fixation at the oral stage of development can result in the emergence of certain "oral" characteristics in adulthood. Describe these characteristics below.

"Oral" characteristics: _____

B.   How Do Other Psychodynamic Explanations Differ from Freud's?, 55

Exercises in this subsection of the workbook cover three of the most influential psychodynamic theories: ego theory, object relations theory, and self theory.

1.   What is the basic assumption of ego theorists?

_____

_____

2.   What is the basic assumption of self theorists?

_____

_____

3.   What is the basic assumption of object relations theorists?

_____

_____

C.   Psychodynamic Therapies, 55

1.   List two of the primary goals of psychodynamic therapy.

_____

_____

2.   What is the therapeutic purpose of **free association?**

_____

_____

3.   The following terms describe some of the phenomena that psychodynamic clinicians attempt to **interpret** during the course of therapy. Define each term.

a.   **Resistance** is the unconscious block in a patient's _____ _____ , or a change of subject so as to avoid a potentially painful discussion.

b.   **Transference** is when a patient acts toward the _____ much as he or she did toward important figures such as his or her parents.

4.   Freud considered **dreams** to be the "royal road to the unconscious" because he believed _____ and other defense mechanisms operate less completely during sleep.

5.   Psychodynamic therapists translate the _____ content of dreams into symbolic, or _____ , content.

6.   Define **catharsis:**   _____

7.   "_____ _____" is the process of examining the same issues over and over again in psychodynamic therapy—each time with a deeper level of clarity and insight.

8.   Traditional psychodynamic therapies can take many months, even years, to complete. In more recently developed short-term dynamic therapies, patients choose a single problem, called a _____ _____ , that they would like to work on in therapy.

9.   A contemporary school of psychodynamic therapy, _____ _____ therapy, argues that therapists' reactions and beliefs should be included in the therapy process.

D.   Assessing the Psychodynamic Model, 58

1.   Strengths of Freud's psychodynamic theory include the fact that it provided an alternative to _____ theories and treatments of abnormality and that for the first time theories and techniques were applied _____ to treatment.

2.   A reason why this model has received little research support is that processes such as id drives and ego defenses are abstract and operate at a(n) _____ level, making it nearly impossible to determine if they are occurring.

III. The Behavioral Model, 58–62

1.   What is the basic assumption of the behavioral model about abnormal behavior?

_____

_____

2.   The behavioral model was the first perspective to be developed in _____ . Psychologists in these laboratories conducted experiments on learning that takes place through _____ .

3.   Behavioral principles established by research psychologists were applied to clinical problems in part because clinicians were becoming frustrated with _____

_____ .

A.   How Do Behaviorists Explain Abnormal Functioning?, 59

1.   The three types of conditioning described in your text include (a) **operant conditioning** and (b) **modeling.** Briefly describe these types of learning/conditioning.

a. Operant conditioning: _____

_____

b. Modeling: _____

_____

2.   The textbook states that classical conditioning is a process of *learning by temporal association.* Briefly explain what this means.

_____

_____

After reviewing Pavlov's famous experiments with dogs in your text, read and respond to the following case study relating to classical conditioning.

Case Study

Thirteen-year-old Diane was riding her bicycle home one day after school while listening to her favorite Foo Fighters song on her headphones. She was thinking about what to wear to a party her friend Jackie was having that night and paid more attention to the song than to the traffic around her. She glided through a red light at a busy intersection. Her preoccupation was suddenly interrupted by the sounds of a car screeching to a halt and blaring its horn. Diane swerved around the car, narrowly avoiding a collision. As she walked her bike home, Diane's entire body trembled with fear—she thought she might vomit. Later, when Diane arrived at the party, her friend Jackie put on the CD of the same Foo Fighters song, which she knew Diane liked. Jackie was surprised to see Diane turn pale and rush to the bathroom. "I guess she doesn't like this song," thought Jackie as she went to check on her friend.

3.   Complete this diagram by providing the **unconditioned stimulus** and the **conditioned stimulus** in the preceding case study.

$$\underline{\hspace{4cm}} \longrightarrow \text{fear, nausea}$$
Unconditioned stimulus   **Unconditioned response**

$$\underline{\hspace{4cm}} \longrightarrow \text{fear, nausea}$$
Conditioned stimulus   **Conditioned response**

Demonstrate your knowledge of classical conditioning by explaining the following case of a young boy named Abe.

Case Study

Five-year-old Abe developed an intense fear of the dark after experiencing horrible nightmares for a period of three months. Abe's fear of the dark was classically conditioned: nightmares (UCS) resulting in a fear response (UCR) were repeatedly paired with the darkness of his bedroom (CS). Darkness eventually evoked a fear response (CR) in Abe even when he did not have a nightmare. Abe's parents are puzzled, however, when their child starts screaming every time he sees a stuffed animal (just like those that sit on Abe's bed).

4.   Briefly explain how classical conditioning principles could explain Abe's fear of stuffed animals.

_____

_____

B.   Behavioral Therapies, 60

1.   Complete the following flowchart by providing missing information relating to the steps in **systematic desensitization,** a classical conditioning technique frequently used with people who suffer from phobias.

Step 1:	Client learns _____ over the course of several sessions.
Step 2:	Client constructs a _____ , which is a list of least to most anxiety-arousing situations.
Step 3:	Client either imagines or is physically exposed to situations on the list while maintaining a state of _____ .
Step 4:	Client moves up the hierarchy until he or she can _____ .

C. Assessing the Behavioral Model, 61

1. Complete the following list of strengths and limitations of the behavioral model as described in the textbook.

   Strengths:

   a. Behavioral explanations can be tested in the laboratory and predicted effects can be observed and measured.

   b. _____

   c. _____

   Limitations:

   a. It is not certain that abnormalities are ordinarily acquired in the same way as clinically induced symptoms.

   b. _____

   c. _____

2. Some behaviorists believe that the traditional focus on overt (observable) behaviors does not adequately capture the complexities of human behavior. For example, Albert Bandura argues that one's behavior is affected by one's sense of _____ , an assessment of whether one can master and perform necessary behaviors.

3. Behaviorists who take into account covert (unobservable) behaviors such as thoughts and beliefs represent the _____ model.

IV. The Cognitive Model, 62–64

The cognitive model suggests that in order to understand human behavior we must investigate WHAT and HOW people think—the CONTENT and PROCESS of human thought.

A. How Do Cognitive Theorists Explain Abnormal Functioning?, 62

According to cognitive psychologists, we create representations of the world in our minds that dictate the way we perceive and understand events in our lives. "Errors" or inaccuracies in these mental representations can lead to maladaptive functioning.

1. Cognitive theorists suggest that some people hold *assumptions* and *attitudes* that are maladaptive and inaccurate. Read through the excerpt from a cognitive therapy session on page 63 of your text. Identify at least one maladaptive assumption that the patient seems to hold in this case.

   _____

   _____

2. Cognitive theorists also focus on the **illogical thinking process**—based on maladaptive assumptions—that some people demonstrate. Look again at the cognitive therapy excerpt on page 63. Can you identify an example of the patient's illogical thinking processes (e.g., overgeneralization)?

   _____

   _____

   _____

B. Cognitive Therapies, 63

    1.   Cognitive therapists help their clients develop new, more adaptive ways of thinking about themselves, others, and the world. Specifically, cognitive therapists help clients to

        a. recognize the _____ thoughts, biased _____ , and logical errors that lead to dysfunction; and

        b. _____ their dysfunctional thoughts, and try out and apply new interpretations in their day-to-day lives.

C. Assessing the Cognitive Model, 64

    1.   Describe two strengths and two limitations of the cognitive model.

      Strengths:

        a. _____

        b. _____

      Limitations:

        a. _____

        b. _____

    2.   One example of the new wave of cognitive therapies that have emerged in recent years is the _____ and _____ therapy (ACT).

    3.   ACT and other new-wave cognitive therapies often employ _____-_____ techniques to help clients achieve _____ of their troublesome thoughts without judgment, in the hopes that the thoughts will eventually trouble the clients less.

V. The Humanistic-Existential Model, 64–70

    1.   Humanistic and existential perspectives of behavior focus on broader dimensions of human existence such as: _____

      _____

    2.   Humanistic models assert that human beings are born with a natural drive to fulfill their innate potential for goodness and growth. This is known as the drive to _____ .

    3.   Which perspective (humanistic or existential) is considered to be more pessimistic, and why?

      _____

      _____

    4.   Carl Rogers called this humanistic approach _____ therapy.

    5.   The existential perspective is based on the ideas of existential philosophers who believed that people attempt to derive the meaning of their existence through their _____ .

A. Rogers's Humanistic Theory and Therapy, 65

    1.   Describe the humanistic theory according to Carl Rogers.

        a. The road to _____ begins in infancy.

b. All of us have a basic need to receive positive _____ from the significant people in our lives (primarily our parents).

c. Those who receive unconditional _____ _____ early in life are likely to develop unconditional _____ .

d. Children who do not, acquire **conditions of worth** as a result.

2. Rogers's client-centered therapy requires clinicians to demonstrate three important characteristics when they are working with clients. Describe each characteristic below:

a. Unconditional positive regard: _____

_____

b. Accurate empathy: _____

_____

c. Genuineness: _____

_____

_____

3. Although the effectiveness of Rogers's therapy has received mixed research support, his approach did open up the practice of psychotherapy to new _____ and to psychologists (before, psychotherapy was the "exclusive territory" of _____).

B. Gestalt Theory and Therapy, 67

1. Gestalt theory and therapy were developed by Frederick (Fritz) _____ in the 1950s and are part of the humanistic approach.

2. Both client-centered and gestalt therapists help their clients move toward self-recognition and self-_____ , but gestalt therapists achieve this goal by _____ and challenging clients.

3. Gestalt therapists urge clients to become increasingly self-aware through several techniques. Complete the table below by briefly describing each gestalt technique and the specific goal of each technique.

Technique	Description	Goal
Skillful frustration		
Role-playing		
Rules		

C. Spiritual Views and Interventions, 67

1. Clinicians only recently began to view spirituality as a positive factor in mental health. What was the reason for Freud's belief that religion could be potentially damaging?

_____

_____

_____

2. Recent research suggests people who view God as warm and caring are less _____, pessimistic, _____ , or _____ than those who view God as cold and unresponsive.

D. **Existential Theories and Therapy, 68**

1. Complete the following flowchart that illustrates the existential explanation of psychological distress and abnormal behavior.

A person hides from personal responsibility and choice when he or she becomes engulfed in constant change, confusion, and the emotional strain of present-day society, as well as the particular stress of his or her immediate environment.

BECAUSE OF THIS,

he or she overlooks his or her personal _____ and won't take _____ for his or her own life. This abdication can be a form of refuge, but can

LEAD TO

the person being left with an empty, "inauthentic" life and experiencing

- ____anxiety____   • _____   • _____   • _____

---

2. What are the goals of existential therapy?

_____

_____

PsychWatch: Cybertherapy: Surfing for Help, 69

1. What are the possible advantages of Internet support groups in coping with depression, substance abuse, anxiety, eating disorders, and other psychological disorders?

_____

_____

_____

_____

2. What are possible drawbacks to "chat group therapy"?

_____

_____

_____

3. What do advocates point to when arguing that computer software programs may help those suffering from emotional distress?

_____

4. Describe audiovisual e-therapy, which is on the rise. Identify key advantages and disadvantages to this type of therapy.

_____

_____

_____

E. Assessing the Humanistic-Existential Model, 70

1. Among the strengths of the humanistic-existential model of abnormal behavior is that it emphasizes issues with which people struggle (e.g., existence, meaning, values, and choices) that are important to effective (or ineffective) psychological functioning. List two other strengths of this model.

   a. _____

   b. _____

2. What is a primary limitation of the humanistic-existential model?

   _____

VI. The Sociocultural Model: The Family-Social and Multicultural Perspectives, 70–78

1. Sociocultural theorists are particularly interested in answering questions about a person's social and cultural environment in order to understand his or her abnormal behavior. Complete the following list of questions that are posed by the sociocultural model.

   a. What are the _____ of the person's society?

   b. What _____ does the person play in the social environment?

   c. What kind of _____ background or _____ structure is the person exposed to?

   d. How do other people _____ and react to the person?

A. How Do Family-Social Theorists Explain Abnormal Functioning?, 71

Sociocultural explanations of abnormal behavior focus on three areas: social labels and roles, social connections and supports, and family structure and communication. The following exercises parallel the textbook's coverage of these areas.

1. Social Labels and Roles, 71

1. Complete the following diagram that depicts the "vicious cycle" that contributes to the development of mental illness according to sociocultural theorists.

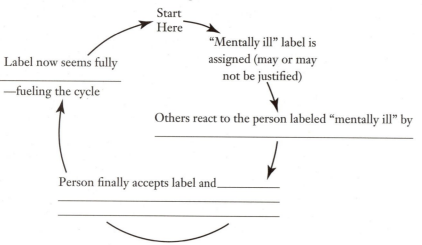

Start Here

"Mentally ill" label is assigned (may or may not be justified)

Label now seems fully
_____
—fueling the cycle

Others react to the person labeled "mentally ill" by
_____

Person finally accepts label and_____
_____
_____

2. Complete the following statements related to the method and findings of David Rosenhan's study of the effects of diagnostic labeling on psychiatric "pseudopatients."

    Rosenhan's "Pseudopatient Study"

    Method:

    *Eight normal people ("pseudopatients") went to several psychiatric hospitals and complained of the following symptom:

    _____

    _____

    *All the pseudopatients were admitted to the hospitals with diagnoses of _____ .

    *Once they were admitted, the pseudopatients behaved normally (i.e., did not exhibit any "symptoms").

    Findings:

    *The pseudopatients' hospitalization ranged from _____ to _____ days, despite the fact that they showed no symptoms of mental disorder while in the hospital.

    *The diagnostic label seemed to influence the way that the _____ viewed and dealt with the pseudopatients.

    *The pseudopatients reported the following feelings during their hospital stay:

    _____

2. Social Connections and Supports, 71

1. Sociocultural theorists believe that the quality of a person's social and professional relationships is sometimes linked to abnormal behaviors. Researchers have identified certain qualities that characterize the social relationships of people who become depressed under stressful conditions. Describe these qualities below.

    _____

    _____

2. Some clinical theorists believe that people who do not communicate and develop relationships in their everyday lives will find meaningful contacts online through social networking sites like Facebook. Describe research findings mentioned in your textbook that appear to contradict this line of thinking.

    _____

    _____

3. Family Structure and Communication, 72

1. How, according to family systems theorists, do some families force individual members to behave in ways that society at large would deem abnormal?

    _____

    _____

    _____

2. Families whose members are grossly overinvolved in each other's lives have a(n) _____ structure, whereas families with overly rigid boundaries between members are said to display a structure of _____ .

3. Even if only one member of the family is identified as "sick," family therapists treat the family system as a whole. Based on your knowledge of family systems theory, why do you think this is the case?

   _____

   _____

   _____

B. Family-Social Treatments, 72

The following exercises follow the textbook's structure of coverage of four special sociocultural strategies: group, family, couple, and community treatment therapies.

1. Group Therapy, 72

1. List some of the important benefits experienced by clients in group therapy.

   _____

   _____

   _____

2. Research findings indicate that group therapy is often just as effective as _____ therapy for people with a range of psychological problems and educational needs.

3. In the self-help group format, people who share similar problems meet without the leadership of a professional _____ .

4. In the United States today there are between _____ and _____ self-help groups attended by _____ to _____ percent of the population.

2. Family Therapy, 73

1. Regardless of their theoretical orientation, family therapists adhere to the principles of family system theory. Describe the principles of this theory.

   _____

   _____

   _____

2. **Structural family therapists** focus on the family _____ structure, the role each family member plays, and the _____ between family members.

3. Therapists pay special attention to family communication patterns in the _____ family therapy approach.

3. Couple Therapy, 74

1. Describe the goals of the following two forms of couple therapy.

   a. Cognitive-behavioral couple therapy:

   _____

   _____

   _____

  b. Integrative couple therapy:

  _____

  _____

  _____

2. Although couples who receive therapy show more improvement in their relationship than couples who do not receive therapy, fewer than _____ percent of treated couples report they are "happily married" at the end of therapy.

4. Community Treatment, 75

1. In 1963, President John F. Kennedy called for a "bold new approach" to the treatment of mental illness, and the Community Mental Health Act was passed by Congress soon after. Describe how the **community mental health movement** changed the way that people with severe psychological problems received treatment services.

  _____

  _____

2. Complete the following statements relating to the three types of prevention practiced in community treatments. Then, give an example of each.

  a. _____ *prevention* consists of efforts to improve community attitudes and policies with the goal of preventing mental disorders altogether.

  Example: _____

  b. The goal of *secondary prevention* is to _____ and _____ mental disorders at their earliest stages.

  Example: _____

  c. In *tertiary prevention,* treatment providers try to prevent severe disorders (that already exist) from becoming _____ problems.

  Example: _____

3. Community programs have often failed to provide tertiary services needed by severely disturbed persons. Why?

  _____

  _____

C. How Do Multicultural Theorists Explain Abnormal Functioning?, 76

1. *Culture* is the set of _____ , attitudes, _____ , _____ and behaviors shared by a group of people.

2. Eating disorders are more prevalent in Western cultures than in non-Western cultures. How does this evidence support a multicultural explanation of the development of eating disorders?

  _____

  _____

3. The _____ perspective suggests that an individual's behavior, whether normal or abnormal, is best understood in the context of his or her unique cultural context.

4. Poorer people are more likely to suffer from severe psychological problems than wealthier people. What are some of the unique pressures that exist for the former group that could be related to higher levels of stress and a greater potential for psychological dysfunction?

   _____

   _____

   _____

   _____

5. *"Racial and sexual prejudice contribute to abnormal functioning."* For each of the following groups of people, list a piece of evidence that supports this statement.

Group	Evidence
Women	Women in Western societies are diagnosed with anxiety and depressive disorders at least twice as often as men.
African Americans	
Hispanic persons	
Native Americans	

D. Multicultural Treatments, 77

1. Research has illuminated several differences in how people from ethnic and racial minority groups respond to and utilize therapy. What are these?

   a. People from ethnic and racial minority groups seem to make fewer improvements in clinical treatment than people from majority groups.

   b. Members of ethnic and racial minority groups use mental health services _____ than members of majority groups.

   c. _____

      _____ .

2. Approaches geared toward the unique issues and special pressures of being a person of color or a woman in Western society are called _____ and _____ therapies, respectively.

3. Name eight of the typical elements of culture-sensitive therapy approaches.

   a. _____

   b. _____

   c. _____

   d. _____

   e. _____

f. _____

g. _____

h. _____

E.   Assessing the Sociocultural Model, 78

1.   The sociocultural model has influenced clinicians to take into account family and societal issues and has highlighted the impact of diagnostic labels. However, two important limitations of this model are:

a. _____

_____

b. _____

_____

V.   Putting It Together: Integration of the Models, 78–80

1.   Contemporary models of abnormality take into account the biological, psychological, and sociocultural aspects of abnormal behavior; likewise, contemporary clinicians are increasingly utilizing _____ theories as they conceptualize and treat their clients'/patients' problems.

2.   Many contemporary theorists and clinicians adhere to a **diathesis-stress model** of abnormal functioning. Complete the diagram on the next page, which depicts this model.

A person has a diathesis—a biological, _____ ,
or sociological _____ to develop a disorder.

↓

The person then experiences episodes of extreme _____ .

↓

Onset of the psychological disorder is "triggered."

MULTIPLE CHOICE

1. A paradigm is
   a. a specific law of behavior.
   b. another name for a theory.
   c. a set of the basic assumptions that organize one's approach to an area under study.
   d. a research study that determines the fundamental causes of a specific mental disorder.

2. A part of the brain that is involved in memory is the
   a. amygdala.
   b. basal ganglia.
   c. hippocampus.
   d. corpus callosum.

3. Neural information gets from one neuron to another via
   a. a chemical messenger.
   b. an electrical nerve impulse.
   c. the movement of receptors across the synapse.
   d. direct contact between an axon and a dendrite.

4. The originator of psychoanalysis was
   a. Jung.
   b. Freud.
   c. Breuer.
   d. Charcot.

5. Which of the following terms is used to describe a person's instinctual needs, drives, and impulses?
   a. id
   b. ego
   c. superego
   d. conscience

6. Focusing on past traumatic events, particularly from childhood, as causes of one's abnormal behavior is a major part of treatment in
   a. psychoanalysis.
   b. cognitive therapy.
   c. behavioral therapy.
   d. biological treatment.

7. Short-term psychodynamic therapies usually
   a. work well with alcoholics.
   b. are best for severely disturbed patients.
   c. focus on a single problem.
   d. demonstrate better outcome than longer, traditional therapy.

8. If you close your eyes and imagine biting into a big, juicy, sour lemon, you are likely to salivate. The image of the lemon is the
   a. conditioned stimulus.
   b. conditioned response.
   c. unconditioned stimulus.
   d. unconditioned response.

9. Which of the following is a cognitive concept?
   a. behavior
   b. self-efficacy
   c. reinforcement
   d. unconditional positive regard

10. Carl Rogers is considered the pioneer of the
    a. behavioral model.
    b. cognitive model.
    c. existential theory.
    d. humanistic theory.

11. What is the type of therapy in which a psychologist treats several unrelated clients together?
    a. psychodrama
    b. group therapy
    c. couple therapy
    d. a self-help group

12. The divorce rate in the United States and Canada is close to
    a. 10 percent.
    b. 25 percent.
    c. 50 percent.
    d. 75 percent.

13. Which of the following would be an example of tertiary prevention of mental health problems?
    a. establishing a suicide hot line
    b. building a sheltered workshop where psychiatric outpatients can work
    c. advocating for establishing a day-care center for neighborhood children
    d. consulting with teachers to identify children who may benefit from services

4 CLINICAL ASSESSMENT, DIAGNOSIS, AND TREATMENT

REVIEW EXERCISES

I.   Clinical Assessment: How and Why Does the Client Behave Abnormally?, 83–98

1.   Complete the following list of the uses of clinical assessment techniques.

   a.   to determine how and why someone behaves abnormally.

b. _____

c. _____

2. A clinician's _____ orientation will influence his or her decision about what type of assessment technique to use.

A. Characteristics of Assessment Tools, 84

1. How would you **standardize** the scores of an alertness test for airline pilots?

_____

_____

_____

2. Each of the following exercises relates to one of four kinds of clinical test **reliability** described in the textbook.

a. The reliability of a test refers to the _____ of assessment measures and test results.

b. How would you go about demonstrating that the "Glass Is Half-Empty Test," a measure of pessimism, has adequate test–retest reliability?

_____

_____

c. Interrater, or interjudge, reliability is demonstrated when several evaluators (or "judges") independently _____ on how a test should be _____ .

3. An assessment tool's **validity** is the _____ with which it measures what it is intended to measure.

4. Each of the following exercises relates to one of five kinds of validity described in the textbook.

a. _____ validity means that the items on a test "look like" they are measuring what they are supposed to measure; this kind of validity, however, does not necessarily establish that the test is _____ .

b. Imagine that the "Glass Is Half-Empty Test," which is designed to measure pessimism, is being considered as a tool to identify people who are at risk for developing clinical depression later in life. What kind of validity would the test need to demonstrate in order for it to be used for this purpose?

_____

c. Concurrent validity is the degree to which test scores agree with

_____

B. Clinical Interviews, 85

1. What pieces of information are typically gained through clinical interviewing?

_____

_____

2. The textbook describes how clinicians give special attention to topics that are important to their particular theoretical orientation. Complete the following table by providing the name of the orientation that fits each description of topics.

Interview Topics	Orientation
Try to discover assumptions and interpretations that influence the way a person acts and feels	
Pinpoint signs of any biochemical or neurological dysfunction	
Elicit relevant information about the stimuli that trigger the abnormal functioning, the precise nature of the abnormal responses, and the consequences of the responses	
Discuss the person's needs and fantasies, relevant memories about past events and relationships	
Discuss the person's self-concept and unique perceptions	
Discuss the person's family, living arrangements, and work relationships	

3. Unstructured interviews are comprised of open-ended questions (questions that cannot be answered with a simple "yes" or "no"). The textbook gives the example "Would you tell me about yourself?" Try to think of two more open-ended questions that might be asked in an clinical interview.

    a. _____

    b. _____

4. Clinicians who use _____ interview strategies sometimes rely on published interview _____ that provide a standard set of questions.

5. List some of the areas of functioning assessed on a mental status exam.

    _____

    _____

    _____

6. Complete the description of four of the limitations of clinical interviews.

    a. Information gathered at the interview is—to some extent—preselected by the client and may be self-serving and less than accurate.

    b. Some clients are simply unable to provide _____ information in an interview.

    c. _____

        _____

    d. Clients respond differently to different interviewers. List some characteristics of clinicians that clients may respond to in one way or another.

        _____

C.   Clinical Tests, 87

Coverage in this important subsection is broken into six parts, devoted to each of the six most prominent kinds of clinical tests.

   Be sure you understand the coverage of reliability and validity, as these concepts serve as a basis for "testing" the usefulness of each type of test.

I.   Projective Tests, 88

1.   The primary assumption of projective tests is that clients will "project" aspects of their own
_____ into the _____ , which is to interpret ambiguous stimuli.

2.   Look at the **Rorschach inkblot** depicted in Figure 4–1 on page 88. This is similar to the 10 inkblots
that Hermann Rorschach selected for use in the assessment of personality. Below, write a response to
the question "What might this be?"

_____

_____

_____

_____

3.   Rorschach believed that the images seen in the inkblots corresponded to a person's
_____ condition. *(After reading over your own response in #2 above, do you agree?)*

4.   Most clinicians who use the Rorschach method today pay primary attention to the "style" of patients' responses to inkblots, such as whether they respond to the whole blot or specific details of it.
Give two examples of the kinds of "styles" that different people demonstrate in their responses.

a.   _____

b.   _____

5.   Complete the following flowchart relating to the questions a clinician using the **Thematic Apper-
ception Test** would ask.

People who take the TAT are shown one picture at a time
and asked to make up a dramatic story about it, stating . . .

↓

1. What is happening?	3. What are the characters_____ and _____
2. _____	4. _____

↓

Clinicians then interpret the stories as an expression of
the person's own circumstances, needs, emotions, etc.

---

6.   Other projective tests include the _____-completion test and the Draw-
a-_____ Test, which is the most prevalent drawing test.

7.   List three of the reliability and validity problems of the projective tests.

a.   _____

_____

b.   Studies that "test" how well clinicians can describe personalities based on the results of projective tests have repeatedly shown inaccuracies.

c.   _____

_____

2.   Personality Inventories, 90

1.   Currently there are two versions—original and revised—of the MMPI, or the Minnesota

   _____   _____   _____ .

2.   Complete the following table by matching the MMPI clinical scales with the letter corresponding to the content description from the list following the scales.

Number	Scale	Content Description
1 or HS	Hypochondriasis	
2 or D	Depression	
3 or Hy	Conversion Hysteria	
4 or PD	Psychopathic deviate	
5 or Mf	Masculinity-femininity	
6 or Pa	Paranoia	
7 or Pt	Psychasthenia	
8 or Sc	Schizophrenia	
9 or Ma	Hypomania	
0 or Si	Social introversion	

Content descriptions:

a.   Obsessions, compulsions, fears, and guilt

b.   Suspicion, delusions of grandeur, persecutory delusions

c.   Excessive concern with bodily functions

d.   Shyness, insecurity, little interest in people

e.   Conventional masculine and feminine styles

f.   Emotional shallowness, disregard for social norms

g.   Pessimism, hopelessness, lethargy

h.   Bizarre thoughts and behavior, hallucinations

i.   Use of symptoms to avoid conflicts and responsibilities

j.   Excitement, overactivity, racing thoughts

3.   People can score from 0 to _____ on each MMPI scale, with scores of _____ or above indicating clinical significance or deviance.

4.   Identify a reason that the MMPI-2 is considered a more accurate indicator of personality and abnormal functioning than the original MMPI.

   _____

   _____

5.   Complete the following list of advantages of structured personality inventories over projective tests

    a. short administration time

    b. _____

    c. _____

    d. _____

    e. greater validity (although it is still limited)

6.   In addition to limited validity, a criticism of personality inventories is that they often fail to consider _____ differences in people's responses.

Table 4-1: Multicultural Hot Spots in Assessment and Diagnosis, 91

Reread Table 4-1 on page 91 in your textbook. Incorporating some of the multicultural "hot spots" described in the table, create a case study in which a dominant-culture assessor attempts to assess, diagnose, and treat an ethnic-minority client.

_____

_____

_____

_____

_____

_____

_____

_____

_____

_____

_____

3.   Response Inventories, 92

1.   Complete the following table by describing the purposes of the listed response inventories.

Inventory	Purpose
Affective inventories	
Social skills inventories	
Cognitive inventories	

4.   Psychophysiological Tests, 93

1.   Psychophysiological tests have become important assessment tools since the discovery that certain _____ responses—such as changes in heart rate or blood pressure—often indicate _____ problems—such as anxiety disorders.

2.   Describe how **polygraphs** are used.

_____

_____

3. One limitation of psychophysiological assessment methods is that the equipment is expensive and must be expertly maintained. List two more limitations.

    a. _____

    b. _____

5. Neurological and Neuropsychological Tests, 94

1. List several causes of neurological damage in the brain that can result in psychological or behavioral problems.

    _____

    _____

    _____

2. In recent years, technological advances have allowed clinicians and researchers to get a closer, more detailed look at the brain in order to pinpoint potential sites of brain dysfunction. Describe each of the following neurological tests:

    a. Electroencephalogram (or EEG): _____

    _____

    b. Computerized axial tomogram (or _____ scan): _____

    _____

    c. Positron emission tomogram (or _____ scan): _____

    _____

    d. Magnetic resonance imaging (or _____): _____

    _____

3. **Neuropsychological tests** can identify subtle brain abnormalities by measuring skills such as visual _____ , recent _____ , and visual-motor _____ .

4. Describe the procedure used to detect neurological impairment by the **Bender Visual-Motor Gestalt Test.**

    _____

    _____

5. Because no single neuropsychological test can distinguish between specific kinds of impairment, clinicians often use a _____ of tests to measure multiple skill areas.

PsychWatch: The Truth, the Whole Truth, and Nothing but the Truth, 95

Although movies and television shows portray polygraphs (lie detectors) as being very accurate, actually they do not work as well as we would like. Research shows that _____ out of 100 truths, on average, are labeled lies by polygraph testing.

6. Intelligence Tests, 96

1. Why is it impossible to measure intelligence directly?

    _____

    _____

2. The overall score on an intelligence test is called the _____ _____ or _____ .

3.   Intelligence tests generally demonstrate high validity and reliability, but they do have several short-comings. Describe two of these important limitations.

a. _____

_____

b. _____

_____

D.   Clinical Observations, 96

1.   Describe how clinicians use the following strategies to observe behavior.

a. Naturalistic observations: _____

_____

b. Analogue observations: _____

_____

2.   Describe how the following factors can limit the validity of clinical observations.

a. Observer drift: _____

_____

b. Observer bias: _____

_____

c. Subject reactivity: _____

_____

3.   Why may clinical observations lack cross-situational validity?

_____

_____

4.   Imagine that you are a clinician and that a 26-year-old man suffering from obesity comes into your clinic for help. You would like him to begin **self-monitoring** immediately. What are some of the things that you would like him to record?

_____

_____

MediaSpeak: Tests, eBay, and the Public Good, 97

1.   To date, eBay has denied all requests to restrict the sale of Wechsler intelligence tests through its Web site. Identify several ways in which these tests might be misused if their sale is not limited to clinical psychologists and trained professionals.

_____

_____

II.   Diagnosis: Does the Client's Syndrome Match a Known Disorder?, 98–106

A.   Classification Systems, 99

1.   A clinician makes a **diagnosis** when he or she determines that a person's pattern of symptoms (or _____) constitutes a particular _____ .

2.   What are the (a) ICD and (b) DSM-IV-TR?

   a. _____

   _____

   b. _____

   _____

B.   DSM-IV-TR, 99

1.   The DSM-IV-TR includes descriptions of approximately _____ mental disorders.

2.   Each entry in the DSM-IV-TR contains numerous pieces of information. What are they?

   _____

   _____

   _____

3.   The following table relates to the five axes (branches of information) of DSM-IV-TR. Match each of the first four axes with the appropriate examples (there are none for Axis V) from the list of entries following the table, then give a short description for each axis. The numbers in parentheses under "Examples" are the number of examples you should choose for that particular axis.

Axis	Examples	Description
Axis I	(6) m, c, h	an extensive list of clinical syndromes that typically cause significant impairment
Axis II	(3)	
Axis III	(3)	
Axis IV	(3)	
Axis V	(none)	

Examples:

a. Major depression

b. Recent death of a spouse

c. Schizophrenia

d. Antisocial personality disorder

e. Leukemia

f. Obsessive-compulsive disorder

g. Mental retardation

h. Autism

i. Ongoing sexual abuse

j. Bipolar disorder

k. Dependent personality disorder

l. AIDS

m. Anorexia nervosa

n. Epilepsy

o. Chronic unemployment

PsychWatch: Culture-Bound Abnormality, 101

1. Briefly describe the culture-bound forms of abnormality described in the textbook on page 101.

    _____

    _____

    _____

C. Is DSM-IV-TR an Effective Classification System?, 102

1. What does "reliability" mean in the context of a diagnostic classification system?

    _____

    _____

    _____

2. Describe the two steps taken by the DSM-IV-TR task force to maximize the reliability of the DSM-IV-TR system.

    a. _____

       _____

    b. _____

       _____

3. A diagnostic classification system that is most useful to clinicians is one that demonstrates _____ validity in that it helps predict future symptoms.

4. A growing number of theorists believe the two fundamental problems that weaken the DSM-IV-TR are

    a. its basic assumption that clinical disorders are _____ different from normal behavior rather than different in degree only.

    b. its use of _____ diagnostic categories, with each category of pathology considered to be separate from all the others.

D. Call for Change: DSM-5, 103

1. Identify eight of the key changes proposed in the 2011 draft of the DSM-5, which will further undergo multiple rounds of revisions and, once adopted, is scheduled for publication in 2013. We will continue to explore these proposed changes throughout this workbook.

    a. _____

    b. _____

    c. _____

    d. _____

    e. _____

    f. _____

    g. _____

    h. _____

E.   Can Diagnosis and Labeling Cause Harm?, 105

    1.   List some examples of how clinicians, in interpreting assessment data, may be "flawed information processors."

_____

_____

_____

    2.   Some theorists believe that diagnostic labels may be self-fulfilling prophecies. Explain the reasoning behind this belief.

_____

_____

_____

III.   Treatment: How Might the Client Be Helped?, 106–109

A.   Treatment Decisions, 106

    1.   What factors influence or contribute to clinicians' treatment decisions? Complete the list of factors below.

       a.   Information about the _____ and _____ of a client's problems that is gained through the assessment process.

       b.   _____ information that includes which techniques have been helpful for the particular type of problem.

       c.   The clinician's theoretical _____ .

       d.   Other sources of information, such as _____ results, colleagues, workshops, and books.

B.   The Effectiveness of Treatment, 107

    1.   One of the problems with answering the question, "Is treatment 'X' successful?" is that researchers and clinicians can define "successful" in many different ways. What is one other problem with answering this question?

_____

_____

    2.   According to reviews of hundreds of studies on the effectiveness of therapy, the average person who receives therapy is better off than _____ percent of those who do not receive treatment.

    3.   The _____ _____ describes the false belief that all therapies are the same despite differences in therapists' theoretical orientation, personality, etc.

    4.   List some of the "common therapeutic strategies" that seem to characterize all effective therapies.

_____

_____

5. Complete the following table by identifying the most effective treatment approach(es) for the listed psychological problems/disorders.

Disorder	Effective Treatment Approach(es)
Schizophrenia	
Phobic disorders	

PsychWatch: Dark Sites, 108

1. It has been reported that there are currently more than _____ pro-anorexia Internet sites.

2. Identify an argument that has been made in favor of allowing pro-suicide Web sites to exist unimpeded.

_____

_____

_____

IV. Putting It Together: Assessment and Diagnosis at a Crossroads, 109–110

1. During the 1960s and 1970s, many therapists lost confidence in the degree to which assessment and diagnosis could benefit clinical practice. More recently, however, assessment and diagnosis are again viewed by therapists as being an integral part of their clinical work. List three reasons for this shift.

a. _____

b. _____

c. _____

MULTIPLE CHOICE

1. In order to understand a client's problems, a clinician uses a process that includes
   a. behavioral analysis and functional analysis.
   b. projective testing and interviewing.
   c. structured observation and classification.
   d. assessment and diagnosis.

2. Jillian is a participant in a study to evaluate a new measure of depression. She takes the depression test once, waits one month, then takes the test again. Her scores are almost identical. If other participants also have near identical scores, the test likely has good
   a. test-retest reliability.
   b. interrater reliability.
   c. predictive validity.
   d. concurrent validity.

3. If a test accurately measures what it claims to measure, that test is said to have
   a. concurrence.
   b. reliability.
   c. validity.
   d. standardization.

4. A clinician who looks for information concerning assumptions, interpretations, and coping skills during an interview probably takes the _____ approach.
   a. biological
   b. behavioral
   c. cognitive
   d. humanistic

5. Current users of the Rorschach now pay attention mostly to the
   a. style of the response.
   b. affect of the responder.
   c. thematic content of the response.
   d. symbolic meaning of the response.

6. Simone is afraid of people and not at all assertive. Which MMPI-2 scale would she most likely score high on?
   a. schizophrenia
   b. psychasthenia
   c. social introversion
   d. psychopathic deviate

7. The PET scan makes a picture of the brain
   a. using X-rays that are projected at several different angles.
   b. that reflects the degree of activity of the various areas scanned.
   c. that reflects the magnetic properties of the atoms in the cells scanned.
   d. using a recording of the electrical impulses produced by the neurons in the brain.

8. One of the drawbacks of clinical observation is that the very presence of an observer might influence the behavior of the subject being observed. This is called
   a. reactivity.
   b. observer bias.
   c. observer drift.
   d. external validity.

9. Who developed the first influential classification system for abnormal behavior?
   a. Sigmund Freud
   b. Emil Kraepelin
   c. the American Psychiatric Association
   d. the American Psychological Association

10. What does Axis V include?
    a. a global assessment of functioning
    b. any relevant general medical condition
    c. any relevant psychosocial or environmental problem
    d. vivid clinical syndromes that typically cause significant impairment

5 ANXIETY DISORDERS

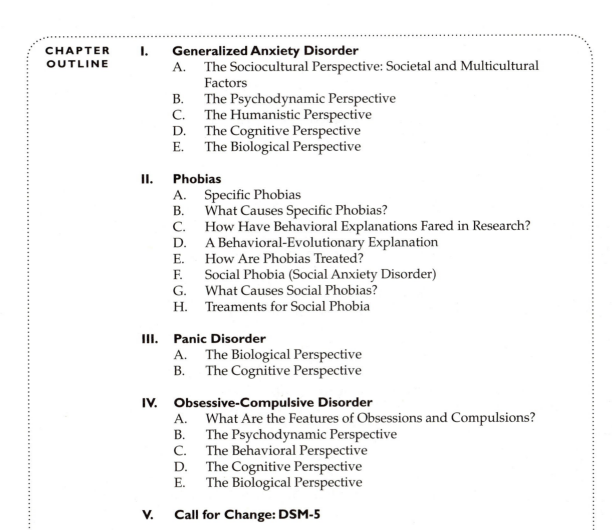

I.   Generalized Anxiety Disorder, 114–126

1.   People with generalized anxiety disorders are often described as having _____ anxiety because they experience worries about so many things in their lives.

2.   In order to qualify for a diagnosis of generalized anxiety disorder, individuals must experience anxiety about numerous activities, situations, or events, and they must have symptoms that are present for at least how long?

    _____

3.   List four of the symptoms of generalized anxiety disorder.

    a. _____

    b. _____

    c. _____

    d. _____

4.   Generalized anxiety disorder usually emerges in _____ or _____ , and _____ times as many women as men are diagnosed with this disorder.

A.   The Sociocultural Perspective: Societal and Multicultural Factors, 115

1.   Sociocultural theorists suggest that people who are confronted with societal situations that are truly _____ are more likely to develop generalized anxiety disorder.

2.   Several important studies suggest generalized anxiety disorder is more prevalent among individuals who live in poverty or face other societal pressures. Sociocultural factors, however, do not completely explain GAD. Why not?

    _____

    _____

3.   Hispanics in both the United States and Latin America suffer from _____ , a culture-bound disorder that bears great similarity to generalized anxiety disorder.

Table 5-2: Eye on Culture: Anxiety Disorders, 115

1.   Compared to the general population, people who earn low incomes suffer a _____ rate of generalized anxiety disorders, specific phobias, social phobias, obsessive-compulsive disorders, and panic disorders.

2.   Compared to the rate in the total population, women suffer the disorders listed in question 1 at a higher rate, with the exception of _____ , which they suffer at the same rate as the total population.

3.   Hispanic Americans suffer all of the disorders listed in question 1 at the same rate as the total population, with the exception of _____ , which they suffer at a higher rate.

B.   The Psychodynamic Perspective, 116

1.   Define the three kinds of anxiety delineated by Freud.

    a. Realistic anxiety: _____

    _____

     b. Neurotic anxiety: _____

_____

     c. Moral anxiety: _____

_____

2.   Freud suggested that people can develop generalized anxiety disorder when their defense mechanisms break down. The textbook lists two ways that this breakdown can occur and result in generalized anxiety disorder; describe them.

_____

_____

3.   The textbook cites two lines of research that appear to support the psychodynamic explanation of generalized anxiety disorder. Briefly state the findings of studies on each of them.

     a. Excessive use of defense mechanisms: _____

_____

     b. Extreme punishment for id impulses: _____

_____

4.   List a major criticism of research on psychodynamic explanations of generalized anxiety disorder.

_____

_____

5.   Describe the goals of the following two types of psychodynamic therapists in the treatment of generalized anxiety disorder.

     a. Freudian therapists: _____

_____

     b. Object relations therapists: _____

_____

C. The Humanistic Perspective, 117

1.   According to Carl Rogers, people can develop generalized anxiety disorder when, as children, they

_____

_____

_____

_____

2.   Rogers's treatment approach is called _____-_____ therapy.

3.   Humanistic therapists believe that if they provide an atmosphere of genuine acceptance and caring, clients will experience relief from their anxiety or other symptoms of psychological distress. How would providing this type of atmosphere result in client change?

_____

_____

D. The Cognitive Perspective, 118

1.   Initially, cognitive theorists believed that generalized anxiety disorders are caused by _____

_____ .

2.   The letters a–e represent a jumbled set of steps in the process of how a person could develop generalized anxiety disorder according to the work of cognitive theorist **Albert Ellis.** Demonstrate that you understand this process by numbering the steps 1–5 in the order that fits Ellis's explanation.

_____ a. Maladaptive assumptions are applied to more and more life situations.

_____ b. A stressful event such as an exam or a date occurs.

_____ c. A person holds a maladaptive assumption, such as "It is catastrophic when things are not the way one would very much like them to be."

_____ d. The person develops generalized anxiety disorder.

_____ e. The event is interpreted as highly dangerous and threatening, leading a person to overreact and experience fear.

3.   Identify and briefly describe the three "new-wave cognitive explanations" of generalized anxiety disorder.

a. _____

_____

_____

b. _____

_____

_____

c. _____

_____

_____

4.   Albert Ellis's **rational-emotive therapy** consists of three important components. Complete the list.

a. The therapist points out the client's irrational assumptions.

b. _____

c. _____

5.   In _____-_____ cognitive therapy, therapists help clients to become aware of their troubling thoughts as they occur and to accept them as mere events of the mind.

E. The Biological Perspective, 122

1.   Biological theorists believe that **family pedigree studies** will shed light on the question of whether a biological predisposition toward generalized anxiety disorder (GAD) might be inherited. In this exercise, (a) describe this research method and (b) describe a research finding that supports the notion that GAD might be heritable.

a. _____

_____

_____

b. _____

_____

_____

2. Researchers have focused on the role of **gamma-aminobutyric acid** (GABA) and GABA receptors in fear reactions. Study the following "scenario" relating to normal fear reactions. (This diagram for study only).

Threatening stimulus perceived

↓

Key neurons throughout the brain
fire rapidly creating . . .

↓

. . . a state of hyperexcitement in the
brain and body

↓

Person experiences
fear and anxiety ——————————————→ Feedback system is triggered

Excitement is thereby reduced
and fear and anxiety subside

↑

GABA binds to GABA receptors on receiving
neurons and induces those neurons to stop firing

↑

GABA-producing neurons throughout
the brain release GABA

↑

Fear Reaction ——————————————→ **Feedback System**

---

3. Researchers believe that people with generalized anxiety disorders may have a problem in their anxiety feedback system. List two possible problems that researchers have speculated may be causing this problem.

a. _____

b. _____

4. Several discoveries have complicated the possibly overly simplistic explanation that GABA plays the central role in generalized anxiety disorders. Complete the following list of these complicating factors.

a. GABA is one of several chemicals that can bind to _____ receptors.

b. No _____ relationship has been established. In other words, it is possible that chronic anxiety eventually leads to poor _____ _____, rather than the other way around.

5. Recent research has indicated that the brain circuit that produces anxiety reactions includes the _____ _____, the _____ _____ _____, and the _____. According to recent studies, it often functions improperly in people with generalized anxiety disorder.

6. Until the 1950s, _____ drugs were the primary drug treatment for anxiety disorders. What were some of the problems associated with these drugs?

_____

_____

7. Benzodiazepines are effective on anxiety disorders because the receptor sites that receive them also receive _____ , a neurotransmitter that _____ neuron firing. What happens when benzodiazepines bind to these receptor sites?

_____

8. Complete the following statements that address the potential risk of benzodiazepine use.

    a. When anxious people stopped taking the drugs, the anxiety returned.

    b. People who take them in large doses over a long period of time can become _____ on them and can experience many undesired side effects, such as drowsiness, memory loss, and depression.

    c. Although they are not toxic by themselves, they seem to _____ the effects of other substances, such as alcohol.

9. Name two kinds of drugs that in recent decades have been found to help people with generalized anxiety disorder.

    a. _____

    b. _____

10. The basic premise of **relaxation training** is that _____ relaxation will eventually lead to _____ relaxation, especially after continued practice.

11. In biofeedback training, the _____ (EMG) device provides visual and/or auditory feedback that informs the client when his or her _____ are more or less tense.

12. The goal of biofeedback training is for people to become skilled at voluntarily _____ muscle tension through a process of trial and error.

13. **Biofeedback** techniques seem to be more helpful in the treatment of _____ problems than psychological problems.

II. Phobias, 126–135

1. A **phobia** is defined as a persistent and _____ fear of a particular _____, _____, or _____ .

2. Complete the following statements. They relate to the characteristics that, according to the DSM-IV-TR, differentiate normal fears from phobic fears.

    a. Fear experienced in a phobic disorder is more intense and _____.

    b. The phobic person's desire to _____ the object or situation is more compelling.

    c. People with phobias experience such distress that their fears often interfere dramatically with their personal, social, or occupational functioning.

A. Specific Phobias, 126

1. The three categories of phobias distinguished by the DSM-IV-TR are agoraphobia, social phobias, and specific phobias. Complete the table below by describing characteristics of each of these disorders, as discussed throughout the "Phobias" section of this chapter.

Phobias	Characteristics
Agoraphobia	
Social phobia	
Specific phobia	

3.   In several studies, African American and Asian American participants have scored _____ on surveys of social anxiety and other social concerns.

B.   What Causes Specific Phobias?, 127

I.   Behavioral Explanations: How Are Fears Learned?, 127

1.   One behavioral explanation of phobias is that fear is acquired through _____ conditioning.

Read the following case study and answer the questions pertaining to it.

Case Study

It was 1:00 AM and Malcolm was driving home to North Dakota for his sister's wedding. It was snowing heavily, and the roads were icy; he was driving as fast as he safely could, but the trip had already taken two hours longer than it normally would. As Malcolm was fiddling with the radio dial, he looked up to see a huge semitrailer swerving dangerously in front of him. Malcolm pumped his brakes, but his car began to spin toward the truck, which was now facing him head-on. Malcolm leaned on the steering wheel and swerved into the ditch. His small car crashed into a fence by the ditch, but fortunately he suffered no physical injuries. Malcolm's heart was pounding, and he had never been so frightened in his life. Since his near-fatal accident, Malcolm cannot travel in a car. Simply contemplating a short drive fills him with panic and dread. In short, Malcolm has developed a phobia.

2. Using the case study and adhering to the behavioral explanation, complete this diagram.

_____	→	fear response
Unconditioned stimulus (US)		**Unconditioned response (UR)**
_____	→	_____
Conditioned stimulus (CS)		**Conditioned response (CR)**

3. Why would one fear-provoking experience (such as Malcolm's accident) develop into a long-term phobia?

    _____

    _____

4. Behaviorists posit that phobias could develop into a generalized anxiety disorder through

    _____ _____ .

5. Describe how Malcolm's phobia specifically could develop into a generalized anxiety disorder through the process identified in item 4.

    _____

    _____

    _____

C. How Have Behavioral Explanations Fared in Research?, 128

1. Describe the findings of the "Little Albert" experiment.

    _____

    _____

2. Experiments have also produced evidence that fear can be acquired through **modeling.** Describe the (a) method and (b) findings of the research in this area by Bandura and Rosenthal in 1966.

    a. _____

        _____

    b. _____

        _____

3. Findings from several studies (particularly studies that have attempted to replicate previous findings) have failed to support the behavioral view of specific phobias. What is the conclusion that the textbook draws in light of this failure?

    _____

    _____

    _____

D. A Behavioral-Evolutionary Explanation, 130

1. "_____" is the idea that human beings, as a species, are predisposed to develop some fears (e.g., of snakes, lightning, heights) rather than others (e.g., of trees, rabbits, candy).

2. The textbook describes a possible explanation of why humans might be predisposed to certain fears. Identify this theory, and describe its underlying arguments.

_____

_____

3. The textbook describes two possible explanations of why humans might be predisposed to certain fears. Briefly, describe the underlying arguments of each.

   a. Evolutionary predisposition: _____

   _____

   b. Environmental predisposition: _____

   _____

E. **How Are Phobias Treated?, 130**

  1. **Treatments for Specific Phobias, 130**

    1. _____ therapy appears to be the most effective form of treatment for specific phobias.

    2. **Systematic desensitization, flooding** and **modeling** are known collectively as _____ treatments because clients are _____ to the object or situation they dread.

    3. Provide a description of each of the three phases of **systematic desensitization**

      a. Relaxation training: _____

      _____

      b. Construction of fear hierarchy: _____

      _____

      c. Graded pairings: _____

      _____

    4. Behavioral therapists who use **flooding** techniques believe that when clients with specific phobias are repeatedly _____ to feared stimuli, they will see that the stimuli are quite _____ .

    5. Unlike desensitization strategies, flooding procedures do not use _____ training or a _____ approach to confronting a feared object or situation.

    6. In **modeling** procedures, the _____ confronts the feared object or situation while the _____ watches.

    7. Actual exposure to the feared object or event (also known as _____ desensitization) is more effective than imaginal or observational exposure (also known as _____ desensitization).

    8. A growing number of therapists are using _____ _____ , which simulates real-world objects and situations, as an exposure tool for treating specific phobias.

F. **Social Phobia (Social Anxiety Disorder), 132**

    1. In several studies, African American and Asian American participants have scored _____ on surveys of social anxiety and other social concerns.

2. Poor people are _____ percent _____ likely compared with wealthier people to experience social phobia.

3. Social phobia may be _____ , such as a fear of talking in public, or _____ such as a general fear of not functioning well in front of others.

G. What Causes Social Phobias?, 133

1. The leading explanation for social phobia has been proposed by researchers from the _____ theoretical orientation.

2. List some of the beliefs and expectations that such researchers believe people with social phobia hold—beliefs and expectations that consistently work against them:

   a. _____

   b. _____

   c. _____

   d. _____

   e. _____

   f. _____

3. This explanation for social phobia suggests that those with social phobia repeatedly perform _____ and _____ behaviors to prevent or reduce anticipated social disasters. Name one example of each behavior.

   _____

4. How does social phobia continue to affect the thinking of those who suffer from it even after a social event has ended?

   _____

5. Although research findings have supported the notion that people with social phobias indeed hold the beliefs, expectations, and feelings discussed in items 1—4, why do researchers still disagree about the causes of social phobia?

   _____

H. Treatments for Social Phobia, 133

1. People with social phobia have incapacitating social fears. What is the second distinct component of social phobia?

   _____

a. How Can Social Fears Be Reduced?, 133

1. Unlike specific phobias, social phobia appears to respond to _____ medications.

2. Gradual _____ therapy, often coupled with homework assignments, helps people with social phobia learn to face the situations they dread most.

3. What makes group therapy an ideal setting for exposure-based treatment of social phobias?

   _____

   _____

4. Cognitive approaches such as Ellis's _____ - _____ therapy help clients challenge and confront underlying assumptions and beliefs that can lead to social anxiety.

b. *How Can Social Skills Be Improved?, 135*

1. Complete the following flowchart that depicts basic elements of social skills training.

Therapists	Clients	Therapists provide
_____	_____	_____
appropriate social behavior	social behaviors with the therapist or other clients	to clients regarding their "performance"

III. Panic Disorder, 135–140

1. Panic attacks usually reach a peak within _____ minutes.

2. List some symptoms of panic attacks.

_____

_____

3. People diagnosed with a panic disorder experience panic attacks without apparent _____ , recurrently, and _____ .

4. The DSM-IV-TR states that a diagnosis of panic disorder is warranted if, after having at least one unexpected panic attack, the person spends one month or more

a. worrying persistently about _____ ,

b. worrying about the _____ ,

c. and/or planning his or her _____ .

5. How are panic disorder and **agoraphobia** linked together?

_____

_____

_____

A. The Biological Perspective, 136

1. Unexpectedly, it was found that people with panic disorders seem to respond most favorably to antidepressant drugs, rather than to _____ drugs.

2. There are a large number of neurons that utilize **norepinephrine** in the area of the brain known as the _____ _____ . When this area is electrically stimulated in monkeys, the monkey displays a paniclike reaction.

3. Name four brain areas included in the brain circuit that produce panic reactions.

a. _____

b. _____

c. _____

d. _____

4. Some people may have an inherited biological predisposition to develop panic disorder. Describe one research finding that supports this hypothesis.

_____

_____

5. _____ percent of patients who experience panic attacks improve somewhat with drug treatment.

6. Antidepressant drugs and alprazolam are also helpful in treating panic disorder with

_____.

PsychWatch: Panic: Everyone Is Vulnerable, 137

1. After reading the news account in this section, reflect on a time in your life when you might have experienced a sensation of panic. Describe how you felt and how you reacted.

_____

_____

B. The Cognitive Perspective, 139

Read the following case study of Dave, a 34-year-old male suffering from panic attacks.

Case Study

Dave woke up early one April morning feeling good. While eating his usual breakfast he noticed in the newspaper that a run was being held on Memorial Day to raise money for a charity. Although he hadn't run much in two years, he decided that he would participate in the event and that he would begin training for it that very morning. Dave felt really winded after three miles, but pushed himself to run two more. When he got home, he was sweating profusely, his heart was pounding, and his legs felt shaky and slightly numb. Fearing that he was having a heart attack, Dave began to hyperventilate and had a panic attack that lasted for approximately 20 minutes. Dave went to his doctor and was assured that his heart was very healthy. Two weeks later, he went to a new restaurant with a friend. They both ordered extra spicy dinners. Midway through the meal, Dave and his friend both complained of stomach pain and nausea. Dave became increasingly upset and told his friend that he had to leave right away because he was certain a panic attack was imminent.

---

1. Briefly describe how Dave's escalating anxiety and panic can be explained by the cognitive perspective of panic disorders.

_____

_____

_____

2. What are some of the factors that may be related to why some people are more prone to misinterpret bodily sensations than others?

_____

_____

3. What is **anxiety sensitivity**, and how it is related to panic disorders?

_____

_____

_____

4. Cognitive therapists teach clients about the nature of panic attacks, the actual causes of their bodily sensations, and their tendency to _____ them.

5. In this exercise, (a) define the biological challenge procedure, and (b) state the purpose of such procedures in the context of therapy.

    a. _____

    _____

    b. _____

    _____

6. A number of recent studies have shown that _____ percent of subjects with panic disorders significantly improved after receiving cognitive therapy (compared to only 13 percent of control subjects who improved).

7. How did cognitive therapy fare in research comparing it to drug therapies as a treatment for panic disorders?

_____

IV. Obsessive-Compulsive Disorder, 140–148

1. Complete the following list of DSM-IV-TR diagnostic criteria for **obsessive-compulsive disorder.** The diagnosis is appropriate when a person's obsessions and compulsions:

    a. feel excessive, _____ ;

    b. cause significant _____ ;

    c. are very _____ ; or interfere with daily functions.

A. What Are the Features of Obsessions and Compulsions?, 141

1. Obsessions are not the same as excessive worries about real problems. They are thoughts that feel both intrusive and _____.

2. What may happen when people try to resist their obsessions?

_____

Match the numbers 3–7, which list terms clinicians use to distinguish various kinds of obsessions, with the appropriate option from the list a–e, which are examples of these obsessions.

3. _____ obsessive wishes

4. _____ obsessive impulses

5. _____ obsessive images

6. _____ obsessive ideas

7. _____ obsessive doubts

    Examples:

    a. A student sees himself starting an arson fire in his dormitory.

b. A man dwells on the notion that he should have stayed in the Navy in 1954.

c. A woman incessantly worries that the mosquitoes in her backyard will give her malaria.

d. A girl wishes her older sister would have a car accident.

e. A man worries that one day he will purposely spill hot coffee onto his co-worker's lap.

8. Complete the following table by listing and giving examples of the types of compulsive rituals.

Type	Example
cleaning compulsion	washing hands 30 or 40 times a day

9. Most people with an obsessive-compulsive disorder experience _____ obsessions and compulsions.

10. What is perhaps the greatest fear of people with obsessive-compulsive disorder? Is this fear usually warranted?

_____

_____

_____

MediaSpeak: Dining Out: The Obsessive-Compulsive Experience, 142

1. In the first-person account in this section, Jeff Bell describes his experience of obsessive-compulsive disorder, and the success he has experienced after receiving exposure and response prevention therapy. Describe how you imagine the course of Bell's therapy.

_____

_____

B. The Psychodynamic Perspective, 143

1. According to psychodynamic theorists, three ego defense mechanisms are commonly used by people with obsessive-compulsive disorder. Complete the table below by first defining each ego defense mechanism, then giving an example of each relevant to someone with obsessive-compulsive disorder.

Mechanism	Definition	Example
Isolation		
Undoing		
Reaction formation		

Freud explained obsessive-compulsive disorders within the framework of his theory of psychosexual development. Study this diagram of his conceptualization.

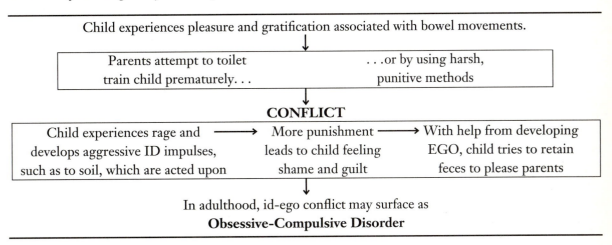

Child experiences pleasure and gratification associated with bowel movements.
↓

| Parents attempt to toilet train child prematurely. . . | . . .or by using harsh, punitive methods |

↓
CONFLICT

| Child experiences rage and develops aggressive ID impulses, such as to soil, which are acted upon | → | More punishment leads to child feeling shame and guilt | → | With help from developing EGO, child tries to retain feces to please parents |

↓
In adulthood, id-ego conflict may surface as
Obsessive-Compulsive Disorder

2. In Freud's conceptualization, depicted above, the child's aggressive impulses will now be countered by the child's strong desire to _____ them.

C. The Behavioral Perspective, 144

1. Give a brief explanation of the behavioral perspective of obsessive-compulsive disorders.

_____

_____

_____

2. In the treatment of obsessive-compulsive disorder, **exposure and response prevention** (or **exposure and ritual prevention**) procedures ask clients to confront dreaded objects or situations that would normally elicit anxiety, _____ fears, and _____ behaviors. Clients are then prevented from performing these behaviors.

Read the following case study and complete the exercise that follows.

Case Study

Patricia is obsessed with counting rituals, and specifically with the number 3. Although she is not distressed when, for example, her dishes sit unwashed on the counter, Patricia does feel compelled to order them in groups of three—three plates in a stack, three glasses lined in a row, etc. Patricia answers the telephone only after the third ring, and must buy three of any item on her grocery list. She also checks compulsively, always in increments of three. For example, she is not satisfied that her front door is locked until she turns the key three times, counting "one-two-three" aloud.

3. Complete this exercise by writing three more response prevention homework assignments for Patricia in addition to the one already given.

    a. buy only one of each item on the grocery list

    b. _____

    c. _____

    d. _____

4. Between _____ and _____ percent of obsessive-compulsive clients treated with exposure and response prevention show significant improvement.

5. As many as 25 percent of people with obsessive-compulsive disorder fail to improve at all with exposure and response prevention. What is another limitation of this technique?

    _____

    _____

D. The Cognitive Perspective, 145

1. The cognitive view of obsessive-compulsive disorder begins with the basic premise that everyone has repetitive, unwanted, unpleasant, and intrusive thoughts. List two examples of these thoughts from the textbook.

    _____

    _____

2. Compared with most people, how do those with obsessive-compulsive disorder interpret their intrusive, unwanted thoughts?

    _____

    _____

3. "Neutralizing" is when a person seeks to eliminate unwanted, intrusive thoughts by thinking or behaving in a way meant to put matters "right" internally. Why is this central to the cognitive explanation of obsessive-compulsive disorders?

    _____

    _____

4. Researchers have found that people with obsessive-compulsive disorder have certain characteristics that could be related to why they find normal intrusive thoughts so disturbing. Complete the list of these characteristics:

    People with OCD

    a. seem to be more _____ than others,

    b. have unusually high standards of _____ and _____ ,

c. believe that their negative thoughts can _____ themselves or others, and must take _____ for eliminating the "danger" their thoughts pose, and

d. tend to believe that they should have perfect _____ over all thoughts and behaviors.

5. What is the course of treatment that cognitive therapists employ in the treatment of obsessive-compulsive disorder?

_____

_____

_____

6. Briefly describe the course of treatment that a client with obsessive-compulsive disorder would undergo with a therapist who practices a combination of cognitive and behavioral therapy, which research suggests is often more effective than either cognitive or behavioral therapy alone.

_____

_____

_____

_____

_____

_____

_____

_____

E.   The Biological Perspective, 146

1. Two sets of findings support the notion that biological factors play a role in obsessive-compulsive disorders. Complete the statements related to them.

a. Obsessive-compulsive symptoms are reduced with the _____ drugs clomipramine and fluoxetine, which seem to increase _____ activity in the brain. The implication of this finding is that obsessive-compulsive disorder is associated with _____ _____ activity.

b. Two areas of the brain—the orbitofrontal cortex and the caudate nuclei—may be functioning abnormally. These parts of the brain control the conversions of _____ input into thoughts and _____ .

Study the following diagram.

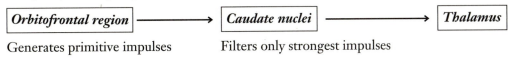

| **Orbitofrontal region** | ⟶ | **Caudate nuclei** | ⟶ | **Thalamus** |

Generates primitive impulses   Filters only strongest impulses

c. List two of the primitive impulses that the orbitofrontal region generates.

_____

d. Researchers believe that the orbitofrontal region or the caudate nuclei may be functioning too _____ , leading to constant "breakthrough" of distressing thoughts and behavior.

2.   Research has found that antidepressant drugs such as _____ help to raise _____ activity in the brain, thus bringing improvement in 50 to 80 percent of those who suffer from obsessive-compulsive disorder.

V. Call for Change, DSM-5, 148

1.   The DSM-5 task force, in its 2011 draft of the DSM-5, recommended a number of significant changes that could have a major impact on the study and classifications of anxiety disorders. Identify four of the significant changes that would occur if the final version of the DSM-5, scheduled for publication in 2013, were to adopt all of these recommendations. Briefly explain the task force's reasons for recommending these changes.

a. _____

_____

b. _____

_____

c. _____

_____

d. _____

_____

VI. Putting It Together: Diathesis-Stress in Action, 149

1.   Increasingly, clinicians and researchers are examining anxiety disorders within the framework of the diathesis-stress model. After reading through this section, create a plausible "scenario" that depicts how an individual might develop GAD. (Be sure to describe both diathesis and stress!)

_____

_____

_____

_____

_____

_____

_____

_____

MULTIPLE CHOICE

1. The most common mental disorders in the United States are the
   a. anxiety disorders.
   b. conversion disorders.
   c. personality disorders.
   d. dissociative disorders.

2. The Freudian view is that generalized anxiety disorder appears when a person is overwhelmed by
   a. realistic anxiety.
   b. neurotic anxiety.
   c. disintegration anxiety.
   d. an ego defense mechanism.

3. Anxiety disorders develop as a consequence of irrational or maladaptive assumptions or automatic thoughts that influence a person's understanding of life events. This illustrates which perspective?
   a. cognitive
   b. existential
   c. behavioral
   d. psychodynamic

4. The benzodiazepines seem to exert their anti-anxiety effect by
   a. facilitating GABA at receptor sites.
   b. blocking serotonin at receptor sites.
   c. blocking acetylcholine at receptor sites.
   d. facilitating norepinephrine at receptor sites.

5. TJ is terrified of going into crowded stores or anywhere else, unless she is accompanied by her sister. A diagnostician would probably diagnose her behavior as
   a. agoraphobia.
   b. a social phobia.
   c. a general phobia.
   d. generalized anxiety disorder.

6. According to the behavioral view, phobias may develop when a person learns a fear response to a specific object by the process of
   a. repression.
   b. reinforcement.
   c. operant conditioning.
   d. classical conditioning.

7. The most effective treatment of specific phobias seems to be
   a. cognitive therapy.
   b. biological therapy.
   c. behavioral therapy.
   d. psychodynamic therapy.

8. Which of the following is not true of panic disorder?
   a. The diagnosis is half as common in men as in women.
   b. A panic attack always has a specific cause.
   c. The disorder develops between late adolescence and the mid-30s for most sufferers.
   d. In any given year, as many as 2.7 percent of all people suffer from it.

9. The apparent mechanism of action of the drugs useful in treating panic attacks is their ability to
   a. block norepinephrine.
   b. block the action of serotonin.
   c. mimic the action of serotonin.
   d. restore the activity of norepinephrine.

10. Max's physician had him breathe deeply and often until he was lightheaded. Max became very anxious. This procedure describes
    a. meditation.
    b. anxiety sensitivity.
    c. systematic desensitization.
    d. a biological challenge test.

11. Most studies on obsessions and compulsions among people with obsessive-compulsive disorder indicate that
    a. obsessions and compulsions generally occur together.

b.   there is no relation between obsessions and compulsions.

c.   obsessions generally occur in the absence of compulsions.

d.   compulsions generally occur in the absence of obsessions.

12.   Psychodynamic theorists believe that the ego defense mechanisms of isolation, undoing, and reaction formation are particularly common in people with

a.   mood disorders.

b.   personality disorders.

c.   dissociative disorders.

d.   obsessive-compulsive disorders.

13.   According to the cognitive explanation of obsessive-compulsive disorder, the elimination or avoidance of repulsive and stressful thoughts is known as

a.   neutralizing.

b.   ego defense reactions.

c.   covert-response prevention.

d.   constructing a strict code of acceptability.

CHAPTER

6   STRESS DISORDERS

REVIEW EXERCISES

I.   Chapter Introduction and Stress and Arousal: The Fight-or-Flight Response, 153–156

1. Whenever we are confronted with situations that require us to change in some way, we experience a state of threat known as **stress.** List and briefly define the two components of a state of stress:

    a. _____ , _____

    b. _____ , _____

2. Complete the following statements, which are paraphrased from the textbook:

    a. The fear response is initiated by the brain structure called the _____ .

    b. The hypothalamus activates the _____ _____ _____ (ANS), which connects the _____ _____ _____ (the brain and the spinal cord) to all the other organs of the body.

    c. After a situation is perceived as dangerous, the _____ nervous system increases the heart rate and produces other fear responses; when the danger has passed, the _____ nervous system returns body processes to normal.

    d. The hypothalamus also stimulates the _____ gland to release adrenocorticotropic hormone (ACTH), which in turn signals the _____ glands to release the stress hormones _____.

3.   Define (a) trait anxiety and (b) state anxiety.

    a. _____

        _____

    b. _____

        _____

II. The Psychological Stress Disorders: Acute and Posttraumatic Stress Disorders, 157–169

1.   According to the DSM-IV-TR, acute stress disorders and posttraumatic stress disorders differ primarily in onset and duration. Complete the following table to fit the DSM-IV-TR.

	Acute Stress Disorders	**Posttraumatic Stress Disorders**
Onset	Symptoms begin within _____ weeks of the traumatic effect.	Symptoms begin anywhere from shortly after to many _____ after the event.
Duration	Symptoms last from 2 to _____ days.	Symptoms have continued for _____ days or more.

Read the following case study and answer the questions pertaining to it.

Case Study

Sarah is a 23-year-old female who works as a pediatric nurse. At 3 A.M. one night, Sarah finished her shift and walked to her car in the parking garage adjacent to the hospital. As Sarah approached her car, she heard footsteps behind her. Before she was able to react, she was thrown down and pinned to the cement floor by a man with a stocking mask over his face. Brandishing a knife, the attacker threatened to kill Sarah if she made any noise or attempted to fight or run. She was brutally raped and knocked unconscious. When she regained consciousness several minutes later, the perpetrator had fled the scene. Sarah drove home in a state of shock and managed to call a close friend, who immediately drove her to the emergency room.

---

2.   Four types of symptoms Sarah might manifest if she developed a stress disorder are listed below as a–d. In the spaces provided list two examples of each symptom specific to Sarah's case. (Symptom "a" is provided.)

a. Reexperiencing the traumatic event:
   Sarah has nightmares in which she "relives" the rape
   Sarah often imagines that she hears the footsteps of her attacker when she goes outside

b. Avoidance:

_____

_____

c. Reduced responsiveness (also called psychic numbing or emotional anesthesia):

_____

_____

d. Increased anxiety, arousal, and guilt:

_____

_____

A. **What Triggers a Psychological Stress Disorder?, 158**

   I. **Combat and Stress Disorders, 158**

   1. This exercise refers to the syndrome involving symptoms of anxiety and depression in soldiers during combat.

      a. At the time of the American Civil War, it was thought that the syndrome was caused by extended absence from home. It was called nostalgia.

      b. During World War I, the syndrome was called _____. Clinicians thought its cause was minute brain hemorrhages or concussions triggered by artillery explosions.

      c. During World War II and the Korean War, the syndrome was called _____

      _____.

   2. After the Vietnam War, approximately _____ percent of all soldiers suffered a stress disorder, and _____ percent still experience posttraumatic symptoms such as flashbacks and nightmares.

   3. According to the RAND Corporation's 2008 assessment of the psychological needs of military service members, nearly _____ percent of the Americans deployed to the wars in Iraq and Afghanistan have reported symptoms of posttraumatic stress disorder.

   2. **Disasters and Stress Disorders, 159**

   1. Natural disasters and serious accidents actually account for more stress disorders than combat. Why?

   _____

   _____

   2. List two natural and/or accidental disasters that might lead to a stress disorder.

      a. _____

      b. _____

   3. **Victimization and Stress Disorders, 160**

   1. Define *rape.*

   _____

   _____

   _____

2. Complete the following statements related to rape and rape victims:

   a. _____ percent of victims are under age 11, _____ percent are between age 11 and 17, and _____ percent are between age 18 and 29.

   b. Approximately 70 percent of rape victims are assaulted by _____ or _____, *not* strangers.

   c. Close to 95 percent of rape victims, when they were examined an average of 12 days after the assault, qualified for a diagnosis of _____.

3. List some of the psychological aftereffects of rape that can linger for months and years after the assault.

   _____

   _____

   _____

4. Surveys estimate that in the days immediately following September 11, 2001, 90 percent of people living in the United States experienced at least some level of increased stress; five months later, 25 percent continued to experience significant symptoms.

   a. How were you, your family, your friends, and/or your community affected by the attacks?

   _____

   _____

   _____

   _____

   b. What kinds of acute or posttraumatic stress symptoms did you see or hear about in the weeks and months after the attacks?

   _____

   _____

   _____

   _____

5. Please give examples of each of the four major types of torture people across the world are subjected to.

   a. Physical torture _____

   b. Psychological torture _____

   c. Sexual torture _____

   d. Torture through deprivation _____

B. Why Do People Develop a Psychological Stress Disorder?, 162

1. Researchers have focused on five sets of factors in their attempts to answer the question "Why do some people develop stress disorders following a traumatic event while others do not?" Describe these factors in the following table.

Factor	Description/Explanation
a. Biological/genetic factors:	
b. Personality:	
c. Childhood experiences:	
d. Social support:	
e. Multicultural factors:	
f. Severity of trauma:	

2. List two possible reasons why Hispanic Americans may be more vulnerable to posttraumatic stress disorder than other cultural groups.

    _____

    _____

C. **How Do Clinicians Treat the Psychological Stress Disorders?, 165**

1. List the three common goals of all treatment programs for trauma survivors. They all seek to help the survivor:

    a. _____

    b. _____

    c. _____

1. **Treatment for Combat Veterans, 165**

1. List the symptoms that were successfully minimized in Vietnam veterans by the following treatments: (a) antianxiety drugs, (b) antidepressant drugs, and (c) flooding and desensitization.

    a. _____

    b. _____

    c. _____

2. Describe **eye movement desensitization and reprocessing** (EMDR), a new treatment for stress disorders.

    _____

    _____

    _____

3. Most clinicians believe that trauma survivors cannot fully recover until they gain _____ into the traumatic experience itself and the continuing _____ of those experiences on their lives.

4. "_____ groups" provide a safe place for trauma survivors to share experiences and feelings, and to give support to other group members.

5.   Identify some of the painful feelings expressed by Vietnam War veterans in the groups mentioned in Exercise 4 and other forms of PTSD therapy.

_____

_____

2.   Psychological Debriefing, 168

1.   Many clinicians believe that people who are traumatized by disasters, victimization, or accidents will benefit greatly from immediate community mental health interventions. The leading approach of this sort is _____ debriefing, or _____ _____ stress debriefing.

2.   Why is this form of crisis intervention commonly applied to victims who have not manifested any symptoms of stress reactions or trauma? _____

3.   Briefly describe a typical group session of the intervention approach identified in question 1 above.

_____

_____

3.   Does Psychological Debriefing Work?, 168

1.   Some studies have suggested that trauma victims who undergo rapid psychological debriefing may experience the same or even higher rates of posttraumatic stress disorder as trauma victims who do not undergo psychological debriefing. Identify two reasons suggested by clinicians why this might be so.

a.   _____

b.   _____

III.   The Physical Stress Disorders: Psychophysiological Disorders, 169–184

Physicians and psychologists have long recognized that some physical conditions result from an interaction of physical and psychological/behavioral factors. These disorders, unlike the somatoform disorders, are characterized by actual medical conditions.

In the textbook and workbook, the term "psychophysiological disorders" is used to indicate those medical conditions that are significantly affected by psychological factors, rather than the current "psychological factors affecting medical condition" diagnostic term delineated by DSM-IV-TR.

A.   Traditional Psychophysiological Disorders, 170

1.   This exercise focuses on the traditional psychophysiological disorders: ulcers, asthma, chronic headaches, hypertension, and coronary heart disease. Complete the table. It was designed to assist in organizing the information in the section.

Ulcers	
Description	lesions that form in the wall of the stomach (gastric ulcers) or in the duodenum (peptic ulcers) cause pain, vomiting, and stomach bleeding
Psychosocial factors	environmental stress, intense anger and/or anxiety, dependent personality traits
Physiological factors	bacterial infections

Asthma

Description

Psychosocial factors	generalized anxiety, dependency traits, environmental stress, dysfunctional family relationships

Physiological factors

Insomnia

Description

Psychosocial factors

Physiological factors

Chronic Headaches

Description	muscle contraction (tension): pain to back or front of head or back of neck; migraine: severe or immobilizing aches on one side of the head

Psychosocial factors

Physiological factors

Hypertension

Description

Psychosocial factors

Physiological factors	diet high in salt; dysfunctional baroreceptors (nerves in the arteries that signal the brain that blood pressure is too high)

Coronary Heart Disease

Description	blockage of coronary arteries; myocardial infarction or heart attack

Psychosocial factors

Physiological factors

1. Biological Factors, 172

Review pages 154–156 of your text as well as the corresponding workbook exercises regarding how the autonomic nervous system (including the sympathetic and parasympathetic systems) works.

1. The textbook provides several explanations of how biological reactions to stress could lead to psychophysiological illnesses. Complete the following statements, explaining how each factor implicated might be related to a physical disorder.

    a. The ANS is stimulated too easily, which could easily result in certain organs being damaged and a psychophysiological disorder developing.

    b. Specific biological problems, such as "weak" gastrointestinal and respiratory systems, result in

    _____

    c. A psychophysiological disorder may ultimately result from individual biological reactions to stress such as

    _____

2. **Psychological Factors, 174**

1. Certain needs, _____, emotions, and coping styles may increase a person's susceptibility to psychophysiological disorders.

2. The link between "_____" coping styles (characterized by pent-up and unexpressed negative emotions) and poor physical health is supported by research.

3. Type _____ personality style is the best known psychological condition that can lead to _____ _____ disease.

4. Describe the behaviors of people who exhibit (a) **Type A personality style** and (b) **Type B personality style**.

    a. _____

    _____

    b. _____

    _____

5. Describe (a) the method and (b) the findings of the Friedman and Rosenman study of the relationship between personality style and coronary heart disease.

    a. _____

    _____

    b. _____

    _____

6. What are the Type A characteristics most associated with coronary heart disease?

    _____

3. **Sociocultural Factors: The Multicultural Perspective, 174**

1. Give three examples of environmental stressors that may open the door for a psychophysiological disorder:

    a. natural disasters or wars

    b. _____

    c. _____

2. For an African American, the inability to successfully hail a cab late at night might be an example of a _____ stressor, while waiting in line at the post office when late for an appointment might be an example of a _____ stressor.

B.   New Psychophysiological Disorders, 177

Like the textbook, the workbook will study the areas of "new" psychophysiological disorders separately.

1.   Are Physical Illnesses Related to Stress?, 178

1.   In the late 1960s, researchers _____ and _____ developed the _____ _____ Rating Scale, which assigned a numerical value to life stressors that people commonly experience (see Table 6–5).

2.   In the scale the stressor is assigned a certain number of _____ _____ _____ (LCUs) that corresponds to the degree that both positive and negative life events have an impact on people; the scale allows researchers to estimate the total amount of stress a person has experienced in a given time period.

3.   In your own words, describe (with an example) the primary shortcoming of the Social Adjustment Rating Scale.

_____

_____

_____

2.   Psychoneuroimmunology, 179

1.   _____ (viruses, bacteria, parasites, etc.) and cancer cells "invade" the body and trigger the immune system to go into action.

2.   Lymphocytes are white _____ _____ manufactured in the lymph system that help the body overcome antigens.

3.   In this exercise, describe the functions of the three groups of lymphocytes in the body's immune system that are described in the textbook.

a.   Helper T-cells identify antigens and then _____ and trigger the production of other immune cells.

b.   What is the function of natural killer T-cells?

_____

_____

c.   B-cells produce _____ , which are protein molecules that recognize and bind to a specific antigen and mark it for _____.

4.   Stress can interfere with lymphocyte activity, which leads to increased _____ to viral and bacterial infections.

5.   Researchers have found compromised lymphocyte activity among people who have experienced stressors such as the recent loss of a _____ and providing ongoing care for loved ones with _____ disease.

Questions 6–9 deal with the four sets of factors that can result in a "slowdown" of the immune system: biochemical activity, behavioral changes, personality style, and degree of social support.

6.   Biological researchers have discovered that:

a.   Under stress the activity of the sympathetic nervous system increases and results in increased secretion of _____ throughout the brain and body.

b. At low levels or in the early stages of stress, this neurotransmitter "tells" lymphocytes to _____ activity, but when stress levels become high or prolonged, the same neurotransmitter gives lymphocytes a(n) _____ message to stop their activity—potentially leading to health problems.

7. In a similar fashion, the so-called stress hormones called _____ give different messages (to increase or decrease activity) to lymphocytes depending on the level and duration of an individual's stress.

8. Recent research indicates that corticosteroids trigger an increase in the production of _____ , proteins that bind to receptors throughout the body. As stress increases and more corticosteroids are released, the spread of these proteins can lead to chronic _____ throughout the body.

9. Stress can also lead to certain behaviors that are known to suppress immune system functioning. List three of these behaviors.

_____

_____

_____

10. Research indicates that people with "hardy" personality styles are better at fighting off illnesses. Describe this hardy style.

_____

_____

_____

11. Poorer cancer prognoses have been found in people who show a _____ coping style and who have difficulty expressing emotions such as _____.

12. Research findings indicate that the immune system functioning of people who have few social supports and feel _____ is poorer in times of stress compared to people who do not share these characteristics.

C. Psychological Treatments for Physical Disorders, 182

1. _____ medicine is the field that combines physical and psychological strategies to treat or _____ medical problems.

2. Complete the table, which summarizes the most common psychological treatments for the psychophysiological disorders.

Intervention	Description	Illnesses Treated
Relaxation training	Patients taught to relax muscles, which curbs anxiety by reducing sympathetic nervous system activity	Essential hypertension, headaches, insomnia, asthma, effects of cancer treatment, and surgery
Biofeedback training		
Meditation		
Hypnosis		
Cognitive interventions		
Emotion expression and support groups		
Combination approaches		

IV. Call for Change: DSM-5, 184–185

1. List four of the disorders that would fall under the proposed new grouping "Trauma and Stressor Related Disorders," which was recommended in the 2011 draft of the DSM-5, if that suggested change is adopted.

   a. _____

   b. _____

   c. _____

   d. _____

2.   Identify several reasons that the proposed grouping "Trauma and Stressor Related Disorders" was recommended to replace the current DSM-IV-TR classifications for these disorders.

   _____

   _____

   _____

   _____

3.   List two other disorders that would join the psychophysiological disorders in the proposed new grouping "Somatic Symptom Disorders," which was recommended in the 2011 draft of the DSM-5.

   a. _____

   b. _____

V.   Putting It Together: Expanding the Boundaries of Abnormal Psychology, 185–186

   In this chapter you have read about how stress contributes to both psychological disorders and physical illnesses. Researchers have learned the value of considering sociocultural, psychological, and biological factors when treating mental illness. Additionally researchers have learned the value that mental health plays in illness prevention and health promotion. What sorts of coping mechanisms do you use to promote your own physical and mental health? Think of a time when you, or someone close to you, experienced a relatively serious physical or mental illness. Describe psychological and/or environmental influences that you believe played a role in the length or severity of this illness.

   _____

   _____

   _____

   _____

   _____

MULTIPLE CHOICE

1. Megan loves riding roller coasters, bungee jumping, skiing, and hang gliding. These activities scare her husband silly. This difference reflects
   a. trait anxiety.
   b. state anxiety.
   c. personality anxiety.
   d. generalized anxiety.

2. If you had forgotten about your abnormal psychology exam on stress disorders and had failed to prepare, you likely would experience such symptoms as a racing heart and sweaty palms. Furthermore, you might not know that the _____ nervous system is responsible for producing those symptoms.
   a. central
   b. parasympathetic
   c. sympathetic
   d. peripheral

3. Difficulty concentrating, sleep problems, and being easily startled are symptoms in which of the four symptom categories of acute and posttraumatic stress disorders?
   a. reexperiencing the traumatic event
   b. avoidance
   c. reduced responsiveness
   d. increased arousal, anxiety, and guilt

4. Salina was terrified during the San Francisco earthquake of 1989. For a couple of weeks after, she did not sleep well or feel comfortable inside a building. However, gradually the fears diminished and disappeared within a month. Her reaction to the earthquake was
   a. a panic attack.
   b. an acute stress disorder.
   c. a phobic reaction.
   d. a posttraumatic stress disorder.

5. Research after the terrorist attacks of September 11, 2001, found
   a. almost all people living in America experienced severe stress symptoms up to a month after the attacks.
   b. almost half of adults in the United States experienced substantial stress symptoms in the first few days after the attacks.
   c. likelihood of developing a stress disorder was unrelated to previous mental health problems.
   d. those individuals who watched less television coverage of the attacks experienced more symptoms because they had less information.

6. The age of a female most likely to be raped is
   a. under 11 years old.
   b. between 11 and 17 years old.
   c. between 17 and 29 years old.
   d. over 29 years old.

7. The rage and guilt that are part of the posttraumatic stress syndrome exhibited by many Vietnam veterans have been successfully treated with
   a. antianxiety drugs.
   b. antidepressant drugs.
   c. a form of group therapy.
   d. the exposure and response prevention procedure.

8. Psychophysiological disorders are different from factitious disorders in that psychophysiological disorders
   a. are caused by hidden needs.
   b. are intentionally produced.
   c. bring about actual physical damage.
   d. are learned through reinforcement.

9. The body's network of activities and cells that identify and destroy antigens and cancer cells is
   a. psychoneuroimmunology.
   b. the immune system.
   c. the psychophysiological response.
   d. biochemical activity.

10. What are the characteristics of someone with a Type A personality?
    a. calm, patient, and tolerant
    b. cold, withdrawn, and intolerant
    c. impatient, easily frustrated, and aggressive
    d. warm, outgoing, with high frustration tolerance

11. A technique of turning one's concentration inward and achieving a slightly changed state of consciousness is called
    a. meditation.
    b. self-hypnosis.
    c. relaxation training.
    d. biofeedback.

7

SOMATOFORM AND DISSOCIATIVE DISORDERS

REVIEW EXERCISES

Stress and anxiety can lead to a wide variety of psychological responses. In the somatoform disorders, unrecognized emotions are expressed as physical symptoms. In the dissociative disorders, stress leads to major losses or changes in memory, conciousness, or identity.

I. Somatoform Disorders, 190–202

A. What Are Hysterical Somatoform Disorders? 190

1. Complete the following table summarizing three types of hysterical somatoform disorders.

Type	Description	Symptoms
Conversion disorder	Expression of psychological problems in the form of one or more motor or sensory symptoms	Called "pseudoneurological": include paralysis, blindness, anesthesia
Somatization disorder		
Pain disorder associated with psychological factors		

2. The textbook discusses several distinctions between symptoms of hysterical somatoform disorders and "true" medical conditions. Provide an example of a hysterical somatoform symptom after each distinction listed.

   a. Symptoms of hysterical somatoform disorders are inconsistent or impossible when compared to the manner in which the nervous system actually functions.

   Example:

   _____

   _____

   b. The physical effects of the hysterical somatoform disorder are very different from the corresponding "true" medical condition.

   Example:

   _____

   _____

3. A person is said to be _____ when he or she "fakes" an illness in order to achieve an external gain such as financial compensation. (*Note:* This is *not* considered a factitious disorder.)

4. People with factitious disorder _____ produce symptoms as well, but they are motivated by internal rewards of maintaining a sick role.

5. Describe two ways that people with factitious disorder might create physical symptoms.

   a. _____

   b. _____

6. _____ syndrome is the most extreme and chronic form of factitious disorder. *(Be sure to read through "PsychWatch" on page 195 of the text, which describes a variant of this disorder.)*

B. **What Are Preoccupation Somatoform Disorders?, 194**

1. People diagnosed with preoccupation somatoform disorders misinterpret and _____ to bodily _____ or features.

2. People diagnosed with _____ become preoccupied with unrealistic misinterpretations of the seriousness of minor or nonexistent physical symptoms.

3. People suffering from **body dysmorphic disorder**, or _____, become preoccupied with imagined or exaggerated _____ in their appearance.

4. List some of the aspects of appearance that are of most concern to people diagnosed with body dysmorphic disorder.

    _____

    _____

5. List some of the differences between normal worries about appearance and the experiences of someone suffering from body dysmorphic disorder.

    _____

    _____

6. _____ percent of people with body dysmorphic disorder are housebound.

C. **What Causes Somatoform Disorders?, 196**

1. Explanations for the preoccupation somatoform disorders are most similar to the cognitive and behavioral theories of _____ disorders.

2. The ancient Greeks believed that hysterical disorders were experienced when the _____ of a sexually _____ woman would wander throughout her body in search of fulfillment, producing a physical symptom wherever it lodged.

1. **The Psychodynamic View, 197**

1. Complete the statements about Freud's view of hysterical somatoform disorders.

    a. Freud believed that because hysterical somatoform disorders could be treated with hypnosis, these disorders represented a _____ of underlying _____ conflicts into physical symptoms.

    b. According to Freud, if parents overreact to a girl's "sexual" feelings toward her father during the _____ stage, she will not adequately resolve the emotional conflict (or Electra complex).

    c. If the Electra conflict goes unresolved, the girl could experience sexual _____ throughout her adult life.

    d. Specifically, what did Freud propose would happen when the adult woman's sexual feelings are triggered, which could lead to a hysterical disorder?

        _____

        _____

2. Although today's psychodynamic theorists agree with Freud that hysterical disorders reflect an unconscious, anxiety-arousing conflict that is converted into more tolerable physical symptoms that symbolize the conflict, they now focus on two mechanisms that seem to be involved in the development of the hysterical somatoform disorders. Define the mechanisms (a) **primary gain** and (b) **secondary gain**.

a. _____

_____

b. _____

_____

2. The Behavioral View, 197

1. The behavioral view of the hysterical somatoform disorders emphasizes the _____ gained by the patient when he or she displays symptoms of the disorder.

2. A main tenet of the behavioral view is that humans can receive a benefit from being in a "sick" role. Was there ever a time when you benefited in any way from being sick (particularly as a child)? If so, write about it. (*Note: This is not to suggest that you had a hysterical disorder.*)

_____

_____

_____

3. What is the primary difference between the behavioral view and the modern psychodynamic view of hysterical disorder?

_____

_____

3. The Cognitive View, 199

1. Cognitive theorists suggest that the hysterical somatoform disorders serve to _____ distressing emotions such as anger, _____, depression, guilt, and jealousy in a physical language that is familiar and comfortable to the patient.

2. According to adherents of the cognitive view, people who have difficulty acknowledging their emotions or expressing them to others are candidates for a hysterical disorder. Who else do they believe is susceptible to this disorder?

_____

_____

4. The Multicultural View, 200

1. Somatization, the development of somatic symptoms in response to personal distress, is generally considered _____ in Western countries, while it is _____ in most non-Western cultures. This difference underscores the importance of the influence of culture on an individual's response to stress.

2. Individuals in Latin America seem to display the _____ number of somatic symptoms. Even in the United States, people from Hispanic cultures display _____ somatic symptoms while under stress than do other populations.

3. Can you suggest one reason why recent Latin immigrants to the United States may display a lower rate of posttraumatic stress disorder than other people throughout the United States?

    _____

    _____

5. **A Possible Role for Biology, 200**

    1. Substances with no known medicinal value, _____, have relieved the suffering of patients for centuries.

    2. While placebos used to be thought of as "magical" treatments, recent research suggests placebos may cause the release of a variety of chemicals in the body. Explain, in your own words, Howard Brody's idea comparing the placebo effect to a visit to a pharmacy.

        _____

        _____

D. **How Are Somatoform Disorders Treated?, 201**

    Hysterical somatoform disorder sufferers tend to resist psychotherapy because they believe they have physical rather than psychological ailments. These exercises relate to treatments used when they give up on the medical alternatives.

    1. People with body dysmorphic disorders are usually treated with interventions that are also utilized for people suffering from _____ disorders (especially _____ disorders); for example, antidepressant (SSRI) drugs and _____ and _____ prevention appear to be effective.

        Read the following case study.

        > **Case Study**
        >
        > Rita has sought treatment for her mysterious physical symptoms from six medical professionals at four hospitals. Her symptoms include a sensation of numbness that "travels" across her scalp and face, frequent abdominal pain, and paralysis of her legs. The last doctor she visited could find no organic (physical) basis for her condition, even after an extensive series of tests, and finally advised Rita to seek psychotherapy. Although she initially resisted, Rita decided that she had better do what the doctor advised or she might not be able to receive further medical services from the hospital.

    2. Complete the following table by writing in the names of the therapeutic techniques used for addressing *physical* symptoms of hysterical somatoform disorder described in the textbook, as well as sample statements you might use for each technique if you were the therapist assigned to treat Rita.

Technique	Sample Therapeutic Statement
Suggestion	
	"Rita, I notice that you walked very quickly into my office today. It's just wonderful that you've been able to suppress the paralysis."

3. Which disorders are more and less likely to benefit from psychotherapy, according to the results of case studies?

    _____

    _____

4. Describe the cognitive-behavioral treatment that is offered to those suffering from hypochondriasis.

    _____

    _____

II. Dissociative Disorders, 202–217

1. Memory connects our _____ to our present and _____.

2. Major changes in memory without any physical causes are called **dissociative disorders**. Complete the following table with brief definitions of the various dissociative disorders.

Disorder	Definition
Dissociative amnesia	Inability to recall important personal events and information
Dissociative fugue	
	The existence of two or more separate identities

A. Dissociative Amnesia, 203

1. People with **dissociative amnesia** manifest an inability to remember important information, usually of a stressful or _____ event in their lives, which cannot be attributed to _____ factors.

Read this case study, which is the basis for an exercise following it relating to the different kinds of amnesia.

Case Study

Clara, the proprietor of a popular inn on the beach, was quite busy one fateful June day. The inn was at full capacity with 60 guests—all of whom seemed to be making requests at the same time for more towels and pillows, extra room keys, and use of the fax machine. Clara managed to get through dealing with an angry guest, a Mr. Barnes, who demanded to have a "bigger room facing the ocean," and then decided it would be an ideal time to escape the chaos and obnoxious guests by running to the bank to make a deposit.

Standing in line, Clara became lost in her thoughts about the big dinner that evening at the inn. She heard a scream behind her, and turned to see four men wearing Richard Nixon masks and carrying guns. The gunmen shot out the cameras on the walls and ordered everyone to drop to the floor. One of them threatened to shoot all of the bank tellers if any of them activated the alarm. Face down on the floor, Clara shut her eyes and silently prayed. She was so frightened that she had trouble breathing. Suddenly, more shots were fired and Clara felt a man falling on top of her. She opened her eyes to see the man all bloody and writhing on the floor next to her. Clara screamed, for which she received a sharp kick to the shoulder and a threat that if she didn't "shut the hell up" she would "be next." The next few minutes were a blur. Clara heard the gunmen running shortly before the police swarmed into the bank.

After waiting what seemed like hours, Clara was checked out by a doctor and then interviewed by police. She was finally allowed to return to the inn—six hours after she left for what she thought would be a brief errand. For the next few weeks, Clara felt as if she were in a fog and had difficulty remembering details about the traumatic event she had experienced.

---

2. Using this case, apply a description of the pattern of forgetting that would illustrate the kinds of amnesia listed.

   a. *Localized amnesia:* Clara is able to recall her hectic day at the inn, including her run-in with Mr. Barnes, but can't remember a thing about being in the bank. She can recall everything after waking up at the inn the day after the robbery.

   b. *Selective amnesia:* _____

   _____

   _____

   c. *Generalized amnesia:* _____

   _____

   _____

   d. *Continuous amnesia:* _____

   _____

   _____

3. People with dissociative amnesia can typically remember abstract or _____ information, but cannot remember _____ information.

4. Many cases of dissociative amnesia emerge during _____ or natural _____, when people's health and safety are threatened.

5. Give an example of an event more ordinary than military experiences that might precipitate dissociative amnesia.

_____

_____

Dissociative amnesia has been linked to child sexual abuse as well. This link has stirred considerable controversy over the reality of "repressed" memories, which is examined in "Repressed Childhood Memories or False Memory Syndrome?" on page 206. Read this material and think about your reaction to the controversy.

B. Dissociative Fugue, 205

1. People with **dissociative fugue** forget their personal _____, flee to a different _____, and might even establish an entirely new identity.

2. For some people with dissociative fugue, the disorder is relatively brief—lasting only a few hours or days. In others, the fugue is more extensive. List three characteristics of those who have the more extensive fugue state.

_____

_____

3. List two ways in which dissociative fugue and dissociative amnesia are similar.

   a. _____

   b. _____

4. Complete these questions about the aftereffects of dissociative fugue.

   a. Usually fugues end _____.

   b. People usually regain most or all of their memories and never experience a _____.

   c. People away for months or years often have trouble adjusting to _____ that occurred during their absence.

   d. Some must also face the consequences of illegal acts committed during the fugue.

C. Dissociative Identity Disorder (Multiple Personality Disorder), 207

1. A person with **dissociative identity disorder** manifests _____ or more distinct subpersonalities, one of which—the primary or _____ personality—dominates the others and appears more frequently.

2. The transition from one subpersonality to another can be _____ and dramatic, and is typically precipitated by a _____ event.

3. Complete these statements relating to the onset and prevalence of dissociative identity disorder.

   a. Most cases of dissociative identity disorder are first diagnosed in late _____ or young _____.

   b. However, symptoms of dissociative identity disorder usually appear in childhood before the age of _____, after the child experiences some form of _____.

   c. For every man diagnosed with dissociative identity disorder, there are at least _____ women diagnosed with the disorder.

4. Complete the brief descriptions of the characteristics of the three kinds of relationships between subpersonalities in this table.

Type	How the Subpersonalities Relate to Each Other
Mutually amnesic	they have no awareness of each other
Mutually cognizant	
One-way amnesic	

5. Research indicates that the average number of subpersonalities per dissociative identity disorder patient is about _____ for women and _____ for men.

6. The dissociative identity disorder case depicted in the book and movie _____ illustrates the fact that therapists typically discover increasing numbers of subpersonalities as a patient's therapy progresses.

7. Complete this table by giving examples of the differences between and among the subpersonalities in people who suffer from dissociative identity disorder.

Types of Differences	Examples of Differences
Personality characteristics	one subpersonality might be fun-loving, spontaneous, and optimistic; another might be hostile and aggressive; a third might be shy, withdrawn, and passive
Identifying features	
Abilities and preferences	
Physiological responses	

8. Some researchers suggest that cases of dissociative identity disorder are actually **iatrogenic,** or unintentionally caused by therapists. Complete the list of ways in which they say therapists create dissociative identity disorder during therapy.

a. Therapists subtly _____ the existence of alternate personalities.

b. While the patient is under _____, therapists elicit the personalities.

c. Therapists may _____ multiple personality patterns by becoming more interested in a patient when he or she displays symptoms of dissociation.

9. Although a diagnosis of dissociative identity disorder is still rare, its prevalence rate has risen dramatically in the past several decades. What two factors might account for this increase?

a. _____

_____

b. _____

_____

D. How Do Theorists Explain Dissociative Disorders?, 210

Explanations for dissociative disorders have been offered by psychodynamic and behavioral theorists. Newer theories that explain these disorders in terms of state-dependent learning and self-hypnosis combine aspects of the cognitive, behavioral, and biological perspectives. Each of these views will be covered separately.

1. The Psychodynamic View, 210

1. The psychodynamic view posits that people with dissociative disorders use _____ excessively in order to prevent painful memories from reaching conscious awareness.

2. According to psychodynamic theorists, people with dissociative amnesia and fugue unconsciously use a _____ episode of repression to avoid confronting a very traumatic event.

3. Dissociative identity disorder is a style of coping characterized by _____ use of repression that is triggered by extremely _____ childhood experiences, according to psychodynamic theory.

4. In order to escape an abusive and dangerous world, children take to flight symbolically by regularly _____ to be another person who is _____ looking on from afar.

Study this diagram relating to the psychodynamic view of dissociative identity disorder.

Abused children try to be "good" and repress the "bad" impulses, which they believe cause the abuse	→	When the "bad" impulses break through, the child tries to disown them by . . .	→	. . . unconsciously assigning all unacceptable thoughts, impulses, and emotions to other personalities

5. The bulk of support for the psychodynamic view of the dissociative disorders is provided by _____ _____.

2. The Behavioral View, 211

1. Complete these questions about the behavioral view of dissociative disorders.

   a. The view holds that dissociation is a response acquired through _____.

   b. Those affected have learned that momentarily forgetting a horrible event leads to a reduction of _____.

   c. The relief resulting from this reduction _____ the act of forgetting and increases the likelihood of more forgetting in the future.

2. Here is a statement representing a belief of the psychodynamic theorists about dissociative disorders. Explain the difference between this statement and the behavioral view of these disorders.

   A hardworking unconscious is keeping the individual unaware that he or she is using dissociation as a means of escape.

   _____

   _____

3. What is one significant limitation of the behavioral view of dissociative disorders?

    _____

    _____

3. State-Dependent Learning, 211

1. What are the central processes underlying state-dependent learning?

    _____

    _____

2. One explanation for state-dependent learning phenomena is that a certain _____ level has a set of remembered thoughts, events, and skills "attached" to it.

Study this diagram that depicts an example of the state-dependent learning explanation of dissociative identity disorder.

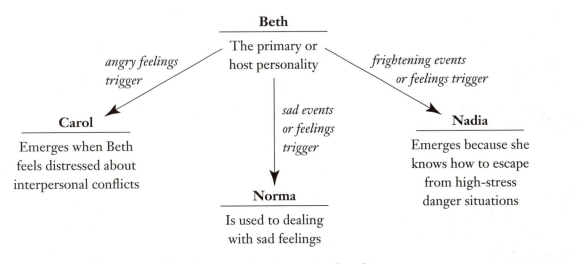

3. People prone to dissociative disorders may have very rigid and _____ state-to-memory links in which certain thoughts, memories, and skills are tied _____ to certain arousal states.

4. Self-Hypnosis, 212

1. Hypnosis is defined as the deliberate induction of a sleeplike state in which the person shows a very high degree of _____.

2. Complete this list of the two parallel features of hypnotic amnesia and dissociative disorders that provide support for the hypothesis that dissociative disorders represent a form of self-hypnosis.

    a. _____

    b. _____

3. The self-hypnosis view of dissociative identity disorder is supported by the fact that the disorder usually begins at a time when children are excellent hypnotic _____ and are very _____ ; perhaps they learn self-hypnosis very early as an attempt to cope with a threatening world.

4. Two different schools of thought about the nature of hypnosis have generated two distinct explanations of how "hypnosis" might be involved in the development of dissociative disorders. Complete the following table that summarizes these contrasting views.

School of Thought	Nature of Hypnosis	Explanation of Dissociative Disorders
Special process	Hypnosis is an out-of-the-ordinary, special trance state of consciousness	
Common social and cognitive process		

E.   How Are Dissociative Disorders Treated?, 213

   1.   How Do Therapists Help People with Dissociative Amnesia and Fugue?, 214

   1.   The primary goal of psychodynamic therapy in treating dissociative disorders is to guide patients to _____ their unconscious in the hope of bringing repressed experiences back to the level of consciousness.

   2.   In **hypnotic therapy** or _____ for dissociative disorders, therapists hypnotize patients and then guide them to recall the forgotten events.

   3.   Less common treatments involve injections of _____ drugs that may help some people recall forgotten events because of their calming and disinhibiting effects.

   2.   How Do Therapists Help Individuals with Dissociative Identity Disorder?, 214

   1.   As you have done before, this exercise calls upon you to imagine that you are a clinician. This time you have been called upon to create a treatment plan for a patient named Maggie N., who suffers from dissociative identity disorder.

City Hospital Department of Psychiatry

Treatment plan for: Maggie N.
Diagnosis: Dissociative Identity Disorder

Treatment Phase I: Recognizing the Disorder

Goals and Strategies

Treatment Phase II: Recovering Memories

Goals and Strategies

Treatment Phase III: Integrating the Subpersonalities

Goals and Strategies

Treatment Phase IV: Postintegration

Goals and Strategies   Through continuing therapy, help Maggie develop the social and coping skills she needs so that she won't have to dissociate in order to function in the world.

F.   Depersonalization Disorder, 215

1.   Depersonalization disorder is quite different from the other dissociative disorders in that the key symptom involves an alteration in one's _____ of self such that one's _____ or body feels _____ or foreign.

2.   Define the following potential symptoms of depersonalization disorder.

a. *Doubling*: _____

_____

_____

b. *Derealization*: _____

_____

3.   While very few people develop a depersonalization disorder, many people experience brief episodes of depersonalization. For example, many people in auto accidents describe the events as "moving very slowly" during the seconds before or during the crash. Other people experience depersonalization during meditation. Think of a time when you or someone you know experienced a depersonalization episode. Describe the event and the accompanying sensations.

_____

_____

_____

_____

_____

4.   What is the primary difference between most people's depersonalization experiences and depersonalization disorder?

_____

_____

_____

_____

5.   Depersonalization symptoms are also seen in other disorders such as _____ or PTSD.

III. Call for Change: DSM-5, 217

The DSM-5 task force, in its 2011 draft, recommended a number of significant changes that, if adopted in the scheduled DSM-5 in 2013, would greatly impact the way the mental health field approaches many of the disorders discussed in Chapter 7. Reflect on whether you agree with the logic behind these various proposed changes.

Complete the following items regarding a number of these proposed changes.

1.   Discuss the proposed new disorder called "complex somatic symptom disorder." How would it affect the classification of some of the disorders discussed in this chapter? What is the logic behind its proposal?

   _____

   _____

2.   What would happen to body dysmorphic disorder if the task force's recommendations were adopted?

   _____

   _____

3.   What would happen to the dissociative fugue category if the task force's recommendations were adopted?

   _____

   _____

IV. Putting It Together: Disorders Rediscovered, 218–220

1.   While somatoform and dissociative disorders were among the first identified psychological disorders, the clinical field began to ignore these disorders. In fact, some questioned the existence of such disorders. In the last 25 years, however, interest in the somatoform and dissociative disorders has increased again. Certainly, the increased interest will be beneficial in finding explanations of and treatments for these disorders. Unfortunately, gains are rarely without costs. What are some potentially problematic side effects of the new interest in and focus on the somatoform and dissociative disorders?

   _____

   _____

   _____

   _____

   _____

MULTIPLE CHOICE

1. The psychogenic disorders called hysterical disorders include:
   a. malingering.
   b. factitious disorder.
   c. conversion disorder.
   d. Munchausen syndrome.

2. Which of the following is a correct pairing?
   a. conversion disorder—heart disease
   b. factitious disorder—somatization disorder
   c. somatoform disorder—conversion disorder
   d. psychophysiological disorder—"glove anesthesia"

3. A person who interprets minimal symptoms as signs of serious physical problems and suffers significant anxiety and depression as a result might be diagnosed with a
   a. conversion disorder.
   b. somatoform pain disorder.
   c. hysterical somatoform disorder.
   d. preoccupation somatoform disorder.

4. People who feign illness because they like "being sick" are diagnosed with a _____ disorder.
   a. factitious
   b. somatoform
   c. psychogenic
   d. psychophysiological

5. Preoccupation somatoform disorders are usually explained by theorists in the same way that they explain
   a. mood disorders.
   b. anxiety disorders.
   c. personality disorders.
   d. dissociative disorders.

6. Teresa was examined for her arm paralysis (conversion disorder). Her physician brought her into his consultation room and carefully explained the etiology of her paralysis (he made it up). He told her that this serious disorder would run its course and "heal itself" in about a month. This therapy was based on
   a. insight.
   b. suggestion.
   c. confrontation.
   d. reinforcement.

7. Karen experienced a mugging and robbery in which her prized Siamese cat was kidnapped. Eventually the cat was found and returned. However, she was able to recall only certain events that occurred between the attack and the safe return of her cat, such as conversations with friends and phone calls from the police. This is a classic example of
   a. selective amnesia.
   b. localized amnesia.
   c. continuous amnesia.
   d. generalized amnesia.

8. Cameron had the traumatic experience of seeing his wife run over by a truck. Two days later, he doesn't remember this event or who he is. He ends up in another town working in a fast-food restaurant under a new name and identity. His overall reaction would probably be diagnosed as
   a. amnesia.
   b. displacement.
   c. dissociative fugue.
   d. dissociative identity disorder.

9. What event most often precipitates the onset of dissociative identity disorder?
   a. head trauma
   b. physical and/or sexual abuse
   c. personal stress
   d. natural disasters

10. What has been found out about the subpersonalities of people with dissociative identity disorder?
    a. They have similar abilities to one another.
    b. They differ in age and family history but not gender or race.
    c. They rarely exhibit a unique pattern of physiological responses.
    d. They differ from one another in age, sex, race, and family history.

11. Glenda experiences a horrifying event. She lets her mind drift to other subjects, reducing her anxiety. She does this more often, and each time the behavior is reinforced by the reduction in anxiety. This pattern may be used by behaviorists to describe the development of
    a. mood disorders.
    b. anxiety disorders.
    c. personality disorders.
    d. dissociative disorders.

12. Self-hypnosis has been offered as an explanation for
    a. personality disorders.
    b. dissociative disorders.
    c. schizophrenic disorders.
    d. impulse control disorders.

13. Which class of drugs has been used to treat dissociative amnesia and fugue?
    a. barbiturates
    b. antipsychotics
    c. antidepressants
    d. antianxiety drugs

14. The following cultures all exhibit high rates of somatization except:
    a. Chinese culture.
    b. Latin cultures.
    c. Arab cultures.
    d. United States culture.

8   MOOD DISORDERS

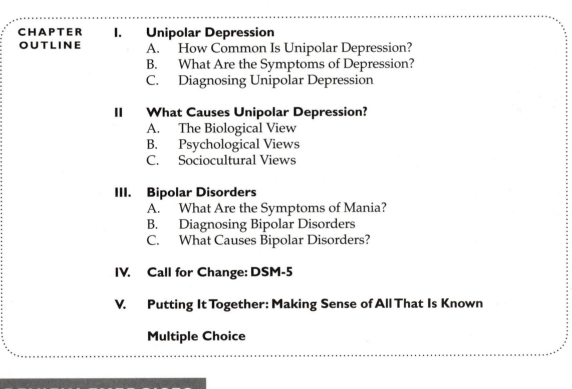

CHAPTER
OUTLINE

I.   **Unipolar Depression**
- A.   How Common Is Unipolar Depression?
- B.   What Are the Symptoms of Depression?
- C.   Diagnosing Unipolar Depression

II   **What Causes Unipolar Depression?**
- A.   The Biological View
- B.   Psychological Views
- C.   Sociocultural Views

III.   **Bipolar Disorders**
- A.   What Are the Symptoms of Mania?
- B.   Diagnosing Bipolar Disorders
- C.   What Causes Bipolar Disorders?

IV.   **Call for Change: DSM-5**

V.   **Putting It Together: Making Sense of All That Is Known**

Multiple Choice

REVIEW EXERCISES

I.   Unipolar Depression, 224–228

A.   How Common Is Unipolar Depression?, 224

1.   Complete the following statements about the prevalence of unipolar depression.

     a.   Each year, almost 8 percent of adults in the United States suffer from a severe unipolar pattern of depression, and another 5 percent suffer mild forms.

     b.   As many as _____ percent of adults worldwide experience a severe depressive episode during their lifetime.

     c.   It appears that the risk of experiencing depression has _____ in the last 100 years.

d. _____ are two times more likely to suffer depression than the other gender.

e. Few differences in prevalence have been found among ethnic or age groups.

f. While _____ percent of severely depressed people recover, _____ percent of those who have been depressed at some point become depressed again.

2. The median age for the onset of unipolar depression in the United States is _____ years.

B. What Are the Symptoms of Depression?, 224

Complete the table below by giving three key words or phrases that describe the symptoms of depression in the listed areas of functioning.

Area of functioning	Key words or phrases
Emotional	miserable, loss of pleasure, anxiety
Motivational	
Behavioral	
Cognitive	
Physical	

MediaSpeak: The Crying Game: Male vs. Female Tears, 226

1. Describe how the results of the Penn State research study support the theory that men who cry in public are taken more seriously than women who cry.

_____

_____

2. Reflect on the media coverage of Hillary Clinton's moments of public emotion during the 2008 Democratic Presidential primary season compared with public displays of emotion by Bill Clinton and John Boehner. Do you feel that this coverage supports the idea that women who cry publicly are not taken seriously?

_____

_____

C. Diagnosing Unipolar Depression, 228

1. DSM-IV-TR specifies that the diagnosis of a major depressive episode is made when a person experiences at least _____ symptoms of depression that last _____ weeks or more. Furthermore, psychotic symptoms may be present in extreme cases.

People experiencing a major depressive episode are usually assigned a diagnosis of "major depressive disorder." A clinician may clarify this diagnosis by indicating the specific type of depression. This part of a diagnosis will use the following terms: recurrent, seasonal, catatonic, melancholic, and postpartum.

2. Complete this exercise by putting yourself in the place of a clinician clarifying a diagnosis of "major depressive disorder." Match each of the following examples with one of the terms listed in the preceding paragraph.

Example	Diagnosis
Although he feels fine most of the year, Clark feels extremely depressed from Thanksgiving until well past New Year's Day.	
Sherrie has been experiencing symptoms including excessive crying, loss of appetite, feelings of hopelessness, and insomnia since the birth of her son three weeks ago.	
Over the last 10 years, Debbie has experienced seven depressive episodes. She fears that she will never have a "normal" life.	
Marjorie's primary and most debilitating symptom is that she feels unable to move. Her face shows no emotion whatsoever, and she does not speak, even when spoken to. She stays in bed for days on end.	
Until recently, Richard loved to go to basketball games and socialize with friends. Now, Richard takes no interest in any activity. He states that he feels like a robot going through the motions. Richard feels most depressed in the very early morning; he typically wakes up at 3:00 or 4:00 A.M. and is unable to fall back asleep because he feels so terrible.	

3. Complete the following statements regarding dysthymic disorder (see page 228 in the textbook).

   a. It is a more chronic but less _____ pattern of unipolar depression.

   b. Typically, a depressed mood and only two or three other symptoms are present and the depression persists for at least _____ in adults.

   c. If the dysthymic disorder leads to major depression, it is called _____ .

II. What Causes Unipolar Depression?, 228–244

1. Researchers have discovered that across cultures, depressed people experience more _____ life events just before the onset of their disorder than do nondepressed people.

2. Define (a) reactive (exogenous) depression and (b) endogenous depression.

   a. _____

   b. _____

PsychWatch: Sadness at the Happiest of Times, 229

1. Postpartum depression, in which symptoms of clinical depression can last up to _____ following the birth of a child, is experienced by _____ to _____ percent of new mothers.

2. Identify four factors that may, according to various theorists, play important roles in causing postpartum depression.

   a. _____

   b. _____

   c. _____

   d. _____

3. Why do many women suffering from postpartum depression shy away from seeking treatment that could prove very beneficial?

   _____

   _____

   _____

A. **The Biological View, 230**

1. **Genetic Factors, 230**

1. Complete the following statements relating to studies examining the role of genetic factors in the development of unipolar depression.

   a. _____ _____ studies have shown a higher rate of depression in close relatives of depressed people (20 percent) than in the population at large (less than 10 percent).

   b. A recent twin study found that out of 200 pairs of twins, the concordance rate for depression among monozygotic (identical) twins was _____ percent, whereas the concordance rate in dizygotic (fraternal) twins was only _____ percent.

   c. _____ parents of adoptees hospitalized for severe depression had a much higher occurrence of severe depression than _____ parents of nondepressed adoptees.

2. **Biochemical Factors, 231**

1. In the 1950s, two sets of research findings suggested that reduced activity of the neurotransmitters **norepinephrine** and **serotonin** were implicated in unipolar depression. Complete the following diagram.

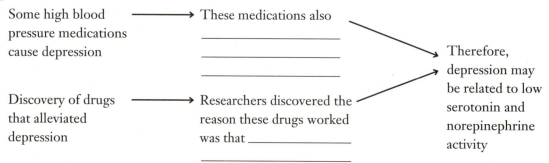

2. Studies have suggested that the explanation depicted in exercise 1 above may be too simplistic. What are three more recent theories about the relation of neurotransmitters to depression?

    a. _____

    _____

    _____

    b. _____

    _____

    _____

    c. _____

    _____

    _____

3. Researchers have found that depression may be related to endocrine system functioning. As you have read, endocrine glands release hormones that affect the activity of various organ systems in the body. What are the two hormones that have been implicated in depression?

    a. _____

    b. _____

4. Give one limitation of research conducted on the biological theories of depression.

    _____

    _____

    _____

3. **Brain Anatomy and Brain Circuits, 232**

1. Name four brain areas believed to be part of the brain circuit responsible for unipolar depression.

    a. _____

    a. _____

    b. _____

    d. _____

2. The brain's _____ _____ is involved in many important brain functions, such as mood, attention, and immune functioning.

3. The hippocampus is one of the few brain areas to perform an activity called _____ , producing new neurons throughout adulthood.

4. PET and fMRI scans indicate that blood flow and activity in the _____ , which is believed to be involved in expression of negative emotions and memories, is 50 percent greater in depressed persons than nondepressed persons.

5. Describe the findings that have caused researchers to believe Brodmann Area 25 is involved in unipolar depression.

    _____

    _____

    _____

4. Immune System, 233

1. When people are under significant stress, their immune system may become dysregulated, leading to lower functioning of _____ _____ cells, called _____ , and increased production of _____ _____ (CRP).

2. Although research support for a relationship between the immune system and depression is circumstantial and such a relationship is subject to multiple interpretations, identify four research findings that seem to lend support for the immune system/depression relationship.

    a. _____

    b. _____

    c. _____

    d. _____

B. Psychological Views, 234

1. The Psychodynamic View, 234

Freud and Abraham's psychoanalytic theory of depression was based on the observation that people's grief reactions are very similar to symptoms of major depression.

1. Study and complete the following chart based on Freud and Abraham's formulation.

A loved one dies or is lost in some way, and a series
of unconscious processes is set in motion

↓

People regress to the oral stage of development in order
to fuse their own identity with that of the person they lost

↓

That is, they introject the loved one and experience feelings
toward the loved one as feelings toward themselves

↓

THE LENGTH OF THE REACTION PERIOD DIFFERS AMONG PEOPLE

For some, the mourning period
lasts a relatively short time

↓

These people reestablish a separate
identity and resume social relationships

For others, the reaction worsens, and
they feel empty and avoid social contact

↓

Introjected feelings of anger create
self-hatred, self-blame, and DEPRESSION

The two kinds of people who are most susceptible to depression
following the loss of a loved one are:

a. _____

b. _____

---

2. Which Freudian concept is illustrated in the following scenario? *A teenager fails to gain admittance to his father's college and becomes depressed because he unconsciously believes that his father will no longer love him.*

   _____

3. Object relations theorists suggest that people whose parents pushed them toward excessive _____ or excessive _____ are more likely to become depressed when faced with the loss of a relationship.

   Several tenets of the psychodynamic perspective of depression have been generally supported by empirical investigations. The next three exercises concern three hypotheses within the perspective and research findings that support them.

4. Complete the following statements regarding research findings that support the hypothesis *Depression is related to early loss.*

   a. Infants and children under age 6 who are separated from their mothers can experience a reaction called _____ depression.

   b. One study found that depressed medical patients were more likely to have lost a _____ during childhood, compared to nondepressed patients.

5. Complete the following statement regarding a finding that supports the hypothesis *People whose needs were not adequately addressed in childhood are more likely to become depressed when they experience loss as adults.*

   Compared to nondepressed people, depressed people were more likely to say that their parents raised them with a(n) "_____ control" style, which is defined as a mixture of low care and high _____.

6. One limitation of psychodynamic research on depression is that findings do not establish that early loss and inadequate parenting are *typically* responsible for the development of depression. List other limitations.

   a. _____

   b. Many components of the psychodynamic view of depression are impossible to test empirically.

2. The Behavioral View, 236

Peter Lewinsohn's behavioral explanation of unipolar depression suggests that some people engage in fewer positive behaviors when the rewards for their positive behaviors start to diminish, and that this is the basis for the development of a depressed style of functioning. Read the following case study relating to Lewinsohn's theory of depression.

Case Study

Saul is a 59-year-old grocery store owner who, through 40 years of hard work, has made his store the biggest in town. He has accomplished this in spite of stiff competition from national chain stores. He has always taken great pride in beating them. Saul has earned the respect of his customers and employees alike. But profits have been down for a few years—a situation he blames on his advancing age. He decides to sell his store when one of the chains offers him a good price. He and his wife retire to the coast of Maine.

> Saul enjoys retirement for about a week, then starts to complain of feeling "empty." He tries improving his golf game, but quits when he is consistently beaten at the sport by his wife and others. He finds himself drinking more alcohol than ever before. He had wanted to take up sailing, but decides not to, figuring he is too old. Within six months of retirement, he is doing little more than watching television, drinking, and going to bed early every night.

1. Apply Lewinsohn's explanation of unipolar depression to the case study.

   a. List some of the rewards for positive behavior Saul received as a store owner.

   _____

   _____

   _____

   b. Saul's eventual depressed style of functioning results from a downward spiral. Which of Saul's activities could be seen as evidence of this spiral?

   _____

   _____

   _____

2. Lewinsohn suggests that _____ rewards decrease as a person becomes more depressed; some studies have indicated that _____ characteristics contribute to the loss of these rewards.

3. Cognitive Views, 237

a. *Negative Thinking, 237*

You should recall from Chapter 3 that theorist Aaron Beck is closely associated with the cognitive perspective. His theory of depression rests on the notion that maladaptive attitudes, the cognitive triad, errors in thinking, and automatic thoughts combine to produce the negative thinking patterns that are characteristic of depression. In this part of the workbook, each of these components will be covered in succession.

1. Beck suggests that some people develop maladaptive attitudes as children. Come up with two original examples of maladaptive attitudes.

   a. _____

   b. _____

2. When people who hold maladaptive attitudes face an upsetting event later in life (such as a failure at work or in a relationship), a series of _____ thoughts are triggered. According to Beck, these thoughts take the form of the "cognitive triad."

3. In this exercise, complete the following figure by supplying the missing "forms" in Beck's cognitive triad.

Negative view of self

The Cognitive Triad

Negative view of
_____

Negative view of
_____

4. Beck's theory of depression states that depressed people commonly use illogical or erroneous logic that results in an even stronger (depressive) cognitive triad. Define each type of error below, then complete the example that illustrates each error.

    a. arbitrary inference: _____

    _____

    Example: The host of an elegant restaurant tells a woman that it will be at least one hour before she can be seated for dinner. The woman concludes that:

    _____

    b. minimization/magnification: _____

    _____

    Example: A man gets an unexpected promotion at work and concludes that:

    _____

    When he accidentally calls his new boss by the wrong name, he concludes that:

    _____

5. According to Beck, people experience (or manifest) the cognitive triad in the form of automatic thoughts, a steady train of unpleasant, "reflexive" thoughts that remind depressed people of their assumed _____ and the _____ of their situation.

    Examine the following flow chart and be sure you understand it. It depicts the feedback system that incorporates all the components of Beck's cognitive theory of depression. Note that Beck believes that the emotional, motivational, behavioral, and somatic aspects of depression all follow from the cognitive process he has described.

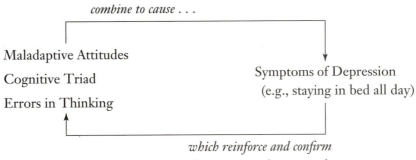

6. Complete the following table summarizing the empirical support for Beck's theory of depression. Provide one example of a research finding that provides evidence for each tenet of the theory listed.

Tenet	Supportive Finding
Depressed people hold maladaptive attitudes	The number of maladaptive attitudes correlates strongly with the degree of depression
Depressed people exhibit the cognitive triad	
Depressed people show errors in logic	
Depressed people experience negative automatic thoughts	

b. *Learned Helplessness, 239*

1. What are the two primary components of Martin Seligman's cognitive-behavioral view of depression?

    a. _____

    b. _____

2. Complete the following exercises relating to Seligman's **shuttle box** experiments on dogs, which were the basis for his original theoretical framework.

    a. Dogs were strapped into hammocks and given _____ electric shocks from which they could not escape.

    b. The dogs were placed in the shuttle box, which had a "shock" compartment and a "safe" compartment.

    c. How did the dogs react when they were placed in the "shock" area?

    _____

    _____

3. Specifically, how did Seligman explain his findings?

    _____

    _____

4. List two research findings that have provided empirical support for the hypothesis that receiving uncontrollable negative reinforcements can result in depressive symptoms.

    a. _____

    _____

    b. _____

    _____

5. A revision of the learned helplessness theory of depression suggests that when people believe events are beyond their control they ask themselves "why?" In other words, they make **attributions** about why they lost control in a particular situation. There are three basic dimensions of these attributions:

    Internal vs. External Attributions: Is the cause of this event located within myself (internal) or elsewhere (external)?

    Global vs. Specific Attributions: Is the cause of this event relevant to many situations (global) or just this one situation (specific)?

    Stable vs. Unstable Attributions: Is the cause of this event enduring (stable), or is it short-lived (unstable)?

    After you have studied the text material related to attributions, try the next exercise. The following table depicts eight possible attributions made by Russell, who has just lost an important tennis match. From the list of Russell's statements after the table, choose the one that best fits each "cell" of the table.

    Event: *"I just lost an important tennis match."*

	Internal		External	
	Stable	**Unstable**	**Stable**	**Unstable**
Global		a.		h.
Specific	d.		g.	

a. "I really didn't feel well today."

b. "I felt especially nervous for this match because so many people were watching."

c. "This sort of competition doesn't prove whether you're a good tennis player or not."

d. "I am a horrible tennis player. I simply have no talent at all."

e. "That line judge really made some lousy calls today; he must not have been paying attention to what was happening."

f. "I am unable to cope with any high-pressure situation no matter what it is."

g. "That line judge has always had it in for me. Every time I play with him up there I lose, no matter how well I play."

h. "No one can play well on a court like this; there are cracks and bumps everywhere!"

6. The combination of attributions that seems to indicate a person is most likely to be depressed is
_____, _____, and _____.

7. Yet another revision of the learned helplessness theory suggests that only attributions that produce a sense of _____ lead to depression.

8. One problem with the learned helplessness theory is that studies reveal mixed findings regarding the relationship between depression and internal, stable, and global attributions. List two other problems with the theory.

a. _____

_____

b. _____

_____

C. Sociocultural Views, 241

1. Sociocultural theorists believe that social factors such as culture, gender and race, and social support are linked to depression. After reading through this section of the text, complete the following table by summarizing at least two research findings that support the link between depression and each factor listed.

Factor	Research Findings
Culture	
Gender and race	
Social support	

1. The Family-Social Perspective, 241

1. Discuss the ways in which the connection between declining social rewards and depression is considered "a two-way street."

_____

_____

2. The study mentioned on textbook page 241 regarding the correlation between marital satisfaction and depression found that the participants who were in unsatisfying relationships were _____ times _____ likely to experience a major depressive episode.

3. The researchers in the same study mentioned in question 2 estimated that eliminating marital stress could prevent _____ of the cases of major depression.

2. The Multicultural Perspective, 242

1. Women around the world are at least _____ as likely as men to be diagnosed with unipolar depression.

2. Name and briefly explain the six theories mentioned in your textbook for the disparity in diagnoses of unipolar depression between men and women.

   a. _____

   b. _____

   c. _____

   d. _____

   e. _____

   f. _____

3. Depressed people in non-Western countries are more likely than their Western counterparts to be troubled by _____ symptoms, less often experiencing _____ symptoms like self-blame, low self-esteem, and guilt.

4. Although researchers in the United States have found few differences in the overall rates of depression among different ethnic or racial groups, researchers have found notable differences in the chronicity of depression between ethnic and racial groups.

   a. Define chronicity.

   _____

   b. Offer a possible explanation for these differences in rates of chronicity.

   _____

   _____

   _____

III. Bipolar Disorders, 244–252

A. What Are the Symptoms of Mania?, 244

1. Rather than feeling sad and apathetic, people in a state of mania experience dramatic and _____ elevations in mood.

2. Complete the table on the next page by giving three key words or phrases that describe the symptoms of mania in the listed area of functioning.

Area of Functioning	Evidence
Emotional	elation, euphoric joy, irritability
Motivational	
Behavioral	
Cognitive	
Physical	

B.   Diagnosing Bipolar Disorders, 245

1.   DSM-IV-TR criteria for a manic episode include experiencing an abnormally _____ or _____ mood, as well as at least _____ other symptoms of mania, for a minimum of one week.

2.   If symptoms of mania are less severe and of shorter duration, the diagnosis would be a _____ episode.

3.   DSM-IV-TR distinguishes between two types of bipolar disorders. Briefly describe (a) bipolar I and (b) bipolar II.

   a.   _____

   _____

   b.   _____

   _____

4.   Complete the following statements regarding the prevalence of bipolar disorders.

   a.   The prevalence of bipolar disorders is the same for men and women, at all socioeconomic levels, and in all _____ classes.

   b.   The age of onset is usually between _____ and _____ years.

5.   A diagnosis of _____ disorder would be assigned to a person who experienced alternating periods of hypomanic and mild depressive symptoms for a period of two or more years.

C.   What Causes Bipolar Disorders?, 249

The most promising clues for an explanation of bipolar disorders comes from three areas of the biological realm — neurotransmitter activity, ion activity, and genetic factors. Each of these is covered separately in this part of the workbook.

1.   Describe one of the two findings that led researchers to believe that mania is related to abnormally high levels of norepinephrine.

   _____

   _____

2. Contrary to the expectations of theorists, research has shown that mania, like depression, is associated with a low supply of _____.

3. Complete the following diagram, which depicts the permissive theory of mood disorders.

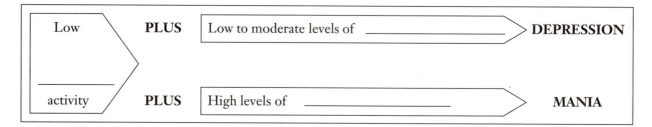

4. Complete the following sequence of events that describe how a neuron "fires" its message to other neurons in the brain.

    a. At rest, the outside of a neuron is positively charged because more _____ ions are outside vs. inside the cell membrane.

    b. The neuron's receptor sites are stimulated, resulting in a "wave" of electrochemical activity down the neuron.

    c. As sodium ions flow *into* the neuron, _____ ions flow *out* of the neuron.

    d. The neuron returns to its resting state.

5. Some researchers believe that improper sodium ion transport that causes neurons to fire too easily results in _____, while that which causes neurons to resist firing results in _____.

6. Name seven brain structures that have been shown to display abnormalities in people with bipolar disorders.

    _____

    _____

    _____

7. Studies involving close relatives and twins of those with bipolar disorders indicate that the more similar the _____ _____ of two people, the more similar their tendency to develop a bipolar disorder.

8. Complete the following description of the method used by researchers in genetic linkage studies.

    a. They select families that have high rates of bipolar disorder over several _____.

    b. They observe the pattern of distribution of bipolar disorder in family members.

    c. They determine whether the bipolar pattern follows the distribution patterns of other family (inherited) traits such as:

    _____

IV. Call for Change: DSM-5, 252–253

1. The DSM task force proposed a number of changes to the "Mood Disorders" grouping in the 2011 draft of the DSM-5. Identify the five major changes to this grouping that would take place if the DSM-5, scheduled for publication in 2013, were to adopt all of these recommendations. Indicate the reason the task force is proposing these changes and, if applicable, why some might be controversial.

a. _____

_____

_____

b. _____

_____

_____

c. _____

_____

_____

d. _____

_____

_____

e. _____

_____

_____

V. Putting It Together: Making Sense of All That Is Known, 253–254

1. Identify and briefly describe four possible relationships between major contributing factors to unipolar depression (such as biological abnormalities, reduction in positive reinforcements, negative thinking, perceived helplessness, life stress, and sociocultural influences) and unipolar depression itself.

_____

_____

_____

_____

_____

_____

2. Clinicians and researchers have come to believe that bipolar disorders can be best explained by a focus on one kind of variable _____ factors.

MULTIPLE CHOICE

1. What role does gender play in the incidence of depression?
    a. Gender is unrelated to the incidence of depression.
    b. Men are twice as likely to suffer from depression as women.
    c. Women are twice as likely to suffer from depression as men.
    d. Depression is more frequent in women but more severe in men.

2. Which of the following would be a cognitive symptom of depression?
    a. lack of desire to eat
    b. a negative view of oneself
    c. experiences of sadness and anger
    d. staying in bed for hours during the day

3. To receive a diagnosis of Major Depressive Episode, Seasonal, the individual must display
    a. repeated episodes of depression.
    b. mood fluctuation during the year.
    c. motor immobility or excessive activity.
    d. onset within four weeks of giving birth.

4. What structure is responsible for secreting cortisol?
    a. pineal gland
    b. hypothalamus
    c. adrenal glands
    d. pituitary gland

5. Which theoretical perspective employs the concept of "symbolic loss" to explain depression?
    a. cognitive
    b. humanistic
    c. existential
    d. psychodynamic

6. What disorder do psychodynamic therapists believe that unconscious grieving over real or imagined loss produces?
    a. conversion disorder
    b. unipolar depression
    c. countertransference
    d. schizotypal personality disorder

7. Who developed a behavioral theory of depression based on insufficient positive reinforcement?
    a. Beck
    b. Freud
    c. Seligman
    d. Lewinsohn

8. Every time Sophie's homework is not done her teacher punishes her. When she does it, she gets a low grade. If she complains about never being recognized for trying, she is given detention. This is an example of a set of conditions that, over time, is most likely to lead to
    a. depression.
    b. schizophrenia.
    c. substance abuse.
    d. bipolar disorder.

9. What critical feature does bipolar II have that is different from bipolar I?
    a. hypomania
    b. mild depression
    c. major depression
    d. full manic episodes

10. Some researchers believe that symptoms of mania can be due to
    a. excessive serotonin.
    b. depleted levels of norepinephrine.
    c. sodium ions increasing a neuron's resistance to firing.
    d. abnormal function of proteins that transport sodium ions.

11. Within the United States, differences in overall depression rates between minority groups are
    a. high.
    b. minimal.
    c. nonexistent.
    d. different at different times of the year.

9 TREATMENTS FOR MOOD DISORDERS

REVIEW EXERCISES

I. Treatments for Unipolar Depression, 258–276

A variety of treatment approaches are available for persons suffering from unipolar depression. In the following section, exercises will cover three general categories of treatments: psychological approaches (psychodynamic, behavioral, and cognitive therapies), sociocultural approaches (culture-sensitive, interpersonal and couple therapies), and biological approaches (electroconvulsive therapy and antidepressant drugs). Additionally, exercises addressing trends in treatment are included at the end of this section.

A. Psychological Approaches, 258

1. Psychodynamic Therapy, 259

1.´ Complete the following chart regarding psychodynamic therapy for unipolar depression.

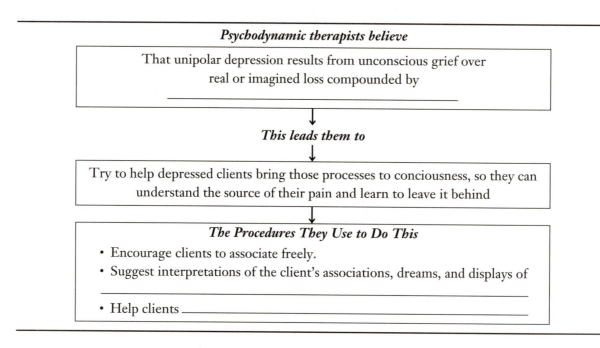

Psychodynamic therapists believe

That unipolar depression results from unconscious grief over
real or imagined loss compounded by
_____

⬇

This leads them to

⬇

Try to help depressed clients bring those processes to conciousness, so they can
understand the source of their pain and learn to leave it behind

⬇

The Procedures They Use to Do This

• Encourage clients to associate freely.
• Suggest interpretations of the client's associations, dreams, and displays of
_____

• Help clients _____

2. List two aspects of psychodynamic therapy described in the textbook that could explain its limited effectiveness in the treatment of depression.

a. _____
_____
_____

b. _____
_____
_____

MediaSpeak: How Well Do Colleges Treat Depression?, 260

Read the article in this section regarding mental health services provided by colleges to their students. Reflect on the mental health services provided by your own school. Do you know if the school offers unlimited therapy, or a full-fledged staff therapist? How accessible would mental health services be to you if you required them?

2. Behavioral Therapy, 261

1. Complete the following table by listing and describing each of the components of Peter Lewinsohn's influential behavioral treatment of depression.

Component	Description
1. Reintroducing pleasurable events	
2.	Contingency management approach that ignores depression behaviors and rewards positive behaviors
3.	

2. Therapies that _____ several of Lewinsohn's strategies seem to reduce symptoms of _____ levels of depression.

3. Cognitive Therapy, 262

1. Complete the following table summarizing the four phases of Beck's **cognitive therapy** of depression.

Phase	Description
1. Increasing activities and elevating mood	Preparation of a detailed weekly schedule that includes behavioral "assignments" designed to gradually involve the client in more activities
2.	
3.	
4.	

2. Hundreds of studies have concluded that _____ to _____ percent of depressed people show a near-total elimination of depressive symptoms after receiving cognitive or cognitive-behavioral therapy.

3. Although Beck calls his treatment approach cognitive therapy, many theorists really consider it a _____ therapy.

4. Many of the new-wave cognitive-behavioral therapists do not agree with Beck's proposition that people must completely _____ their negative cognitions to overcome depression. Some, including those who practice _____ (ACT), see their role as guiding depressed clients to _____ their negative thoughts for what they are and then work around them in their lives.

B. Sociocultural Approaches, 264

1. Many of today's therapists offer _____ therapy for depressed minority clients in combination with a culture-sensitive focus on their economic pressures and related cultural issues.

2. In the United States, minority clients are _____ likely than white Americans to receive helpful antidepressant medication.

3. Complete the following table by first describing the key problem areas addressed in **interpersonal psychotherapy** (IPT), then by giving examples of the therapist's tasks in each of these areas.

Problem Areas	Description	Therapist's Tasks
Interpersonal loss	Feelings of grief and sadness after the loss of a loved one (e.g., through death or divorce)	Explore relationship with lost person, help client express feelings toward lost person, encourage development of new relationships

Problem Areas	Description	Therapist's Tasks
Interpersonal role dispute		
Interpersonal role transition		
Interpersonal deficits		

4. Depressive symptoms were relieved in approximately _____ to _____ percent of clients treated with IPT, according to research findings.

5. Interpersonal psychotherapy appears to be the most effective treatment for what kinds of clients?

_____

6. Research has indicated that as many as _____ percent of all depressed clients are in a dysfunctional relationship.

7. Describe the central goals of the behavioral marital therapist.

_____

_____

C. **Biological Approaches, 266**

1. **Electroconvulsive Therapy, 266**

   1. Complete the following list of characteristics of ECT.

      a. In _____ electroconvulsive therapy (ECT), electrodes carrying 65 to 140 volts of an electrical current are placed on both sides of the patient's head, whereas in _____ ECT, electrodes are placed on only one side of the head.

      b. The electrical current causes a brain _____ that lasts from 25 seconds to a few minutes.

      c. ECT programs consist of _____ to _____ treatments over the course of two to four _____.

   2. Inducing convulsions as a treatment for depression has historical origins in an accident that occurred over 70 years ago. Provide the missing information in the following statements regarding the path that led from this accident to ECT.

      a. Believing that epileptic convulsions prevented psychosis, Joseph von Meduna used the drug _____ to induce convulsions in psychotic patients.

      b. _____ therapy, a related and very dangerous technique, was developed at about the same time by Manfred Sakel, a Viennese physician.

      c. A few years later ECT was developed by _____ and his colleague Lucio Bini.

3. Describe the purpose of (a) barbiturates and (b) muscle relaxants in ECT.

    a. _____

    b. _____

4. Describe the most disturbing side effect observed in some patients after they undergo ECT.

    _____

    _____

5. Approximately 60 to 80 percent of patients improve with ECT. What are some of the symptoms of the patients with the best improvement rates?

    _____

2. Antidepressant Drugs, 269

The primary classes of drugs that are used to treat depression are the MAO inhibitors, the tricyclics, and the second-generation antidepressant drugs. Each of these kinds of drugs will be examined separately in the following exercises.

a. MAO Inhibitors, 269

1. Complete the following exercises related to how researchers believe MAO inhibitors alleviate depression.

    a. Recall (from Chapter 8) that in some people, depression seems to be associated with decreased activity of the neurotransmitter norepinephrine.

    b. The enzyme MAO, which stands for _____, interacts with norepinephrine and breaks it down so that it is no longer effective.

    c. When the antidepressant drug MAO inhibitor is introduced into the system, what is prevented?

        _____

        _____

    d. Summarize why MAO inhibitors act to alleviate depressive symptoms.

        _____

        _____

2. Explain how tyramine can present a danger to people using MAO inhibitors.

    _____

    _____

b. Tricyclics, 270

1. Before it was found to be effective in treating depression, the tricyclic drug _____ was used unsuccessfully in the treatment of schizophrenia.

2. About _____ to _____ percent of mildly to severely depressed patients who take tricyclic antidepressant drugs improve (although the drugs must be taken for at least _____ days before improvement is observed).

3. Complete the following statements related to relapse among depressed patients who take tricyclic drugs.

    a. If they stop taking the drugs immediately after they experience relief, they are at high risk of _____ within 1 year.

b. The risk of relapse decreases significantly if patients continue to take the drugs for a period of at least _____ after depressive symptoms disappear (this is called "_____ therapy").

c. Some studies have indicated that patients who take full dosages of the drugs for _____ or more years after initial improvement—a strategy called "_____ therapy"—reduce their risk for relapse even more.

4. When neurons release neurotransmitters into the synapse, they simultaneously "recapture" some of the neurotransmitter by way of a pumplike mechanism in the nerve ending. Answer the following questions about this process.

a. What is the purpose of this reuptake process?

_____

_____

b. What might be "going wrong" in the reuptake process of depressed people?

_____

_____

c. How are tricyclics thought to alleviate depressive symptoms?

_____

_____

5. This question has two parts: (a) What observation did researchers make about the action of tricyclics on the reuptake mechanism that led them to question how these drugs alleviate depression? and (b) What do researchers now believe about how tricyclics work?

a. _____

b. _____

_____

c. *Second-Generation Antidepressants, 271*

1. Some second-generation antidepressants such as Prozac (fluoxetine) are classified as selective _____ _____ _____ (SSRIs) because they alter serotonin activity specifically but do not affect other neurotransmitters in the brain.

2. List some of the (a) strengths and (b) weaknesses of the second-generation antidepressants compared to older tricyclics.

a. _____

b. _____

PsychWatch: First Dibs on Antidepressant Drugs?, 272

1. According to a 2005 Medicaid study, depressed individuals who were African American, Hispanic American, or Native American were _____ as likely as white Americans to be prescribed antidepressant medication on their initial therapy visit.

2. List three other trends indicating unequal treatment of white and nonwhite depressed individuals that were identified by this study.

_____

_____

3. Brain Stimulation, 273

a. Vagus Nerve Stimulation, 273

1. Vagus nerve stimulation was first developed by depression researchers who were trying to mimic the positive effects of _____ without the accompanying undesired effects and trauma.

2. Briefly describe the procedure of vagus nerve stimulation.

_____

_____

3. Why was vagus nerve stimulation approved by the U.S. Food and Drug Administration?

_____

_____

b. Transcranial Magnetic Stimulation, 274

1. In transcranial magnetic stimulation (TMS), an electromagnetic coil placed on the patient's head sends a current into the _____.

2. Describe the research conclusions about the effectiveness of TMS as a treatment for major depressive disorder.

_____

_____

_____

c. Deep Brain Stimulation, 274

1. In deep brain stimulation, tiny holes are drilled into the patient's skull and electrodes are implanted into _____ in the patient's brain. These electrodes are connected to a battery that sends a stream of low-voltage electricity to this brain region.

2. Although the early test results on deep brain stimulation have been very encouraging, why is it important for scientists to do much more research before assuming that this technique will prove effective and safe for most patients?

_____

_____

D. How Do the Treatments for Unipolar Depression Compare?, 275

1. In comparative outcome studies, _____ , _____ , interpersonal (IPT), and _____ therapies appear to be equally and highly effective at alleviating mild to severe depressive symptoms.

Below is a diagram relating to the ambitious National Institute of Mental Health outcome study of treatments for depression.

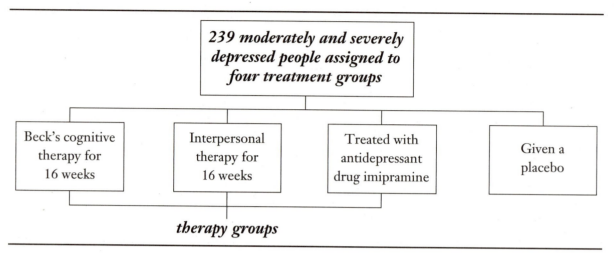

2. Answer the questions below relating to the findings of the National Institute of Mental Health outcome study of antidepressant therapy.

   a. Describe improvements in the three therapy groups.

   _____

   _____

   b. Describe the improvement in the placebo group.

   _____

   _____

   c. What were the differences in how quickly the treatments worked in relieving depression?

   _____

   _____

   d. _____ and _____ therapy may be more effective than _____ therapy at preventing relapses in depression, except when the latter therapy is continued for an extended period.

3. Because as many as _____ percent of depressed patients treated with cognitive or interpersonal therapies relapse, clinicians are now encouraging "continuation" or "_____" cognitive or IPT sessions to prevent relapse among successfully treated patients.

4. Depressed people who experience marital conflict are treated effectively with_____ therapy (with improvement rates similar to cognitive, IPT, and biological treatment rates).

5. _____ therapy is less effective in treating depression (particularly severe depression) than cognitive, interpersonal, or biological therapies.

6. A much disputed finding is that _____ therapy does not appear to be very effective in treating depression.

7. A combination of _____ and _____ therapy may be more helpful to depressed people than any single treatment, although the evidence for this is not consistent.

8. Complete the following statements that relate to biological treatments of unipolar depression.

   a. ECT seems to act more _____ than antidepressant drugs.

b. Clinicians usually treat depressed people with _____ first, and only if that treatment is unsuccessful will they consider _____ .

c. Research findings have indicated that _____ to _____ percent of people who do not respond to drug therapy are helped by ECT.

II. Treatments for Bipolar Disorders, 278–281

A. Lithium and Other Mood Stabilizers, 279

Researchers are not certain about how lithium relieves symptoms of bipolar disorder, but several possible explanations exist. The two most prominent theories involve second-messenger systems and sodium ion transport.

1. Lithium therapy requires that patients undergo regular analyses of _____ and _____ in order for doctors to determine the correct dosage.

2. If the lithium dosage is too low, the drug will be ineffective; however, if the dosage is too high, what are the potential results?

   _____

   _____

3. Improvement rates for people with manic symptoms who take lithium or other mood stabilizers are _____ percent and higher.

4. One study found that the risk of relapse is _____ times greater if patients stop taking mood stabilizers, suggesting that mood stabilizers may be a _____ drug (one that actually *prevents* symptoms from developing).

5. Study this diagram of the role of second messengers in neuronal firing, then complete the exercise that follows.

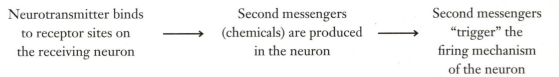

| Neurotransmitter binds to receptor sites on the receiving neuron | → | Second messengers (chemicals) are produced in the neuron | → | Second messengers "trigger" the firing mechanism of the neuron |

   a. Lithium appears to affect second-messenger chemicals called _____ which in turn alter the way certain neurons—presumably implicated in bipolar disorder—function.

6. To the extent that bipolar disorder is triggered by ion instability across the membranes of certain neurons, lithium may work by _____ for sodium ions themselves, or by changing the way that ions are transported across the neuronal membranes.

B. Adjunctive Psychotherapy, 281

1. Most clinicians agree that neither _____ alone nor _____ therapy alone is effective in treating bipolar disorders. In light of these beliefs, some clinicians utilize _____ , _____ , or _____ as adjuncts to mood-stabilizing drugs.

2. What are some of the reasons patients give for why they stop taking mood stabilizers?

   _____

   _____

3. List three objectives of therapies in the treatment of bipolar disorder.

   a. _____

   b. _____

   c. _____

4. Clinical reports suggest that combining psychotherapy with drug treatment for patients with bipolar disorder leads to reduced _____ , better social functioning, and higher _____ rates.

III. Putting It Together: With Success Come New Questions, 282

1. Summarize two explanations for the somewhat surprising finding that a number of **very** different approaches (e.g., cognitive therapy, electroconvulsive therapy, interpersonal therapy, etc.) have been effective in the treatment of unipolar depression.

   a. _____

   _____

   _____

   _____

   b. _____

   _____

   _____

   _____

MULTIPLE CHOICE

1. Why was the use of insulin, camphor, or metrazol to induce convulsions or comas in mentally ill people discontinued?
   a. It did not work.
   b. It was expensive.
   c. It was dangerous.
   d. The treatment was too difficult to manage.

2. What disorders are monoamine oxidase (MAO) inhibitors and tricyclics most effective in treating?
   a. agoraphobia
   b. schizophrenia
   c. bipolar disorders
   d. unipolar depression

3. There is some evidence that tricyclic antidepressant medications help depressed people feel better by
   a. raising monoamine oxidase (MAO) activity.
   b. lowering norepinephrine and serotonin activity.
   c. increasing the level of norepinephrine and serotonin synthesis.
   d. increasing the availability of norepinephrine and serotonin in the synapse.

4. Johnny has recently entered a large university and lately has been feeling depressed. He came from a very small high school with 35 seniors in his graduating class. He knew everyone and was a class leader. He feels lost in the crowd here. According to the premises of interpersonal psychotherapy, his depression stems from
   a. a grief reaction.
   b. an interpersonal conflict.
   c. an interpersonal role transition.
   d. unrealistic expectations regarding his place in his new school.

5. Which intervention is the single most effective current treatment for bipolar disorder?
   a. ECT
   b. lithium and other mood stabilizers
   c. tranquilizers
   d. antidepressant medication

6. George is depressed and has sought therapy. His cognitive therapist is most likely to
   a. test the reality behind his thoughts.
   b. reinforce him only when he says positive things.
   c. ask him to talk about conflicts he had with his parents as a child.
   d. question whether he is actually depressed.

7. The primary goal of the psychodynamic therapist in treating a patient who is depressed is
   a. to challenge depressive styles of thinking.
   b. to explore disputes and conflicts with significant others.
   c. to bring unconscious grief and dependency issues into conscious awareness.
   d. to reward active, non-depressed behavior and punish apathetic, depressed behavior.

8. Monoamine oxidase (MAO) serves the function of
   a. relieving depressive symptoms.
   b. breaking down the neurotransmitter norepinephrine.
   c. relieving manic symptoms.
   d. preventing the reuptake of serotonin.

9. One of the risks associated with the contemporary use of ECT is
   a. memory loss.
   b. death.
   c. stroke.
   d. fractures of limbs.

10. Approximately how many days after a person starts taking tricyclic antidepressant will he/she experience a reduction of depressive symptoms?
    a. 2 b. 5
    c. 10 d. 20

10   SUICIDE

1. Statistics show there are _____ suicides each year in the United States and _____ more unsuccessful attempts, called _____.

2. The textbook suggests that the actual number of suicides could be much higher than the official total. Give two reasons for the difficulty in obtaining accurate suicide statistics.

   a. Suicide is _____ by society, so relatives and friends might not acknowledge that suicide was the actual cause of death.

   b. _____

   _____

I. What Is Suicide?, 286–292

1. Edwin Shneidman defines **suicide** as a self-inflicted death in which the person makes an _____, direct, and _____ effort to end his or her life.

2. Complete the following table by describing the characteristics of Shneidman's four categories of people who attempt or commit suicide. Then, read through the case examples provided and match each with the most appropriate category.

Category	Description of Characteristics	Example
Death seekers		
Death initiators		
Death ignorers		
Death darers		

Cases:

a. Sheldon repeatedly engages in high-risk activities such as drinking and driving, and mixing alcohol and drugs. When his girlfriend pleads with him to stop the dangerous behavior, Sheldon usually retorts with statements like "You wouldn't care if I died, anyway" and "It would serve you right if I did kill myself one of these days."

b. After her suicide attempt by drug overdose, Jackie stated the following to a hospital psychiatric nurse: "I had thought about killing myself on and off for weeks. I would have a really bad day and almost do it, but then I'd feel a little better the next day and decide not to. Today was a really, really bad day—the worst."

c. Six-year-old Marianne is devastated after seeing her family dog, Jo-Jo, killed by a car in front of her house. Her parents try to comfort her by telling her that Jo-Jo is happy in heaven, but later she runs into the busy street and is nearly hit by an oncoming truck. When Marianne's parents ask why she did what she did, she replies, "I wanted to go to heaven to make sure Jo-Jo is okay."

    d. Antonio is a 72-year-old man who is suffering from advanced bone cancer. Certain that his last days will be filled with intolerable pain, Antonio asphyxiates himself in his car.

3. The term **subintentional death** describes a pattern of behavior. Describe this pattern in your own words, then come up with an original example.

    a. Description: _____

    _____

    b. Original example: _____

    _____

4. List some reasons why the behavioral pattern of self-injury or self-mutilation might become addictive to those who engage in it.

    _____

    _____

    _____

5. Why did the DSM-5 task force in the 2011 draft recommend adding a new category called non-suicidal self-injury (NSSI)? How might this new category affect the treatment and prevention of suicide, if it is ultimately adopted as part of the DSM-5?

    _____

    _____

    _____

A. How Is Suicide Studied?, 289

1. Complete the following statements regarding some of the sources of information used by researchers for **retrospective analyses** of suicide, and the limitations of those sources.

    a. Relatives and friends may remember past statements, conversations, and behavior that can be revealing. Unfortunately, grieving and perhaps guilt-ridden friends and relatives may be incapable of objective and accurate recollections.

    b. About half of all suicide victims have never been in _____, which limits this potential data source.

    c. Likewise, less than one-third of victims leave _____ _____.

    d. Because of these limitations, many researchers rely on a useful, albeit imperfect, study strategy. Describe that strategy.

    _____

    _____

B. Patterns and Statistics, 289

1. The United States and Canada have annual suicide rates of about 11.5 per 100,000 persons. List (a) three countries with *higher* rates and (b) three countries with *lower* rates.

    a. _____

    b. _____

2. _____ affiliation, in particular the extent to which people are devout in their beliefs, could account for national differences in suicide rates.

3. The male:female ratio for suicide *attempts* is roughly _____ : _____ , whereas the male:female ratio for suicide *completions* is roughly _____ : _____ .

4. Write a brief response to the question "Why do completed suicide rates differ between men and women?"

   _____

   _____

5. According to research on marital status and suicide, which groups of people are

   a. at higher risk for suicide? _____

   b. at lower risk for suicide? _____

6. The suicide rate of white Americans is _____ as high as the suicide rate for _____ Americans and members of most other nonwhite racial groups. (Be sure to examine Figure 10–1 in the textbook.)

7. The suicide rates of some Native Americans is an exception to the usual rule that white Americans have a higher suicide rate than nonwhite Americans. What are some of the factors that might account for the high suicide rate among Native Americans?

   _____

II. What Triggers a Suicide?, 292–297

A. Stressful Events and Situations, 292

1. Give examples of immediate and long-term stressors that might precipitate suicide.

   Immediate stressors: _____

   Long-term stressors: _____

2. Complete the following table by describing research evidence of the association between suicide and the delineated long-term stressors.

Long-Term Stressor Linked to Suicide	Research Evidence
Social isolation	
Serious illness	
Abusive environment	High suicide rates seen for prisoners of war, Holocaust victims, abused spouses and children, and prison inmates
Occupational stress	

B. Mood and Thought Changes, 293

    1. Increased sadness is one mood change that is associated with suicide. List some others.

        _____

    2. Describe the most salient cognitive changes (shifts in patterns in thinking) that seem to precipitate suicide.

        _____

        _____

        _____

PsychWatch: Can Music Inspire Suicide?, 294

    1. *Reread this section on page 294 of your textbook and reflect on whether you think music should be held accountable for inspiring some teenage suicides, or whether there are inevitably other factors at play. Do you think parents should be concerned about whether their children are listening to music that might inspire them to commit suicide? Explain.*

        _____

        _____

        _____

C. Alcohol and Other Drug Use, 295

    1. Evidence gained from autopsies of suicide victims indicate that about _____ percent of them drank alcohol just before the act, and that one-fourth of these people were legally intoxicated at the time of death.

    2. Alcohol may allow suicidal people to overcome their _____ of committing suicide, lower inhibitions against the expression of underlying _____, and/or impair their ability to make _____ and solve problems.

D. Mental Disorders, 295

    1. The majority of all suicide attempters meet DSM-IV-TR diagnostic criteria for a mental disorder. Which mental disorders are most often linked with suicide?

        _____

        _____

    2. Why might psychiatric staff continue to monitor a patient for suicide risk even after his or her depression seems to be lifting?

        _____

        _____

    3. Although the link between substance-related disorders and suicide is not well understood, there are two distinct possibilities that could explain the relationship. The first possibility is provided. What is the second?

        a. The substance user's tragic lifestyle may lead to a sense of hopelessness that triggers suicidal thinking.

        b. _____

        _____

4.   Among people with schizophrenia, suicide is most often associated with feelings of
      _____, rather than being a response to hallucinations or delusions.

E.   Modeling: The Contagion of Suicide, 296

1.   List the four kinds of models that most often seem to trigger suicide attempts.

      _____

2.   Can you think of people you know or have read about that have modeled suicides or suicide
      attempts? Write a paragraph describing the effects of that model on others' behavior.

      _____

      _____

      _____

      _____

III. What Are the Underlying Causes of Suicide?, 297–301

A.   The Psychodynamic View, 298

1.   Many psychodynamic theorists believe that suicide results from _____ and anger to-
      ward another person that is _____ toward oneself.

2.   Freud and others felt that through introjection, extreme _____ feelings toward a lost
      loved one could lead to unrelenting _____ toward oneself. Suicide could be yet a fur-
      ther expression of this self- _____.

3.   Freud suggested that human beings have a basic "death instinct," called _____, that
      most people direct toward _____ and suicidal people toward _____.

4.   Describe research findings supporting the psychodynamic theory of suicide in relation to (a) child-
      hood losses and (b) the "death instinct."

      a.   _____

           _____

      b.   _____

           _____

B.   Durkheim's Sociocultural View, 299

1.   Emile Durkheim proposed that a person's likelihood of committing suicide is strongly influenced by
      his or her involvement in social institutions and structures. Complete the following chart by provid-
      ing the missing information on social structures and Durkheim's three categories of suicide.

Category of Suicide	Relationship with Society	Characteristics or Examples of People in This Category
Egoistic Suicide		Isolated, alienated, nonreligious
Altruistic Suicide	So well integrated into the social structure that they sacrifice their lives for the well-being of society	
Anomic Suicide		Displaced by economic depression, social disintegration, and great changes in wealth/status

C. The Biological View, 300

The exercises in this subsection together represent an interesting "story" of how the biological view of suicide has evolved with continual research.

Until the 1970s, researchers using family pedigree studies consistently found evidence of higher than normal rates of suicidal behavior among the parents and close relatives of suicidal people. On the basis of this evidence, it was supposed that biological factors contributed to suicide.

1. Twin studies have supported the notion that genetic factors might contribute to suicide. Complete this exercise that relates to one Denmark study that examined suicide rates among the surviving twin in fraternal and identical twin pairs in which one of the pair had previously committed suicide.

   a. Out of the 19 identical twin pairs, _____ of the surviving twins also committed suicide.

   b. Out of the 58 fraternal twin pairs, _____ of the surviving twins also committed suicide.

2. Researchers have found evidence that low activity of the neurotransmitter serotonin is linked to suicide. Describe the results of these studies.

   _____

   _____

   _____

3. Some researchers speculate that low serotonin levels might increase the likelihood of suicide (regardless of the presence or absence of depression) by causing _____ feelings and _____ behavior.

4. Recent PET scan studies have revealed that people who contemplate or attempt suicide display abnormal activity in areas of the brain that are comprised of many _____-using neurons.

IV. Is Suicide Linked to Age?, 301–307

A. Children, 301

   1. Circle the correct answer in the following statements related to suicide among children.

      a. Of the children under the age of 14 who commit suicide each year in the United States, (boys/ girls) are five times more likely to be suicide victims than the other gender.

      b. It is (true/false) that most children who attempt suicide do not understand death and do not really wish to die.

   2. List some of the behaviors that commonly precede suicide attempts among children.

      _____

      _____

   3. What does recent research say about how common suicidal thinking is among "normal" children?

      _____

      _____

B. Adolescents, 302

   1. Suicide ranks _____ among causes of death in people between the ages of 15 and 19 in the United States.

   2. Although white American teenagers are more likely to attempt suicide than are African American teenagers, the suicide rates of these two groups have become more similar in recent years. One rea-

son for this trend may be that African American and white American youths increasingly are facing similar pressures to achieve academically. What are other possible reasons for this trend?

_____

_____

3. Compared to other teenagers, teenagers who attempt suicide seem to be more angry and _____, and have deficient problem-solving abilities.

4. Suicidal behavior in teenagers has been linked to depression, low self-esteem, and feelings of hopelessness, as well as to experiences of both long-term and immediate stress. List some of the (a) long-term and (b) immediate stressors that have been identified.

    a. _____

    b. _____

5. Describe some of the ways in which the period of adolescence itself produces stress that could increase the risk of suicide.

_____

_____

_____

6. The ratio of suicide attempts to fatalities among teenagers is about 200:1, suggesting that teenagers may be more _____ about killing themselves than people from other age groups.

7. Complete the following list of the four perceived societal changes discussed in the textbook that could explain the recent dramatic rise in suicides among adolescents and young adults.

    a. Competition for jobs, college positions, and academic and athletic honors is steadily increasing—leading to high levels of frustration and desperation in some.

    b. Recently weakened ties in the family structure have resulted in alienation and rejection among the young, fitting Durkheim's notion of _____ suicide.

    c. A propensity toward suicide may be increased by the availability of drugs and

    _____

    d. _____

    _____

8. List three or four possible reasons why Native Americans display the highest rates of teenage suicide of any ethnic group in the United States.

_____

_____

_____

PsychWatch: The Black Box Controversy: Do Antidepressants Cause Suicide?, 304

1. Identify one advantage to the mental health field stemming from the controversy over the FDA issuing black-box warnings regarding a potential link between antidepressants and suicide in children and young adults.

_____

_____

_____

C. The Elderly, 305

1. Suicide rates among the elderly are higher than in any other age group; in fact, elderly persons commit _____ percent of all suicides in the United States but account for just _____ percent of the U.S. population.

2. This subsection in the textbook discusses many factors and events that seem to contribute to the high rate of suicide among the elderly. In this workbook you have been presented with several case studies that depict people experiencing a range of problems. Now you will write a case study: one that fits the textbook's discussion of characteristics of the suicidal elderly. Describe the suicide of an 87-year-old woman. Be sure to include information on the victim's *recent life events, particular thoughts* and *feelings*. (*Note:* Writing your own case study will help you to remember the "profile" that is characteristic of elderly persons who attempt suicide.)

Case Study

3. Briefly describe explanations for the lower suicide rates (relative to elderly white Americans) of (a) elderly Native Americans and (b) elderly African Americans.

a. _____

_____

b. _____

_____

V. Treatment and Suicide, 309–313

A. What Treatments Are Used After Suicide Attempts?, 309

1. Studies indicate that most suicidal people do not receive continued _____ after a suicide attempt.

2. The first goal of therapy for people who have attempted suicide is to keep the client alive. What are two other primary goals?

a. _____

b. _____

3. About _____ percent of suicide attempters who receive treatment attempt suicide again, compared with _____ percent who do *not* receive treatment, suggesting that psychological intervention following a suicide attempt is effective.

4. List four ways in which cognitive-behavioral therapies, including mindfulness-based cognitive therapy, are found to be particularly helpful for suicidal people.

    a. _____

    b. _____

    c. _____

    d. _____

B. **What Is Suicide Prevention?, 309**

1. List two programs or services that have developed as a result of the growing emphasis on suicide *prevention* rather than suicide treatment.

    _____

    _____

2. List some of the characteristics of a person who is "in crisis."

    _____

    _____

3. Complete the following table by putting yourself in the place of a crisis-line counselor at the Los Angeles County Suicide Prevention Center. List your primary tasks to accomplish when taking a crisis call. Then match the task with the statement from the following list that is most indicative of that particular task. The first is given.

Task	Statement
1. Establishing a positive relationship	d.
2.	
3.	
4.	
5.	

Statements:

a. "Do you have a suicide plan at this point? Do you have access to a gun or pills?"

b. "What is going on in your life right now that feels difficult to handle? Did something happen that made you think about killing yourself?"

c. "Instead of hurting yourself, I want you to come to the crisis center now. Will you agree to do that?"

d. "I can hear how overwhelmed you feel. I want you to know that I am here to listen to you and help you."

e. "Do you have a friend or family member who you feel you can talk to and trust? Who is that person?"

4. How are online chat rooms and forums to which suicidal people turn different from suicide prevention centers and hot lines? Why are such chat rooms and forums less well-equipped to help people in crisis than hot lines and prevention centers?

_____

_____

C. Do Suicide Prevention Programs Work?, 312

Assessing the effectiveness of suicide prevention centers is difficult. The findings of such studies have not been consistent. While some studies indicate that in some communities, centers have had no effect on suicide rates—or even that rates have gone up after centers were established—these findings are not conclusive.

1. It appears that only a small percentage of suicidal people contact prevention centers; furthermore, whereas the highest rate of suicides is among elderly _____ _____, the typical caller to a suicide prevention center is young, _____, and _____.

2. A study of the Los Angeles Suicide Prevention Center indicated that among _____ people who did call the center, a much higher than expected number were averted from committing suicide.

3. One certain implication of effectiveness studies of suicide prevention centers seems to be that they need to be more _____ to and _____ for people who are harboring thoughts of suicide.

4. Edwin Shneidman has called for broader and more effective _____ _____ about suicide as the ultimate form of prevention.

VI. Putting It Together: Psychological and Biological Insights Lag Behind, 313–314

1. Which of the models of abnormality has made the most progress in terms of shedding light on the dynamics of suicide?

_____

2. The identification of effective strategies for people who are suicidal continues to evade clinicians and researchers, but it is clear that public _____ about suicide will be an important component of any successful intervention program.

MULTIPLE CHOICE

1. In Edwin Shneidman's taxonomy of people who end their own lives intentionally, those who do not believe that their self-inflicted death will mean the end of their existence are called
   a. death darers.
   b. death seekers.
   c. death ignorers.
   d. death initiators.

2. According to a study using a strategy of "hyperlink network analysis," suicidal individuals were least likely to visit Web sites that
   a. were pro-suicide.
   b. were dedicated to suicide prevention.
   c. offered treatment for suicidal individuals.
   d. offered educational suicide-related information.

3. About what percent of people who successfully commit suicide leave suicide notes?
   a. 5 percent–10 percent
   b. 20 percent–30 percent
   c. 40 percent–45 percent
   d. 55 percent–60 percent

4. Why do more men than women commit suicide?
   a. Men use more lethal means.
   b. Men make more attempts at suicide.
   c. Men are more likely to be death initiators.
   d. Women are more likely to be death ignorers.

5. What is the term for the belief that a current negative mood and situation cannot be changed?
   a. anxiety
   b. sadness
   c. hopelessness
   d. dichotomous thinking

6. According to Durkheim's sociological theory of suicide, egoistic suicide occurs when
   a. persons sacrifice themselves for their society.
   b. persons have a close friend who commits suicide.
   c. persons have a history of few ties to their society.
   d. individuals experience a sudden change in their relationship to society.

7. Which neurotransmitter has been linked to suicidal behavior when levels are low?
   a. GABA
   b. serotonin
   c. dopamine
   d. norepinephrine

8. The arguments in favor of a person's right to commit suicide generally focus on the issue of
   a. role conflict.
   b. serious illness.
   c. occupational stress.
   d. abusive environment.

9. Which of the following persons is in a group at highest risk for suicide?
   a. female, African American, single
   b. elderly Native American male, married
   c. adolescent white female
   d. elderly white male, divorced

CHAPTER

11   EATING DISORDERS

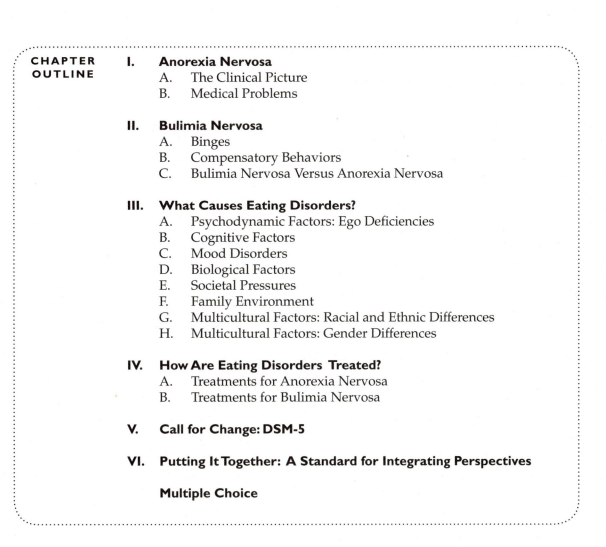

REVIEW EXERCISES

I. Anorexia Nervosa, 318–320

Until recently, anorexia nervosa and bulimia nervosa were viewed as very distinct disorders with different characteristics and causes that required different kinds of treatment. Although it is true that the varieties of eating disorders do have important differences, clinicians now realize that the similarities are significant as well.

1. According to the DSM-IV-TR, the central features of anorexia nervosa are:

    a. a refusal to maintain more than _____ percent of normal body weight,

    b. intense fear of becoming _____,

    c. a _____ view of body weight and shape, and

    d. the cessation of _____.

2. In _____-type anorexia, people move from cutting out sweets and fattening foods to eating very little food at all. *(Note the difference between this type and the binge-eating/purging type.)*

3. Complete the list of facts concerning anorexia nervosa.

    a. _____ to _____ percent of people with anorexia nervosa are female.

    b. The peak age of onset is between _____ and _____ years.

    c. About percent of the Western female population develops the disorder.

    d. The disorder often develops following a particularly _____ event in the person's life.

    e. Between _____ and _____ percent of people with anorexia nervosa die, typically from medical problems associated with _____ or from suicide.

A and B. The Clinical Picture and Medical Problems, 319

1. In the following table complete the summary of the central features of anorexia nervosa by providing an example of each feature.

Features	Examples Illustrating Features
Drive for thinness	The patient fears she will not be able to control her eating and that she will become obese
Preoccupied with food	

Cognitive distortions	
Psychological problems	
Medical problems	

II. Bulimia Nervosa, 320–324

1. Bulimia nervosa is also known as _____-_____ syndrome.

2. Define the following two terms as they relate to bulimia nervosa:

Binge:

_____

_____

Compensatory behavior:

_____

_____

3. Write the appropriate subtype of bulimia next to each description below.

   a. Jessie binges regularly, then does not eat for days and exercises at least four hours each day that she "fasts." _____

   b. Michelle, after consuming huge amounts of food very quickly, forces herself to vomit.

   _____

4. Unlike those who suffer from anorexia nervosa, the weight of people with bulimia nervosa usually fluctuates in the _____ range.

5. _____-_____ disorder, which does not involve compensatory behaviors, has been identified by clinicians but is not an official category of the DSM-IV-TR.

A. Binges, 321

1. Complete the following table by giving a description of the typical aspects of a binge that are listed.

Features	Examples Illustrating Features
Setting of binge	In secret
Types of food chosen	
Feelings at start of binge	Unbearable tension, irritability, removed, powerless
Feelings during binge	
Feelings after binge	

B. Compensatory Behaviors, 323

1. Describe the results of the following kinds of compensatory behaviors: (a) self-induced vomiting and (b) laxative abuse.

   a. _____

   _____

   b. _____

   _____

C. Bulimia Nervosa Versus Anorexia Nervosa, 323

1. List five similarities between anorexia nervosa and bulimia nervosa.

   a. _____

   b. _____

   c. _____

   d. _____

   e. _____

2. In the table below, certain features that seem to distinguish the "typical" person with anorexia nervosa from the "typical" person with bulimia nervosa are presented. Decide which disorder is being described in each column, then write the name of the disorder in the box above the column.

Which disorder is described?

	_____	_____
Physical features	Weight fluctuation, dental and gastrointestinal problems, potassium deficiencies	Very underweight, amenorrhea
Personality and mood	Impulsive, dramatic, mood swings, trusting, need to please others	Less trusting, emotionally over-controlled, obsessive
Behavior	More antisocial behavior, more alcohol and drug use, more likely to be sexually experienced/active	Less antisocial behavior, less likely to be sexually active

III. **What Causes Eating Disorders?, 324–335**

    1.   Today's theorists usually apply a _____ _____ perspective to eating disorders—a view that identifies several key factors that place a person at risk for developing them.

A. Psychodynamic Factors: Ego Deficiencies, 324

    1.   Eating disorders pioneer Hilde Bruch proposed a theory of eating disorders that is in line with the _____ perspective.

    2.   Study the completed diagram that shows how Bruch proposed children of "effective" parents were raised. Then give the missing information in the diagram below it showing how eating disorders can develop in the children of "ineffective" parents.

Effective parents accurately attend to their children's expressions of biological and emotional needs	⟶ Children develop a sense of self-control and are able to differentiate between internal need states	⟶ Children become autonomous, confident, and self-reliant individuals

Ineffective parents: ⟶ _____ _____ _____ _____ _____ _____	Children fail to develop cohesive self-concept and are unable to differentiate between internal need states—children rely on other people (parents) to tell them what they need and when they need it	⟶ As adolescents, children feel _____ because they are unable to establish _____ ⟶ To overcome these feelings, children try to achieve extreme _____ over their body size and shape, and their _____

    3.   Research and clinical reports support Bruch's tenet that parents of adolescents with eating disorders define their children's needs for them. List two other tenets relating to people with eating disorders that have been supported.

        a. _____

            _____

        b. _____

            _____

B. Cognitive Factors, 326

    1.   Cognitive theorists believe that a broad cognitive distortion, or "_____ ," lies at the center of disordered eating.

    2.   Explain the ways in which cognitive theorists believe this type of disordered thinking is on display in anorexia and bulimia nervosa:

        _____

        _____

C. Mood Disorders, 327

    1.   In the following table, summarize the research findings that support the notion that people who suffer from mood disorders are predisposed to develop eating disorders.

Research Topic	Findings
Major depression	
Close relatives	
Neurotransmitter activity	
Medications	The dysfunctional eating patterns of those with eating disorders are often helped significantly by antidepressant drugs

D. Biological Factors, 327

1. Some research findings support the contention that genetic factors contribute to the development of eating disorders. Fill in the missing statistics below.

   a. Compared to the general population, relatives of those with eating disorders are up to _____ times more likely to develop the disorders themselves.

   b. The concordance rate for bulimia nervosa among identical twins is _____ percent, whereas the concordance rate for fraternal twins is only _____ percent.

2. Recently, researchers found a link between abnormally low levels of the neurotransmitter _____ and eating disorders; the specific relationship between these variables is still being studied.

*Biological researchers are also interested in the role that specific brain areas might play in eating disorders. In particular, the **hypothalamus**— a part of the brain that regulates the endocrine system —has been implicated. Complete the following questions related to the ways in which hypothalamic functioning might be related to eating disorders.*

3. The _____ hypothalamus (LH) and the _____ hypothalamus (VMH), the two parts of the hypothalamus that control eating, have become the focus of biological researchers studying eating disorders.

4. Researchers think that the LH, the VMH, and the natural appetite suppressant called GLP-1 set up a "weight thermostat" in the body that predisposes people to maintain a stable body weight, called the weight _____ _____ _____.

5. What are the two things that happen when a person's weight falls *below* his or her weight set point? The _____ is activated and seeks to _____ the lost weight by (1) _____ hunger, and (2) _____ the body's metabolic rate.

6. What are the two things that happen when a person's weight *rises above* his or her weight set point? The _____ is activated and seeks to _____ the excess weight by (1) _____ hunger, and (2) _____ the body's metabolic rate.

E. Societal Pressures, 330

1. The textbook describes several pieces of evidence that since the 1950s, Western culture's image of the "perfect" female form has steadily become thinner. Describe the findings related to "Miss America," "Playboy," or "thin subcultures."

   _____

   _____

   _____

2. Describe the research findings of one of the studies in the textbook that point to Western society's prejudice against overweight people.

    _____

    _____

    _____

3. A recent survey of 248 adolescent girls found that those who spent more time on Facebook, and on fashion and music Web sites, were _____ likely to display eating disorders, experience negative body image, and eat in dysfunctional ways.

F. Family Environment, 331

1. Research findings suggest that as many as half of the people with eating disorders come from families who seem to emphasize _____, physical appearance, and _____.

    Theorist Salvador Minuchin believes that **enmeshed family patterns** can lead to eating disorders. Study the chart on enmeshed family patterns below, then complete the following exercises.

    Characteristics of Enmeshed Family "Set the Stage" for Eating Disorders

    ---

    -   family members are overinvolved with each other's affairs
    -   family members are overconcerned about each other's welfare
    -   little room for family members' individuality and autonomy
    -   parents too involved in the lives of their children
    -   family members are discouraged from speaking about their own ideas and feelings
    -   families can be clinging and foster dependency

    Conflict Arises During Adolescence

    During adolescence, these characteristics come into conflict with the natural tendency toward independence among adolescents

    ---

    As a Result, Problems Can Develop

    The family responds to the conflict by subtly forcing the child to take on a "sick" role (to develop an eating disorder or some other problem)

    ---

2. The chart lists negative characteristics of the enmeshed family. List any aspects of the pattern that could be viewed as positive.

    _____

    _____

3. _____ studies and empirical studies have sometimes, but not always, lent support to this family systems explanation.

G. Multicultural Factors: Racial and Ethnic Differences, 332

1. Briefly compare the attitudes toward their own body image and beauty of young African American women and young white women revealed in a 1995 study at the University of Arizona, and then briefly describe the clinical picture that has been unfolding since then. Suggest some possible reasons for the changes.

    a. Pre-1995 _____

    _____

_____

_____

b. Post-1995 _____

_____

_____

_____

2. Briefly describe the results of the 2006 study in which mental health professionals and clinical psychology graduate students evaluated the diary of a 16-year-old girl—some having been told that the girl was white, some that the girl was African American, and some that the girl was Hispanic American.

_____

_____

_____

H. **Multicultural Factors: Gender Differences, 334**

1. Males account for _____ to _____ percent of all cases of eating disorders.

2. Give two possible reasons for the disparity in eating disorder rates between males and females.

a. _____

b. _____

3. Give two reasons men develop eating disorders.

a. _____

b. _____

4. There is a new eating disorder emerging, found almost exclusively among men, known as _____ , or _____ .

IV. **How Are Eating Disorders Treated?, 335–343**

Current treatments for eating disorders vary depending on the symptoms, behaviors, and circumstances of each client. However, all treatments are comprised of two broad components, or dimensions: (1) correcting the eating pattern that is endangering the client's health and (2) addressing the psychological and situational factors that led to and maintain the eating disorder.

A. **Treatments for Anorexia Nervosa, 335**

Read the following case study to be used in an exercise relating to the treatment of anorexia nervosa.

Case Study

Josie S. is a 15-year-old female who was referred to the City Hospital's Department of Psychiatry because she is believed to be suffering from anorexia nervosa. Josie is 5 feet 6 inches tall. In the last six months, her weight has dropped 59 pounds, from 142 to 83 pounds. She appears emaciated and is physically weak. Josie reached menarche at age 11 but has not had a period in 16 weeks. Her parents state that although they really wanted Josie to lose some weight "because she was too big to wear all the nice clothes" they bought for her, they are now concerned because she is refusing to eat meals at home. Josie reports that she feels fine and "doesn't understand all the fuss because I am still a fat pig."

1. This exercise is designed to give you a thorough understanding of some of the important concepts and issues involved in the treatment of eating disorders. Be sure that you have carefully read pages 335–338 in the textbook before attempting this exercise.

   In this exercise, you will put yourself in the place of the therapist assigned to treat Josie's anorexia nervosa by completing the "treatment plans" on the following pages. For both of the treatment dimensions listed, describe the specific treatment strategies that you might employ as Josie's therapist.

City Hospital—Department of Psychiatry

Treatment Plan for:	Josie S.
Diagnosis:	Anorexia nervosa, restrictive type

Treatment dimension: Weight restoration and resumption of normal eating patterns

---

Treatment Strategy #1: **Medical/biological approaches:** If Josie's life is threatened, use tube and intravenous feedings and/or antidepressant drugs to help restore her weight.

Treatment Strategy #2: **Behavioral approach:**

Treatment Strategy #3: **Supportive nursing care:**

Treatment dimension: Address broader psychological and family issues

---

Treatment Strategy #1: **Self-exploration/insight approach:** Help Josie express her need for independence and control in more appropriate ways; help Josie learn to recognize and trust her internal sensations and feelings.

Treatment Strategy #2: **Cognitive-behavioral approach:**

Treatment Strategy #3: **Family therapy:**

---

2. This exercise summarizes some of the positive and negative outcomes of people who have been treated for anorexia nervosa. Complete the statements below.

Posttreatment Positive Outcomes

When patients are evaluated several years after treatment:

a. As many as _____ percent continue to show improvement.

b. _____ returns and other medical problems improve.

Posttreatment Negative Outcomes

When patients are evaluated several years after treatment:

a. Up to _____ percent continue to show significant anorexic symptoms and behaviors.

b. Approximately _____ percent continue to show emotional difficulties, such as depression, social anxiety, and obsessiveness.

3. This exercise focuses on the recovery rates of people who have been treated for anorexia nervosa and addresses information contained on pages 339–340 of the textbook. In the following paragraph, create a profile for the "ideal" patient with anorexia nervosa from the standpoint of the characteristics that seem to indicate the best chances for recovery. Draw a line through the option within each set of parentheses that represents the *poorer* prognosis or recovery rate.

> Before treatment, the patient lost (a lot of/relatively little) weight. The patient suffered with the disorder for a (long/short) period without successful clinical intervention. (The patient) was a (young adolescent/older person) at the time of treatment. The patient (did/did not) experience pre-onset psychological and sexual problems.

B. Treatments for Bulimia Nervosa, 340

Treatment programs for bulimia nervosa emphasize education as well as therapy. Specific treatment strategies are addressed in the following exercise.

1. Complete this table summarizing treatment strategies for bulimia nervosa. Find two examples of strategies for each type of treatment approach (from the list following the table), and then summarize the effectiveness of each approach.

Treatment Approach	Examples	Effectiveness
Individual insight therapy	b.	Pschodynamic, cognitive, and combined approaches effective
Group therapy		
Behavioral therapy		Decrease in eating anxiety; decreased binging and purging
Antidepressant medications		

Examples

a. Group meals in which clients plan and eat a meal together, while discussing thoughts and feelings

b. Free association and interpretation of clients' underlying conflicts about lack of self-trust and need for control

c. Exposure and response prevention

d. Teaching that having an eating disorder is not "strange" or shameful

e. Evaluation and alteration of maladaptive beliefs toward food, eating, and weight (e.g., "I must lose weight in order to be happy")

f. Keeping diaries of eating behavior, body sensations, thoughts, and feelings

g. Use of Prozac or similar drugs

h. Daily texts to therapists reporting on binge urges and behavior, with encouraging feedback from the therapists

2. Complete the following statements regarding the aftermath of bulimia nervosa.

a. Of clients treated for bulimia, _____ percent almost immediately stop their binge-purge behaviors and stabilize their eating habits, 40 percent show a moderate response to treatment, and the remaining _____ percent show no improvement in bulimic behaviors.

b. Revisited years after treatment, _____ percent of people with bulimia had recovered, according to recent studies.

c. As with anorexia, relapses are usually precipitated by new _____ in the person's life.

d. One study showed that almost one-third of recovered bulimic clients relapsed within _____ years of treatment.

V. Call for Change: DSM-5, 343

1. Identify the three significant changes to the grouping and diagnosing of eating disorders that the DSM-5 task force proposed in 2011. Briefly discuss why the task force has recommended these potential changes for the upcoming DSM-5, which is scheduled for publication in 2013.

a. _____
   _____

b. _____
   _____

c. _____
   _____

VI. Putting It Together: A Standard for Integrating Perspectives, 343–344

1. Describe the multidimensional risk perspective on eating disorders.

   _____
   _____
   _____
   _____

2. As stated in your text, one person who had recovered from bulimia nervosa made a very intriguing comment: **"I still miss my bulimia as I would an old friend who has died"** (Canwels, 1983). Discuss possible meanings of this statement, and explain why it is so important for clinicians to understand feelings like these if they want to provide effective treatments for patients with eating disorders.

   _____
   _____
   _____
   _____
   _____

MULTIPLE CHOICE

1. The relentless pursuit of thinness by starving to lose weight is called
   a. obesity.
   b. obsession.
   c. anorexia nervosa.
   d. bulimia nervosa.

2. The person who will be anorexic usually starts out
   a. underweight.
   b. quite a bit overweight.
   c. just to lose a little weight.
   d. always with normal weight.

3. One reason men are less likely to suffer from anorexia than women is the cultural stereotype that the "perfect" male body is
   a. thin.
   b. tall.
   c. muscular.
   d. much more variable than for women.

4. People who display anorexia nervosa usually display
   a. mania.
   b. a clinical depression.
   c. a preoccupation with food.
   d. generalized anxiety disorder.

5. For people with bulimia nervosa, binge episodes are often preceded by feelings of
   a. mania.
   b. control.
   c. high tension.
   d. guilt and depression.

6. In contrast to people suffering from anorexia nervosa, individuals suffering from bulimia nervosa
   a. are less concerned with food.
   b. don't struggle with anxiety and depression.
   c. tend to be more interested in pleasing others.
   d. feel conflicted about what, when, and how much to eat.

7. According to a survey of women in sports, the weight-control method that is most likely to be used/abused by female athletes in general is
   a. using diet pills.
   b. using a diuretic.
   c. using a laxative.
   d. inducing vomiting.

8. Activation of the _____ appears to produce hunger.
   a. thalamus
   b. lateral hypothalamus
   c. anterior hypothalamus
   d. ventromedial hypothalamus

9. The prognosis for recovery from anorexia nervosa is worse as a function of
   a. the length of time in treatment.
   b. amount of weight lost before treatment.
   c. the weight of the patient at the onset of treatment.
   d. the amount of weight gained by the patient during treatment.

10. Parents who incorrectly interpret their children's actual conditions are:
    a. enmeshed.
    b. ineffective.
    c. dysfunctional.
    d. anticipatory.

11. What is the *first* goal of most treatment plans for anorexia?
    a. weight gain
    b. changing misperceptions about the body
    c. changing eating habits
    d. changing purging habits

12 SUBSTANCE-RELATED DISORDERS

REVIEW EXERCISES

The following exercises cover Chapter 12's introductory material on pages 347–349.

Match numbers 1–6 below with the appropriate letter from the list a–f.

1. _____ Intoxication

2. _____ Hallucinosis

3. _____ Substance abuse

4. _____ Substance dependence

5. _____ Tolerance

6. _____ Withdrawal

   a. Condition in which a person needs increasing doses of a substance in order to keep obtaining the desired effect.

   b. A state of perceptual distortions and hallucinations.

   c. Condition in which people experience unpleasant symptoms when they suddenly stop taking or reduce their dosage of a drug.

   d. Addiction—physical dependence on a drug.

   e. A temporary syndrome in which the person exhibits impaired judgment, mood changes, irritability, slurred speech, and loss of coordination.

   f. An excessive and chronic reliance on drugs, in which the drugs occupy a central place in a person's life.

7. Research indicates that in any given year in the United States, 8.9 percent of all adults have a substance-related disorder, but only about _____ percent of these individuals receive treatment.

8. The highest rate of substance abuse or dependence in the United States is found among American _____, while the lowest is among _____ Americans.

I. Depressants, 349–358

A. Alcohol, 349

1. Almost 7 percent of all persons over 11 years of age are heavy drinkers, which means that they consume at least _____ drinks on at least _____ occasions each month.

2. The ratio of male heavy drinkers to female heavy drinkers is about _____ to one.

Ethyl alcohol consumption affects the physiological, cognitive, and emotional states of people who consume progressively more amounts of it. Study the diagram, which illustrates these progressive effects.

All alcoholic beverages contain ethyl alcohol, which is . . .

↓

Rapidly absorbed into the blood through the lining of the stomach and the intestines

↓

Alcohol is taken by the bloodstream to the central nervous system (CNS)

↓

In the CNS, alcohol acts to depress functioning by binding to GABA receptors

---

Alcohol first affects the higher centers of the CNS, which control judgment and inhibition
- People become less constrained, more talkative, and often more friendly
- As inner control breaks down, they may feel relaxed, safe, self-confident, and happy
- Impairment of fine motor skills, increased sensitivity to light, feeling warm, and having a flushed face and neck also occur

These effects increase, and other CNS areas are depressed, as more alcohol is ingested
- People become still less restrained and more confused
- The ability to make rational judgments declines, speech becomes less guarded and less coherent, and memory falters
- Many become loud, boisterous, and aggressive, and emotions become exaggerated
- Motor impairment increases, reaction times slow, people become unsteady, and vision and hearing problems occur

3. The concentration of ethyl alcohol in the _____ determines its effect on body chemistry.

4. Women have significantly _____ of the stomach enzyme called alcohol _____, the enzyme that breaks down alcohol before it enters the blood.

5. The effects of alcohol decline as it is _____ by the liver; this rate differs among people, so rates of "_____" vary as well.

6. What are the only two things that can help a person sober up?

I. Alcohol Abuse and Dependence, 351

1. About 3 percent of high school _____ say that they use alcohol daily, and approximately 14 percent of those in _____ school say that they have consumed alcohol.

2. At some point in their lives, about 13 percent of all adults in the United States will experience a pattern of alcohol abuse and/or dependence. The male to female ratio of these patterns in adults is at least _____ to 1.

3. Each of the following case studies illustrates one of three broad patterns of alcohol abuse described in the textbook. Make up a name for each pattern that will help you remember it (if your instructor has given names, use those). Then underline the parts of each description that are typical for that pattern.

Case Study

Name of pattern:

Almost every day of Alan's life in the last six years has been built around alcohol. This is his fourth year in college, but he hasn't progressed much since he rarely makes it through the entire term of a class. Alan usually blames "rotten" professors. Most days Alan gets up at lunchtime (he's learned not to attempt morning classes) and meets friends at a fast-food restaurant. Invariably he orders just a jumbo soft drink, which he proceeds to spike with alcohol. If he hasn't drunk too much, and if he isn't too hungover, he might then go to a class or two. Often, however, Alan goes straight from "lunch" to a bar, where he nibbles on the buffalo wings they put out at happy hour and drinks copious amounts of beer until he stumbles home and passes out.

Name of pattern:

There are over 20 times as many people attending Rebecca's college as there are living in her hometown. She is the first member of her family to go to college, and she wants to make everyone proud of her. Rebecca gets excellent grades because she works very hard, never missing a class and spending a good part of the evenings in the library. After a long day of studying, though, she usually goes to her room and drinks alone for at least a couple of hours. Rebecca gets up early on Saturdays to go to the library. However, her Saturday afternoons and Sundays are spent just like her weekday evenings—drinking alone in her room.

Name of pattern:

Ric is probably the most intelligent and hardest working undergraduate in his college's math department. He loves his classes, and he pushes himself tremendously to maintain a near-perfect academic record. Whenever a big test is approaching, he vanishes for several days so he can devote himself entirely to studying. The results are always the same—an A+. Once the test is over, Ric makes up for lost time by partying every bit as hard as he studies. If a test falls on a Thursday, he probably won't draw a sober breath from that night until Monday morning. Stories of these episodes and of his drunken exploits during school vacations have become legendary among his friends. Ric is glad for this, since he himself often remembers little of what he does while drunk.

4. For many, the pattern of alcoholism includes physical dependence. Complete these exercises relating to the effects of physical dependence.

   a. As they use alcohol repeatedly, many build up a _____ , which forces them to drink more to feel any effects.

   b. Describe some of the withdrawal symptoms people dependent on alcohol experience when they stop drinking.

   _____

   _____

   c. Alcohol withdrawal delirium, or _____ _____ (the DT's), is characterized by great mental confusion, clouded consciousness, and terrifying visual _____.

   d. Like most other alcohol withdrawal symptoms, the DT's usually run their course in two to three days.

2. What Is the Personal and Social Impact of Alcoholism?, 354

1. List some of the social costs of alcoholism.

   _____

   _____

2. Write a paragraph about the impact of alcoholism on the 30 million children of alcoholic parents.

   _____

   _____

   _____

   _____

   _____

Take a few moments to consider some of the damaging physical effects of chronic and excessive alcohol consumption. Make sure you understand how alcohol consumption can lead to each of the following physical problems:

- Cirrhosis of the liver
- Heart failure, irregularities of heart functioning
- Immune system impairment, susceptibility to certain diseases
- Malnutrition, Korsakoff's syndrome (see below)

3. Chronic alcohol use can result in malnutrition, since alcohol contains no nutritional value, but lowers a person's desire for food. Furthermore, alcohol-related vitamin and mineral deficiencies can result in mental disorders, such as Korsakoff's syndrome. Complete this diagram relating to these disorders.

Alcohol-related
vitamin B
deficiency   ⟶ *can lead to* ⟶   Korsakoff's
syndrome

*vitamin B is
also called:*

Characteristics

4. Alcohol during pregnancy can result in miscarriage and **fetal alcohol syndrome.** What are some of the characteristics of fetal alcohol syndrome?

_____

_____

B. Sedative-Hypnotic Drugs, 355

1. Sedative-hypnotic drugs produce a sedative or _____ effect at low doses and at high doses are _____ inducers.

1. Barbiturates, 355

1. Low doses of barbiturates reduce anxiety by binding to _____ of the inhibitory neurotransmitter _____.

2. Overdoses of barbituates can result in _____ failure and _____ blood pressure, leading to coma and even death.

3. List some parallels between alcohol dependence and barbiturate dependence.

_____

_____

4. One of the great dangers of barbiturate dependence is that the _____ dose of the drug remains the same even while the body is building up to a _____ for its other effects.

2. Benzodiazepines, 355

1. Complete these items relating to benzodiazepines, the antianxiety drugs discovered in the 1950s that are now the most popular hypnotic drugs available.

    a. What are some of the trade names of benzodiazepines?

    _____

    b. Reasons for their popularity include the fact that, compared to other kinds of sedative-hypnotic drugs, they relieve anxiety while causing less _____, and their use is less likely to lead to death by an _____.

    c. Approximately 1 percent of the adults in the United States abuse or become dependent on anti-anxiety drugs at some point in their lives.

C.   Opioids, 356

Be sure to read the material in the textbook about the many uses and misuses of opioids from the use of opium in ancient times through the development of synthetic opioids in our day.

1.   Write in the correct term that is associated with the following definitions.

    Term   *Definition*

    a. _____   Used in the past as a cough medicine and pain reliever, this highly addictive, illegal substance is derived from morphine.

    b. _____   This is the name for all natural and synthetic opioids that include both illegal and medically prescribed substances.

    c. _____   A natural substance that comes from the sap of poppies.

    d. _____   A synthetic opioid manufactured in laboratories that is sometimes used in the treatment of heroin addiction.

    e. _____   A substance that is derived from opium that is medically prescribed for pain relief but that can lead to addiction.

2.   Narcotics may be smoked, inhaled, injected just beneath the skin, or " _____," which means it is injected directly into the _____.

3.   Name and describe the two phases people experience when they use narcotics.

    a. _____, _____

    b. _____, _____

4.   Opioids generate their effects because they stimulate neuron receptor sites that usually receive _____, neurotransmitters that help to relieve _____ and _____ emotional tension.

1. Heroin Abuse and Dependence, 357

1.   Most heroin abusers develop a dependence on it, quickly building up a tolerance and experiencing withdrawal symptoms when they abstain. Complete these statements relating to heroin withdrawal symptoms.

    a. Initial withdrawal symptoms include _____, restlessness, _____, and rapid breathing.

    b. Symptoms become progressively more serious for two or three days and can be accompanied by twitching, constant aches, fever, vomiting and diarrhea, loss of appetite, higher blood pressure, dehydration, and weight loss.

    c. Unless the person takes more heroin, the withdrawal distress usually peaks by the _____ day and disappears by the _____ day.

2. What Are the Dangers of Heroin Abuse?, 357

1. During a heroin overdose, the drug depresses the _____ center of the brain, virtually paralyzing it.

2. List two major health risks besides overdosing to which heroin users are particularly susceptible.

   _____

   _____

II. Stimulants, 358–363

Cocaine and amphetamine use stimulates activity of the central nervous system, resulting in effects such as increased blood pressure and heart rate, as well as intensified behavioral activity, thought processes, and alertness.

A. Cocaine, 358

1. Cocaine is the most powerful _____ stimulant known and is derived from the _____ plant, found in South America.

2. Processed cocaine is most commonly snorted through the nose, but it is also intravenously injected, or _____.

Be sure to read about the dramatic surge in the number of people in the United States who have tried cocaine over the course of the last few decades. Today 1.6 million people are using cocaine. Many users are young; almost 7 percent of all high school seniors have used cocaine in the past year.

3. Describe the high experienced by those who use cocaine.

   _____

4. Cocaine produces its effects because it overstimulates the central nervous system by releasing excessive amounts of which three neurotransmitters?

   _____

5. What are the symptoms of cocaine intoxication?

   _____

6. If a person with a physical dependence for cocaine decides to stop, what are the withdrawal symptoms that may result from abstinence?

   _____

   _____

7. Newer forms of cocaine have produced an increase in abuse and dependence on the drug. Complete the statements regarding these recent forms.

   a. In the technique called _____, the pure cocaine basic alkaloid is chemically separated from processed cocaine, vaporized by heat from a flame, and inhaled with a pipe.

   b. Almost 1.5 percent of high school seniors say they have used _____ (a form of free-base cocaine) in the past year.

Take some time to consider the many ways in which cocaine can be an extremely dangerous drug to one's health. Be sure you understand how cocaine use can lead to each of the following physical problems:

- Cocaine overdose (effects on the brain and body)
- Irregular heart functioning
- Fetal cocaine syndrome

B. **Amphetamines, 361**

1. Unlike substances such as opium and cocaine, amphetamines are stimulant drugs that are _____ in the laboratory.

2. List some of the uses and misuses of amphetamines since they were first synthesized in the 1930s.

_____

_____

_____

3. Amphetamines are taken in the form of _____, can be injected, or are ingested in such forms as "ice" and "_____."

4. Complete the list of physiological and psychological similarities between the effects of amphetamines and cocaine.

   a. In low doses, they both increase energy and alertness and reduce appetite.

   b. Both cause an emotional _____ as they leave the body.

   c. Both stimulate the central nervous system by increasing the release of the neurotransmitters _____, _____, and _____.

Read the following case study relating to amphetamine abuse.

Case Study

Margaret is a full-time college student, holds a part-time job, and is also on the cross-country team. While competing in a track meet one week ago, Margaret started her race feeling good and full of energy. At the 1-mile mark, however, she felt a wrenching pain in her hamstring muscle. She pushed herself to run, but had to drop out of the race as she approached the 2-mile mark. Margaret felt exhausted, and the pain in her leg was excruciating. After being examined by a physician, Margaret learned that in addition to tearing several ligaments, she had tested positive for amphetamines. She confessed to her coach that she had been using increasing amounts of Dexedrine in order to maintain the energy she needed to keep up with the demands of her life.

---

5. Using the concepts of tolerance and dependence, how would you explain Margaret's increased amphetamine use and subsequent injuries?

_____

_____

_____

6. Almost _____ percent of all Americans over the age of 11 in the United States have used methamphetamine at least once.

7. Compared to men, women are _____ likely to use methamphetamine.

8. One particular health concern associated with methamphetamine use is _____ , which damages nerve endings.

C. Caffeine, 362

1. List the most common forms in which caffeine is consumed.

   _____

2. Caffeine affects the central nervous system by stimulating the release of which three neurotransmitters?

   _____

3. The possible physiological effects of caffeine include disruption of the performance of complex motor tasks and interference with both duration and quality of sleep. Listed below are several physiological processes. Put an "I" before those that caffeine increases, and a "D" before those it decreases.

   _____ Arousal   _____ Fatigue
   _____ General motor activities   _____ Rate of breathing
   _____ Heart rate   _____ Secretion of gastric acid by stomach

4. Describe (a) the method and (b) results of Silverman and colleagues' study on the effects of caffeine withdrawal.

   a. _____

   _____

   b. _____

   _____

III. Hallucinogens, Cannabis, and Combinations of Substances, 363–370

A. Hallucinogens, 363

1. **Hallucinogens** (aka psychedelics) are chemical substances that affect sensory experiences, producing sensations that are sometimes called "_____."

2. Psychedelics include **LSD** (_____ _____ diethylamide), mescaline, psilocybin, and MDMA (also called _____).

3. LSD was derived by the Swiss chemist Albert Hoffman in 1938 from a group of naturally occurring drugs called _____ _____.

4. Describe hallucinogen intoxication, or hallucinosis.

   _____

   _____

5. If a person using LSD has sensations that he or she can "see" musical vibrations in the air, that person is experiencing _____.

6. The immediate effects of LSD wear off in about _____ hours.

Study this diagram that shows how LSD produces the characteristics of a "trip."

Normal Process		LSD-Influenced Process
Serotonin released	*Neurons*	LSD binds to serotonin receptor sites, preventing release of serotonin
↓		↓
Serotonin helps filter incoming sensory information	*The Brain*	Brain is flooded by sensory input
Undistorted Sensory Perception		*Distorted Sensory Perception* (e.g., hallucinations)

7. Even though LSD use does not result in significant tolerance or withdrawal, it poses serious risks— even to first-time users. Complete the following questions relating to the three primary risks related to LSD.

    a. LSD is so remarkably _____ that a dose of any size is likely to elicit powerful perceptual, emotional, and behavioral reactions—which are sometimes extremely unpleasant (i.e., a "bad trip").

    b. _____ sensory and emotional changes that recur long after the LSD has left the body—called _____—are experienced by about a quarter of LSD users.

B. Cannabis, 366

1. Cannabis is harvested from the leaves and flowers of the _____ plant, and its main active ingredient is **tetrahydrocannabinol**, or _____.

2. The most powerful of the cannabis drugs is _____, whereas the most common is _____.

3. Complete this exercise by describing some of the characteristics of cannabis intoxication as they relate to the categories below.

    a. *Mood changes:* Most people feel joyful and relaxed and become contemplative or talkative. Others become anxious, suspicious, apprehensive, or irritated.

    b. *Perceptual distortions:* Many report sharpened perceptions and preoccupation with sounds and sights. _____ seems to slow down, and distances and _____ seem greater than they actually are.

    c. *Physical changes:* _____

4. The effects of cannabis last about _____ to _____ hours, although mood changes can persist.

5. What is the main reason that increased patterns of marijuana abuse and dependence have emerged since the early 1970s?

6. Researchers have become more aware of the potential negative effects of chronic marijuana use, such as how it induces panic attacks in some. Describe other negative effects.

    _____

    _____

    _____

    Read through the material on "Cannabis and Society" on pages 368–369, and consider how you feel about the legalization of medical marijuana, the 2005 United States Supreme Court ruling on the subject, and the 2009 directive from the U.S. Attorney General against prosecuting medical marijuana cases when state laws are followed.

C. **Combinations of Substances, 369**

1. Define **cross-tolerance.**

    _____

    _____

2. A synergistic effect occurs when different drugs are in the body at the same time and they enhance each other's effect. Complete these questions about the two types of synergistic effects.

    a. One type of synergistic effect called **similar actions** is when one or more drugs have the same effects, or similar actions, on the brain and body.

    b. Physiologically, how can the similar actions of alcohol, antianxiety drugs, barbiturates, and opioids lead to death even when mixed in small doses?

    _____

    _____

    c. The other type of synergistic effect is called **opposite** (or _____) **actions.**

    d. Physiologically, why is it dangerous to combine barbiturates or alcohol with cocaine or amphetamines?

    _____

    _____

3. Often, drugs are mixed in ignorance of the dangerous consequences. However, increasingly this kind of multiple drugs use, or _____ use, seems to be done knowingly because the user enjoys the synergistic effects.

IV. What Causes Substance-Related Disorders?, 370–374

A. Sociocultural Views, 370

The sociocultural theories of drug abuse and dependence propose that the people most likely to develop problems are those whose societies create an atmosphere of stress and those whose families value, or at least tolerate, drug taking.

1. Complete the following statements regarding research that has tended to support sociocultural theories regarding substance abuse.

    a. Higher rates of _____ have been found in regions of the United States where _____ is more common.

b. People in lower _____ classes have higher substance abuse rates than other classes.

c. Problem drinking is more common among teenagers whose parents and peers drink than among those whose parents and peers do not.

d. Lower rates of alcohol abuse were found among ethnic and religious groups in which drinking is acceptable *and* the _____ of drinking are clearly defined.

B. Psychodynamic Views, 371

1. Psychodynamic theorists suggest that people who abuse substances were not _____ enough during childhood, and that they subsequently try to meet their need for comfort and support by relying on others, or on drugs.

2. The psychodynamic hypothesis that some people develop a "substance abuse personality" is supported by research findings indicating that, compared to others, people who abuse substances are more likely to have what kinds of personality characteristics?

   _____

3. What is the major problem with studies that have purported to identify personality traits of people with or prone to substance abuse problems?

   _____

   _____

C. Cognitive-Behavioral Views, 371

There are two primary behavioral theories that attempt to explain substance-related disorders: the operant conditioning theory and the classical conditioning theory. Read the following case study. The exercise after the case will ask you to apply it to each of these theories.

Case Study

Glenn started using alcohol at age 15. Always rather shy and socially awkward, he found that drinking helped him "loosen up" enough to interact with his peers, whom he had avoided in the past. By age 18, Glenn was known as a real "partier." He drank nearly every day and often experienced blackouts. Glenn managed to get into college but dropped out at the end of his first semester because his grades were so poor. He got a job at a convenience store but was fired for coming to work intoxicated. Depressed and broke, Glenn asked an acquaintance if he could "crash" at his place until he found another job. It turned out that the acquaintance sold heroin. Glenn continued his heavy drinking, and within three months of moving in, he was also hooked on heroin. He tried to quit, but whenever his roommate brought out his drug paraphernalia, Glenn would succumb to an overpowering urge to shoot up. The fact that he would become depressed, anxious, and physically ill after going without heroin for even a day or two, made it even more difficult to quit.

1. How would each of the following behavioral theories explain Glenn's increasing heroin and alcohol use?

   a. Operant conditioning theory: _____

   _____

   _____

   _____

    b. Classical conditioning theory: _____

_____

_____

_____

D. Biological Views, 373

  1. Genetic Predisposition, 373

    1.   There are several lines of research that have implicated genetic factors in the development of substance abuse and dependence. Complete this table by summarizing the findings from each area of research.

Research area	Study or studies	Summary of findings
Twin studies	Kaij, 1960	In 54 percent of cases where one identical twin abused alcohol, so did the other, compared to a 28 percent concordance rate among fraternal twins.
Adoption studies	Walters, 2002; Cadoret, 1995; Goldstein, 1994	
Genetic linkage	Cosgrove, 2010; Gerlantes and Kransler, 2008 Blum et al., 1996, 1990	

  2. Biochemical Factors, 373

Recent advances in technology have enabled researchers to explore the biochemical underpinnings of drug dependence. The diagram below relates to a line of study that has pinpointed some of the biological processes that produce drug tolerance and withdrawal symptoms.

The normal process . . .	The brain normally produces particular kinds of neurotransmitters, which produce certain reactions (i.e., to sedate, alleviate pain, lift mood, increase alertness)
When on a drug . . .	A particular drug produces the same reaction as the neurotransmitter, making the neurotransmitter less necessary—excessive and chronic ingestion of the drug causes the brain to produce fewer neurotransmitters

	Tolerance	*and*	*Withdrawal*
This leads to . . .	As the drug is taken increasingly, the body's production of the corresponding neurotransmitter decreases, leaving the person in need of more of the drug to achieve its initial effects		Relying on the drug to feel good rather than on neurotransmitters means that discontinuing drug use will lead to a deficient supply of the neurotransmitter for a while; this means the user will feel terrible

    1.   The preceding diagram lists neither specific drugs nor specific neurotransmitters. Complete the table below by providing the names of the neurotransmitters that become deficient when a person abuses the identified substance.

Drug(s)	Neurotransmitter(s)
Alcohol, benzodiazepines	
Opioids	
Cocaine or amphetamines	
Marijuana	

2. One reason why drugs are so rewarding is that they seem to trigger (either directly or indirectly) the _____ center, or "_____ pathway" in the brain, by increasing _____ activity in those areas of the brain.

3. Some theorists believe that people who abuse drugs may suffer from _____ _____ syndrome, which might involve a reward center that is not easily activated by usual events in their lives (so they use drugs to activate it).

4. Describe the incentive-sensitization theory of addiction, which has received some research support in animal studies.

_____

_____

V. How Are Substance-Related Disorders Treated?, 375–382

A. Psychodynamic Therapies, 375

1. Psychodynamic therapies help clients discover and work through underlying needs and _____ in order to foster change in their substance-related lifestyles, but research has not found these approaches to be very _____.

B. Behavioral Therapies, 377

Match the numbers 1–3 below with the appropriate option from the list a–c that follows the numbers. Numbers 1–3 are widely used behavioral treatments for substance-related disorders. Options a–c represent examples of these treatments.

1. _____ Aversion therapy
2. _____ Alternate version of aversion therapy
3. _____ Contingency management

   a. A man who is alcohol dependent is given a nausea-producing chemical injection at the same time he drinks alcohol.

   b. Whenever she takes a drink, a woman who is alcohol dependent imagines gruesome scenes of the carnage after a terrorist bombing.

   c. A woman addicted to cocaine gets rewards whenever she submits drug-free urine samples to her treatment program manager.

4. In general, behavioral strategies appear to be most effective in treating people who are very _____ to continue despite the work these strategies require.

C. **Cognitive-Behavioral Therapies, 377**

    1.   Complete this exercise, which summarizes central steps in **relapse-prevention training (RPT)**, an approach used by clinicians whose aim is to help clients control (but not abstain from) alcohol use.

        a. Clients monitor and record certain aspects of their drinking behavior. Name three of these aspects.

             _____

        b. Why is it so important for clients to become aware of the aspects noted above?

             _____

        c. Clients are then taught how to set and recognize _____ on how much alcohol they will drink to control their _____ of drinking, and to apply coping strategies in situations that might otherwise lead to drinking.

        d. What are the two client characteristics that predict success in RPT treatment programs?

             _____

    2.   In addition to the skills discussed in Item 1, RPT also teaches clients additional skills. What are these skills?

        _____

        _____

D. **Biological Treatments, 378**

    1.   **Detoxification** is the _____ and medically supervised _____ from a drug.

    2.   Briefly describe one method or strategy of detoxification.

        _____

    3.   The relapse rates of people who fail to pursue _____ after withdrawal tend to be high.

    Antagonist drugs are used to avoid a relapse of drug abuse and dependence after a successful withdrawal from drugs.

    4.   Antagonist drugs _____ or _____ the effects of an addictive drug.

    5.   Complete the following statements regarding various antagonist drugs.

        a. Disulfiram, or _____, is given to people being treated for alcohol problems and produces a terrible physical reaction when taken with alcohol.

        b. Although narcotic antagonists are sometimes used for people who are dependent on _____, they are more often considered too dangerous because they result in very severe _____.

    6.   Summarize key points in the current debate (pros and cons) over the usefulness of **methadone maintenance programs.**

    Pros: _____

    _____

    _____

    Cons: _____

    _____

    _____

7. _____ antagonists are now preferred over _____ antagonists by clinicians for use in the treatment approach often called rapid detoxification.

E. **Sociocultural Therapies, 380**

1. **Alcoholics Anonymous (AA)** was founded in 1935 and today has over 2 million members world-wide. Describe two or three of the features and emphases of AA.

   _____

   _____

2. Culture-sensitive treatment programs pay attention to the special pressures faced by people in lower socioeconomic status and ethnic minority groups. Likewise, women might benefit from gender-sensitive treatment programs for several reasons. List two of these reasons.

   a. _____

   _____

   b. _____

   _____

3. Community drug-prevention programs offer education and intervention to people whose lives are affected by substance abuse. Give an example of one strategy that such prevention programs might employ with the following groups.

   a. *Individual:* Provide education about the risks associated with drug use

   b. *Family:* _____

   c. *Peer group:* _____

   d. *Community:* _____

4. Describe various research findings and conclusions that support each side of the highly controversial abstinence versus controlled-drinking debate.

   _____

   _____

   _____

5. What do research results suggest about various community-based prevention programs, such as "The Truth.com" and "Above the Influence?" How do these findings compare with research on the effectiveness of previous anti-drug campaigns?

   _____

   _____

VI. Call for Change: DSM-5, 382–383

1. In the 2011 DSM-5 draft, the DSM task force recommended two changes that would affect the various disorders discussed in Chapter 12. They recommended changing the entire grouping name to "Substance Use and Addictive Disorders," and they recommended consolidating multiple categories into the category "Substance Use Disorder." Briefly describe how each new classification would, if the DSM-5 were to adopt these recommendations, change the way the disorders discussed in this chapter are studied, diagnosed, and treated, and also briefly state some of the reasons for these recommended groupings.

a. Substance Use and Addictive Disorders: _____

_____

_____

_____

b. Substance Use Disorder: _____

_____

_____

_____

VII. Putting It Together: New Wrinkles to a Familiar Story, 383–384

1.   Summarize two things that researchers and clinicians have learned about the causes and treatments of substance-related disorders that have come about as a result of **integrated** efforts to understand these disorders.

a.   _____

_____

_____

b.   _____

_____

_____

MULTIPLE CHOICE

1. Which of the following is not a characteristic of simple substance abuse?
   a. excessive reliance on a drug
   b. physical dependence on a drug
   c. excessive and chronic use of a drug
   d. the possibility of damage to family and social relationships

2. How long does it take to fully sober up, that is, to get all the alcohol out of your body, after a single beer?
   a. about 1 hour
   b. about 3 hours
   c. the same for a 200-pound man as for a 120-pound woman
   d. it depends on the metabolism of the individual.

3. The legal limit for blood alcohol in the operator of a motor vehicle is .10 in most states. How many cans of beer would a 100-pound female need to consume in an hour to be legally drunk (for purposes of driving)?
   a. a little over 1
   b. a little over 2
   c. a little over 4
   d. at least 4

4. Guessing to fill in memory lapses is a symptom of the condition called
   a. delirium tremens.
   b. alcohol intoxication.
   c. Korsakoff's syndrome.
   d. withdrawal from opioids.

5. Death by heroin overdose is often due to
   a. respiratory failure.
   b. neuronal breakdown.
   c. cirrhosis of the liver.
   d. a drop in blood sugar levels.

6. Which of the following are associated with the action of cocaine?
   a. endorphins and dopamine
   b. GABA and norepinephrine
   c. endorphins and norepinephrine
   d. dopamine, norepinephrine, and serotonin

7. Gina was sitting in her living room when she suddenly began experiencing the same pretty, wavy visions as she did in her last trip two years ago. This is an example of
   a. a memory.
   b. a flashback.
   c. LSD psychosis.
   d. a withdrawal symptom.

8. According to psychodynamic theory, substance abuse develops when parents fail to fulfill a child's need for
   a. discipline.
   b. nurturance.
   c. dependence.
   d. independence.

9. Research on the efficacy of psychodynamic therapy for substance use disorders has found it to be
   a. detrimental to patients.
   b. not particularly effective.
   c. more effective than Alcoholics Anonymous.
   d. effective in encouraging alternatives to drug taking.

10. The reason there has been a reawakening of interest in methadone maintenance as a means of managing heroin addiction is
    a. that nothing else seems to work.
    b. fear of AIDS from shared needles.
    c. the development of a new, "less addictive" substitute drug.
    d. the increase in support for such programs because of federal grants.

13 SEXUAL DISORDERS AND GENDER IDENTITY DISORDER

REVIEW EXERCISES

I. Sexual Dysfunctions, 388–399

1. What is the definition of sexual dysfunction given in your textbook?

   _____

   _____

2. DSM-IV-TR categorizes sexual dysfunctions according to the **phase of the sexual response cycle** that is most affected by specific dysfunction. The table below will help you to organize basic information about each phase of the sexual response cycle, as well as dysfunctions that occur in each phase. Information on each of the phases and dysfunctions is scattered throughout the first half of the chapter (pages 388–399). As you read material on each of the cycles and associated dysfunctions, come back to this table and fill in the symptoms and prevalence rates of each dysfunction listed.

Phase: Desire	
Phase characteristics:	
Dysfunction name	**Dysfunction symptoms (and prevalence)**
Hypoactive sexual desire:	
Sexual aversion:	revulsion, disgust, and fear regarding sex (rare in men, more common in women)
Phase: Excitement	
Phase characteristics:	increased heart rate, muscle tension, blood pressure, and respiration; pelvic vasocongestion leads to male erections and female vaginal lubrication and genital swelling
Dysfunction name	**Dysfunction symptoms (and prevalence)**
Male erectile disorder:	
Female sexual arousal disorder:	(formerly called frigidity) failure to lubricate and swell (more than 7 percent prevalence rate)
Phase: Orgasm	
Phase characteristics:	
Dysfunction name	**Dysfunction symptoms (and prevalence)**
Rapid, or premature ejaculation:	
Male orgasmic disorder:	inability to reach orgasm despite adequate stimulation (8 percent prevalence rate)
Female orgasmic disorder:	

Note that the resolution phase has no associated disorders.

A. Disorders of Desire, 388

*Go back to the table that you have just worked on and fill in symptoms and prevalence rates of each dysfunction associated with the **desire phase.***

1. In defining **hypoactive sexual desire,** DSM-IV-TR refers to a "deficient" level of sexual desire without specifying what a "deficient" level is. The statements given in shaded area in this exercise illustrate some of the problems that can arise from this lack of specificity. Below each shaded area statement, see if you can formulate a counterstatement that shows its limitations.

> The average frequency of sex for married couples is two to three times per week, so anything less is "deficient."

    a. _____

        _____

> Frequency of intercourse is a good estimator of sexual desire.

    b. _____

        _____

> When partner A complains that partner B does not want to have sex enough, it is a good indication that partner B has hypoactive sexual desire.

    c. _____

        _____

2. In both men and women, a (high / low / either high or low) level of prolactin, a (high / low / either high or low) level of testosterone, and a (high / low / either high or low) level of estrogen are associated with low sex drive.

3. Recent research has suggested that hypoactive sexual disorder may be linked to excessive activity of the neurotransmitters _____ and _____.

4. List four illicit drugs that can interfere with sex drive.

    _____

5. Complete the following table by giving two examples of each psychological and/or sociocultural factor that could interfere with sex drive or cause sexual aversion.

Psychological or Sociocultural Factors	Examples
Emotional factors	increase in anxiety
Personal attitudes and beliefs	
Psychological disorders	
Situational factors	

Psychological or Sociocultural Factor	Examples
Relationship issues	feeling powerless and very dominated by the other in a relationship
Cultural factors	
Sexual trauma	fears about/aversion to sex

B. Disorders of Excitement, 392

*Go back to the table on page 182 of the workbook and fill in symptoms and prevalence rates of each dysfunction associated with the **excitement phase**.*

I. Female Sexual Arousal Disorder, 392

1.   Female sexual arousal disorder is usually associated with _____ disorder, so it will be covered in the section related to the latter disorder *(on page 182 of this workbook)*.

2. Male Erectile Disorder, 392

Traditionally, the causes of male erectile disorder were assumed to be either psychological or organic. Currently, clinicians believe that this problem is a result of interacting biological, psychological, and sociocultural factors.

1.   _____ abnormalities—which are abnormalities in the structure of the penis and blood flow through the penis—are more commonly the cause of erectile failure than are hormonal problems.

2.   List four factors that could lead to erectile failure related to abnormality in the structure of and blood flow through the penis.

     _____

     _____

3.   Complete the following statements related to techniques used to identify causes of erectile failure.

     a. Evaluation of _____ _____ _____ (NPT), or erections during sleep, in a laboratory is useful in assessing physical factors related to erectile problems.

     b. Healthy men typically have two to three hours of erections, during the usual two to five _____ periods each night.

     c. Abnormal or absent NPT usually indicates some _____ basis for erectile failure.

4.   Certain sociocultural issues such as _____ loss and extreme _____ stress are often associated with erectile failure.

5.   Two relationship patterns seem to be associated with erectile disorder among men. The first is provided. What is the second pattern?

     a. An aging man (who very naturally requires more intense and direct stimulation to achieve erection) is not provided enough stimulation by his partner.

     b. _____

     _____

Examine this diagram, which depicts a primary psychological mechanism that can result in erectile failure: **performance anxiety and the spectator role.** *According to the performance anxiety theory of erectile failure, whatever the initial reason for the erectile failure, the resulting anxious, self-evaluative spectator role becomes the reason for the ongoing problem.*

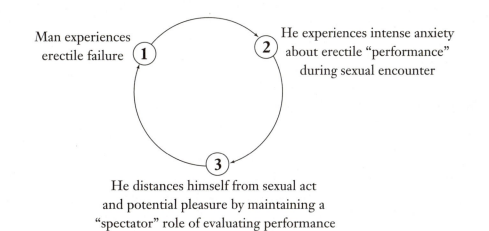

Man experiences erectile failure ①

② He experiences intense anxiety about erectile "performance" during sexual encounter

③ He distances himself from sexual act and potential pleasure by maintaining a "spectator" role of evaluating performance

C. Disorders of Orgasm, 395

Go back to the table on page 182 of the workbook and fill in symptoms and prevalence rates of each dysfunction associated with the **orgasm phase.**

1. Rapid, or Premature, Ejaculation, 395

1. Young men who are sexually _____, and who have not learned to slow down and control their _____, appear to be most prone to premature ejaculation.

2. List three other factors that seem to be related to premature ejaculation among men.

   _____

   _____

   _____

3. List three theories that have been put forward as biological explanations for rapid ejaculation.

   a. _____

   b. _____

   c. _____

2. Male Orgasmic Disorder, 396

1. List (a) three biological factors and (b) three psychological factors that can inhibit ejaculation—i.e., contribute to *male orgasmic disorder*—among men.

   a. _____

   _____

   _____

   b. _____

   _____

3. Female Orgasmic Disorder, 397

1. Studies indicate that women who are more sexually _____ and who feel comfortable _____ have more frequent orgasms.

2. Whereas early _____ theorists held that the failure to achieve orgasm from vaginal intercourse alone was an indication of pathology in women, contemporary clinicians and researchers agree that not only is orgasm *not* a criterion of _____ sexual functioning, but that women who rely on stimulation of the _____ to reach orgasm are completely normal and healthy.

3. A variety of biological causes can affect arousal and orgasm among women. Describe examples in each of the three categories listed below:

   a. physical illness or injury: _____

   b. postmenopausal changes: _____

   c. drugs and medications: _____

4. In one study, several factors that were associated with a lack of orgasm among women emerged, including memories of an unhappy childhood and loss of a parent during childhood. List three factors that seem to be *positively* related to orgasm among women.

   a. _____

   b. _____

   c. _____

5. The traditional explanation for the causes of female arousal and orgasmic dysfunction held that these difficulties result from cultural messages that demand women suppress and deny their

   _____.

6. Describe two characteristics of the upbringing of many women with arousal and orgasmic problems that lend support to the theory described above.

   _____

   _____

7. What is the flaw in the theory described above? _____

   _____

8. Many women who were victims of _____ suffer from arousal and orgasm dysfunction.

D. Disorders of Sexual Pain, 399

Note that sexual pain disorders are not associated with a particular phase in the sexual response cycle.

1. Complete the following statements regarding **vaginismus.**

   a. In this condition, the _____ around the vagina involuntarily _____ to prevent penile penetration.

   b. Most clinicians agree that it is a _____ fear response that is triggered by the fear that vaginal penetration will be _____ and damaging.

2. List three psychological factors that can lead to the fears described above.

   _____

   _____

3. List three biological factors that might be associated with vaginismus.

_____

_____

4. Describe the symptoms of **dyspareunia**.

_____

_____

5. List four causes of dyspareunia.

a. _____

b. _____

c. _____

d. _____

6. Psychogenic dyspareunia usually reflects an underlying condition of _____ .

II. Treatments for Sexual Dysfunctions, 400–406

A. What Are the General Features of Sex Therapy?, 400

In 1970, Masters and Johnson published the book Human Sexual Inadequacy. *It described a revolutionary approach to the treatment of sexual dysfunction that came to be called "sex therapy." Although the approach has been modified, the original components remain intact. In some ways, you can think of this approach as a generic program, and not necessarily focused on any one dysfunction.*

1. This exercise calls for a summary of each component of modern sex therapy. For each component, be sure to include a brief statement regarding the specific issues being addressed and the therapist tasks and/or techniques. The first is done for you.

Component 1

Assessment and conceptualization of the problem

a. Understanding past and current factors that might have caused or maintain the patient's problem is the emphasis. Along with a thorough medical examination, the therapist gathers information on the patient's "sex history" through in-depth interviews and tests.

Component 2

Mutual responsibility

b. _____

_____

_____

Component 3

Education about sexuality

c. _____

_____

Component 4

Emotion identification

d. _____

_____

_____

Component 5

Attitude change

e. _____

_____

_____

Component 6

Elimination of performance anxiety and the spectator role

f. _____

_____

_____

Component 7

Increase sexual communication skills

g. _____

_____

_____

Component 8

Change destructive lifestyles and interactions

h. _____

_____

_____

Component 9

Address physical and medical factors

i. _____

_____

_____

B. What Techniques Are Applied to Particular Dysfunctions?, 402

1. Clinicians employ several kinds of strategies and specific interventions to treat clients with *hypoactive sexual desire* and *sexual aversion*. In the table below, describe the purpose of each set of strategies, then write a specific example of the technique.

Strategy	Purpose	Specific Techniques
Affectual awareness	Uncover negative feelings about sex	
Self-instruction training		
Behavioral approach		
Approach for sexual aversion due to assault	Work through feelings associated with trauma	
Biological intervention		

2. Complete the following descriptions of techniques used to treat *erectile disorder.*

a. During _____ focus exercises, the *tease technique* is taught. One partner _____ the other until he achieves an erection, then stops until he loses his erection.

b. The recent development of the popular drug _____ (sildenafil) increases blood flow to the penis within _____ hour of ingestion, leading to erection.

c. The _____ _____ device (VED) is a hollow cylinder that is placed over the penis; when air is pumped out of the cylinder, _____ is drawn into the penis, causing an erection.

3. Describe one technique used in the treatment of *male orgasmic disorder.*

_____

_____

4. In one treatment for *rapid ejaculation,* the stop-start or _____ procedure gradually increases the man's ejaculation threshold through repeated stimulation to _____, but not to ejaculation.

5. The primary components of treatment for *female arousal and orgasm dysfunction* emphasize _____, enhancement of body _____, and directed masturbation training.

6. Complete the statements about directed masturbation training's success rates.

a. Over 90 percent of women learn to have orgasms during masturbation.

b. Eighty percent of women learn to have orgasms . . .

_____

c. Thirty percent of women learn to have orgasms . . .

_____

7. Sex therapists emphasize that women who are able to reach orgasm in some, but not all, situations should be reassured that they are _____ and probably need _____ rather than treatment.

8. Complete the following statements regarding the treatment of *vaginismus*.

    a. Women who suffer from vaginismus learn to contract and relax their _____ muscles at will until they have gained _____ control over them.

    b. The vaginal insertion of gradually larger _____ helps these women overcome their fear of _____.

    c. Most women treated are able to have pain-free intercourse.

9. What strategies can be recommended by a sex therapist when a medical examination reveals that a patient's *dyspareunia* is caused by scars or lesions?

    _____

C. What Are the Current Trends in Sex Therapy?, 406

1. Complete the following list of new directions in sex therapy:

    a. Partners who _____ but are not married are regularly treated.

    b. Sexual dysfunctions that arise from psychological disorders such as _____, mania, and schizophrenia are treated.

    c. Sex therapists are more likely to provide treatment to clients with severe _____, _____ the elderly, the mentally ill, or the physically _____ .

    d. People with a _____ orientation, those with no ongoing sex partner, and people with sexual _____ are also provided sex therapy.

III. Paraphilias, 406–415

1. According to DSM-IV-TR criteria, to be diagnosed with a paraphilia, a person must

    a. have recurrent, intense sexual urges and sexually arousing fantasies involving either _____ objects, children, _____ adults, or experiences of suffering or _____.

    b. have experienced these urges, fantasies, or behaviors for at least _____ months.

2. Relatively few men (and almost no women) are ever formally diagnosed with a paraphilic disorder. So why do clinicians suspect that the disorder is actually quite prevalent?

    _____

3. Complete the following chart that summarizes the descriptions, causes, and treatments for the paraphilias.

Fetishism	
Description	recurrent, intense sexual urges that involve the use of nonliving objects (e.g., women's undergarments, shoes) that may be smelled or touched
Causes	*psychodynamic:* these are defense mechanisms against anxiety of normal sexual contact; *behavioral:* acquired through classical conditioning

Treatment	*behavioral:* aversion therapy, covert sensitization, masturbatory satiation (which is designed to produce boredom in clients who are told to masturbate for long durations to fetishistic fantasies), and orgasmic reorientation (teaching more appropriate sexual responses)

Transvestic Fetishism (Transvestism, Cross-Dressing)

Description	those with disorder (almost exclusively heterosexual males) have a recurrent need to dress in clothes of the opposite sex in order to become sexually aroused
Causes	*behavioral:* as children, those with the disorder were operantly conditioned, or reinforced, for cross-dressing
Treatment	no specific treatment described in textbook

Exhibitionism

Description	
Causes	no specific cause described in textbook; individuals act on exhibitionistic urges when they have free time or are under stress.
Treatment	

Voyeurism

Description	recurrent and intense sexual urges to spy on people as they undress or have sex; usually begins before age 15 and is chronic
Causes	
Treatment	no specific strategies described in textbook; however, typical strategies used for treatment of paraphilias could be applied (e.g., covert sensitization, masturbatory satiation, orgasmic reorientation)

Frotteurism

Description	
Causes	no specific cause described in textbook; however frotteurism frequently develops after observing another engage in similar behaviors.
Treatment	no specific treatments described in textbook; usually disappears after the age of 25

Pedophilia

Description	

Causes	
Treatment	*behavioral:* orgasmic reorientation, in which clients are conditioned to become sexually aroused by other stimuli; aversion therapy; and masturbatory satiation; *cognitive-behavioral:* relapse-prevention training focuses on identifying triggering situations and the development of healthier coping strategies

Sexual Masochism

Description	recurrent sexual urges and fantasies that involve being made to suffer (e.g., through pain, humiliation)
Causes	
Treatment	no specific treatments described in textbook

Sexual Sadism

Description	
Causes	*behavioral:* as children, the sexually sadistic might have been classically conditioned to become aroused when inflicting pain, or may have seen models engaging in sexual sadism; *cognitive, psychodynamic:* may feel sexually inadequate and insecure; *biological:* evidence of possible brain and hormonal abnormalities
Treatment	aversion therapy, relapse prevention training

4. Briefly explain why some clinicians argue that, except when people are hurt by them, many paraphilic behaviors should not be considered disorders at all.

_____

_____

_____

IV. Gender Identity Disorder, 415–420

1. In _____ , people feel that they have been assigned the wrong sex.

2. The ratio of males to females with this disorder is _____ to 1.

3. List some of the characteristics of people who have gender identity disorder.

_____

_____

_____

4. People with gender identity disorder do not have _____ _____. In other words, they do not cross-dress strictly in order to achieve sexual arousal.

5.   Many adults with this disorder had a gender identity disorder as children, but most children with a gender identity disorder . . .

_____

6.   Findings of a study on the autopsied brains of six people who changed their sex from male to female suggest that biological factors may play a role in gender identity disorder. Complete the following statements related to this study.

   a.   Compared to a control group of autopsied brains of "normal" males, the autopsied brains of six males with gender identity disorder had cells in the _____ called the *bed nucleus of stria terminalis* (BST) that were only _____ as large as in the control group of male brains.

   b.   In effect, the brains of men with gender identity disorder seem to have "_____-sized" BST cells.

   c.   Although the function of human BST cells is not known, researchers have discovered that in rats, BST cells help control _____ behavior.

Although hormone therapy and psychotherapy are effective in helping many with gender identity disorder lead satisfying lives that reflect their "true" gender role, some such individuals undergo sex-reassignment surgery. Sex-reassignment surgery is a highly controversial procedure, and research has not been able to settle the debate regarding its long-term effectiveness.

7.   Complete the following statements regarding sex-reassignment procedures.

   a.   Surgery is preceded by one or two years of _____ therapy.

   b.   For men, the surgery consists of _____ of the penis and restructuring of its parts into a _____ and _____.

   c.   For women, the surgery consists of bilateral _____, hysterectomy, and sometimes _____ (the surgical creation of a functioning penis) or the implantation of a silicone prosthesis.

8.   The long-term psychological outcome of sex-reassignment surgery is not well established. Some believe sex-reassignment surgery is a "humane solution," whereas others view it as a "drastic nonsolution." What do you think?

_____

_____

_____

_____

_____

_____

9.   Briefly define the three patterns of gender dysphoria identified by Richard Carroll.

   a.   female-to-male gender dysphoria _____

   _____

   b.   male-to-female gender dysphoria: androphilic type _____

   _____

   c.   male-to-female gender dysphoria: autogynephilic type _____

   _____

MediaSpeak: A Different Kind of Judgment, 419

Read the article about Judge Victoria Kalakowski, who was formerly a man and is now living as a woman. Reflect on Kalakowski's description of the prejudice those with gender identity disorder encounter, as well as the public's lack of knowledge about the condition. How does Kalakowski's experience relate to the controversy over whether gender identity disorder should be classified as a disorder?

V. Call for Change: DSM-5, 420–421

1. The DSM-5 task force has proposed a number of changes in its 2011 draft of the DSM-5. If adopted, these changes would affect the classification of a number of the disorders discussed in this chapter. Briefly identify the changes recommended by the task force regarding the classification of each of the following disorders, and explain the reason for each recommended change.

   a. Male orgasmic disorder: _____

   _____

   b. Female hypoactive sexual desire disorder/female sexual arousal disorder: _____

   _____

   _____

   c. Dyspareunia/vaginismus: _____

   _____

   d. General paraphilias: _____

   _____

   _____

   e. Pedophilia: _____

   _____

   _____

   f. Gender identity disorder: _____

   _____

VI. Putting It Together: A Private Topic Draws Public Attention, 421

1. Describe three pieces of knowledge, or insight, with regard to the explanation and treatment of sexual disorders that have emerged over the last three decades.

   a. _____

   _____

   b. _____

   _____

   c. _____

   _____

MULTIPLE CHOICE

1. Sexual dysfunction can occur during all of the following phases except
   a. desire.
   b. orgasm.
   c. arousal.
   d. resolution.

2. Hypoactive sexual disorder is a disorder of which phase of the sexual response cycle?
   a. excitement phase
   b. orgasm phase
   c. resolution phase
   d. desire phase

3. Which of the following drugs increases sexual drive at a low level and decreases it at higher levels?
   a. alcohol
   b. antidepressants
   c. antianxiety drugs
   d. antipsychotic drugs

4. Samuel experienced a period of high stress during which he was unable to perform sexually. Thereafter, he was detached and apprehensive during sexual activity and unable to perform. Samuel is displaying
   a. sexual frustration.
   b. performance anxiety.
   c. hypoactive sexual desire.
   d. organically induced male erectile disorder.

5. In a study of female orgasm, women who had higher rates of orgasm
   a. were more aggressive than other women.
   b. behaved in a stereotypically "feminine" way.
   c. had more affectionate parents than other women.
   d. were more passive in their behavior than other women.

6. A major component of sex therapy is
   a. hormone therapy.
   b. elimination of performance anxiety.
   c. relieving depression about the symptoms.
   d. identifying who is responsible for the problem.

7. Paraphiliacs treated by clinicians are usually
   a. male.
   b. young.
   c. female.
   d. ordered into treatment by the court.

8. During which period does frotteurism typically develop?
   a. adolescence
   b. early adulthood
   c. middle adulthood
   d. late adulthood

9. Which of the following used to be, but is no longer, considered a sexual disorder?
   a. transvestism
   b. sexual masochism
   c. homosexuality
   d. pedophilia

10. One characteristic of people with gender identity disorder is that they often feel
    a. heterosexuality is abnormal.
    b. angry and exploited by others.
    c. they were born the wrong sex.
    d. they underwent a sex-change operation during childhood.

14 SCHIZOPHRENIA

REVIEW EXERCISES

The following items cover Chapter 14's introductory material on pages 426–427.

1.   Although the term *schizophrenia* is often misused for multiple personality disorder, it actually denotes these three points:

   a.   a _____ of thought processes,

   b.   a split between _____ and _____, and

   c.   a withdrawal from _____.

2.   Approximately _____ percent of the world's population meets DSM-IV-TR criteria for schizophrenia during his or her lifetime.

3. Figure 14–1 on page 426 illustrates the fact that people in lower socioeconomic groups are more likely to suffer from schizophrenia than wealthier groups. Complete this list of possible reasons for this fact.

    a. The stress of _____ could lead to schizophrenia.

    b. Schizophrenia could cause people to:

    _____

    _____

4. For this exercise, complete the paragraph describing the prevalence of schizophrenia by drawing a line through the incorrect option within each set of parentheses.

    Schizophrenia prevalence rates are higher among people in (lower/higher) socioeconomic groups. Neither gender appears to be at higher risk, but the age of onset is earlier among (men/women). Although divorced people have (higher/lower) rates than either married or single people, the exact reasons for this are not clear.

I. The Clinical Picture of Schizophrenia, 427–434

1. DSM-IV-TR classifies schizophrenia as a single disorder with different "faces." A number of clinicians hold a contrary view. Describe that view.

    _____

    _____

A. What Are the Symptoms of Schizophrenia?, 427

Symptoms of schizophrenia can be grouped into three categories: positive symptoms, so named because they represent bizarre "additions" to or "excesses" of normal behavior; negative symptoms that represent "deficits" of normal behavior; and psychomotor symptoms that reflect unusual or bizarre motor behaviors.

Exercises in this subsection are broken down into one part for each of the three categories of symptoms. Within these category parts, exercises are broken down further into specific symptoms.

1. Positive Symptoms, 427

a. Delusions, 427

1. Delusions are ideas that schizophrenic people believe fervently, but that have no basis in

    _____.

2. Complete this exercise by describing the type of delusion and then by matching the example that best illustrates each type.

Type of delusion	Description	Example
Persecution	irrational belief that one is being threatened, plotted against, spied upon, etc.	
Reference		
Grandeur		
Control		

Examples:

a. Lowell eats at a Chinese restaurant every day. At the end of each meal, he reverently reads the message in the fortune cookie and carefully writes it down in a notebook. He believes that the messages are written specifically for him.

b. [Excerpt from a letter to a newspaper] Beware of the plot of destruction orchestrated by so-called door-to-door salesmen. They come to my home 20 or 100 times a day, always snooping around and wanting to kill me. They say they are selling things, but they lie! They carry guns and knives and explosives. Beware! You could be the next victim!

c. Over the past two years, Lea has become convinced that thoughts are being put in her brain by alien life forms conducting mind-control experiments. Lately she has become certain that the aliens want her to disguise herself as Madonna and appear on television.

d. While watching the national college basketball championship on television, Margaret becomes convinced that she is determining the outcome of the game by manipulating the players with her mind.

PsychWatch: Mentally Ill Chemical Abusers, 428

1. Between ___ and ___ percent of all people with chronic mental disorders may be mentally ill chemical abusers (MICAs).

2. List some common characteristics of MICAs, including gender, age, social functioning, scholastic achievement, treatment outcomes, and others.

   _____

   _____

   _____

3. Why is the relationship between substance abuse and mental dysfunction particularly complex and variable from case to case?

   _____

   _____

4. List two factors that tend to undermine the treatment of MICAs.

   a. _____

   b. _____

5. It is estimated that ___ to ___ percent of the homeless population may be MICAs. List some characteristics of homeless MICAs that differentiate them from other homeless people.

   _____

   _____

b. *Disorganized Thinking and Speech, 429*

3. Many people with schizophrenia display positive formal _____ disorders that are manifested in the form of peculiar _____ and illogical patterns of thinking.

   Match the numbers 4–7 below with the appropriate option from the list a–d below the numbers.

4. _____ loose associations

5. _____ neologisms

6. _____ perseveration

7. _____ clang

    a. Made-up words that have meaning only to the person using them

    b. Using rhyme as a guide to formulating thoughts and statements

    c. Repeating words and statements over and over again

    d. Rapidly shifting from one topic to another, making inconsequential and incoherent statements, and apparently believing them to make sense (also called derailment)

  c. *Heightened Perceptions and Hallucinations, 429*

8. People with schizophrenia often report a heightened sensitivity to _____ and _____, making it difficult for these individuals to attend to relevant stimuli.

9. One study demonstrated that, compared to nonschizophrenic subjects, subjects with schizophrenia were less able to pick out a target _____ when they listened to a recording that also contained distracting _____ speech.

10. Attention problems in people with schizophrenia may be related to smooth _____ eye movement (the ability to keep one's head still and track a moving object back and forth with one's eyes).

11. Define the term **hallucination**.

    _____

12. _____ hallucinations are the most common form of hallucination in schizophrenia and may be experienced as voices talking, or giving _____ or warnings.

13. Research has suggested that people with schizophrenia actually "hear" sounds that they attribute to _____ sources; the area of the brain that is most active during an auditory hallucination is _____ area (the area associated with speech production).

Match the numbers 14–19, representing the types of hallucinations, with the example from letters a–f that best illustrates each type of hallucination.

14. _____ auditory

15. _____ tactile

16. _____ somatic

17. _____ visual

18. _____ gustatory

19. _____ olfactory

    a. While on a cross-country flight, Norman starts to see his fellow passengers as grotesque, green-colored monsters.

    b. Lil, an office worker, quits her job when she can no longer bear the "stench of death" that she can smell coming from her vent. No one else can smell the odor.

    c. While at the mental health clinic, Phil tells the counselor taking information from him that she will have to get rid of her wristwatch if she wants him to be able to answer the questions. "It's ticking so loud that I can't hear your voice," he shouts.

   d. Much to the consternation of her family and doctor, Bernadine insists against all medical evidence to the contrary that she has "grapefruit-sized" tumors throughout her body.

   e. Roger, a guest at a nice hotel, calls the front desk to say that his room is "crawling with spiders." When the hotel investigates and finds no spiders, Roger contends that he could feel the spiders running over his body all night long.

   f. At her nephew's wedding, Fay stands by the punch bowl and warns the other guests not to drink the punch because she tasted poison in it.

d.   *Inappropriate Affect, 431*

20. In some cases, inappropriate affect may come about as a result of another positive symptom of schizophrenia. Give one explanation for this example:

   Jerry, a man with schizophrenia, shows extreme anger at the same time he wins $500 playing the state lottery.

   _____

   _____

2. Negative Symptoms, 431

a. Poverty of Speech, 431

1. Complete these exercises relating to the forms of poverty of speech.

   a. **Alogia** is a reduction in _____ and _____ of speech characterized by brief and meaningless statements.

   b. After reading the diary entry of Vaslav Nijinsky on page 432 of the text, identify one statement from it that best illustrates alogia, in your opinion.

   _____

   _____

   _____

b.   *Blunted and Flat Affect, 432*

2. What is the difference between blunted affect and flat affect?

   _____

3. Blunted or flat affect may reflect_____, a general lack of pleasure and enjoyment.

c.   *Loss of Volition, 432*

4. Schizophrenic people who display **avolition,** or_____, feel drained of energy and _____ in normal goals, are unable to initiate or complete a normal course of action, and commonly also display_____ (conflicting feelings) about most things.

d.   *Social Withdrawal, 432*

5. Schizophrenic people withdraw from the "real" external world and become preoccupied with their own _____ and _____, leading to deterioration in social skills.

3. Psychomotor Symptoms, 432

1. The extreme forms of the *psychomotor symptoms* of schizophrenia are collectively known as **catatonia.** Complete this table by providing the names of the types of catatonia being described.

Type of Catatonia	Description
	assuming awkward, bizarre positions for long periods of time
	being totally unaware of and unresponsive to the external world, remaining motionless and silent for long stretches of time
	moving excitedly, sometimes with wild waving of arms and legs
	remaining in an unmoving, upright posture for hours and resisting efforts to be moved

B. **What Is the Course of Schizophrenia?, 433**

Schizophrenia usually emerges between the late teens and mid-30s. The most typical course the disorder follows is to go through three distinct phases. Study this diagram, which shows these phases and their characteristics.

The Prodromal Phase

- Schizophrenic symptoms are not yet prominent
- The person has begun to deteriorate from previous levels of functioning

The Active Phase

- Schizophrenic symptoms become prominent
- In some instances, the active phase is triggered by stress in the person's life

The Residual Phase

- A return to the prodromal level of functioning
- The florid symptoms of the active phase recede
- Many individuals remain in a general state of decline

1. While approximately _____ percent of schizophrenic patients recover completely, the majority shows signs of residual _____.

2. The several characteristics that are predictive of recovery in schizophrenic patients include good premorbid functioning. List two other characteristics.

C. Diagnosing Schizophrenia, 433

1. Complete these two general DSM-IV-TR diagnostic criteria for schizophrenia.

a. Signs of schizophrenia present for at least _____ months.

b. Deterioration from previous levels of functioning in _____ , _____ re-lations, and self-care.

2. The DSM-IV-TR categorizes types of schizophrenia based on descriptions of patients' behaviors. In the following table, write key words that will help you remember the central features of each type of disorder. Then, match each type with the example that best illustrates it.

Category	Key Words for Central Factors	Example
Disorganized		
Catatonic		
Paranoid		
Undifferentiated		
Residual		

Examples:

a. Daniel lost his job as a corporate attorney about a year ago, which seemed to trigger an intense phase of schizophrenic symptoms. Most of them have passed, but Daniel no longer seems to show much emotion about anything.

b. Jenny excitedly waves her arms about wildly in an attempt to fight off the "evil spirits" who tell her they are going to hurt her.

c. Albert lives in a large city, where he is homeless. He spends most days sitting in a small park, speaking to no one, and quietly laughing and grimacing as thousands of people walk past him.

d. Bob is convinced that government agents are trying to kill him because President Kennedy has "spoken" to him, telling Bob the truth about his assassination.

e. Ellen is a 45-year-old ex-teacher, who had to quit her job when her schizophrenic symptoms took over her life. She can usually be found sitting in her kitchen, where she often will barely move a muscle for hours at a time.

3. List the major characteristics for each of the two types of schizophrenia many researchers believe exist.

   a. Type I schizophrenia: _____

   b. Type II schizophrenia: _____

4. What are the major differences that have been observed between the course of Type I schizophrenia and the course of Type II schizophrenia?

   _____

   _____

II. How Do Theorists Explain Schizophrenia?, 434–445

A. Biological Views, 434

Coverage of this subsection is broken down into its three parts—genetic factors, biochemical abnormalities, and abnormal brain structure.

1. Genetic Factors, 434

1. Although it seems clear that the risk of developing schizophrenia is significantly greater in people who are closely related to schizophrenic probands, the trend does not (in itself) establish a genetic basis for the disorder. Why?

_____

_____

2. If genetic factors were at work in schizophrenia, _____ twins would have a higher concordance rate for the disorder than _____ twins.

3. What have studies shown with regard to the fact stated above in item 2?

_____

_____

4. Other than genetic factors, what is one biological explanation for the concordance patterns found by researchers studying schizophrenia among identical and fraternal twins?

_____

_____

5. In adoption studies, the prevalence of schizophrenic symptoms in both the biological and the adoptive relatives of people with schizophrenia (who were adopted away from their biological parents in infancy) is compared. Complete the following statements related to adoption studies.

   a. _____ influences would be indicated when *adoptive* relatives have symptoms of schizophrenia, whereas _____ influences would be suggested when *biological* relatives have symptoms of schizophrenia.

   b. In adoption studies, _____ relatives of people with schizophrenia are more likely to display symptoms than _____ relatives.

6. Researchers using *genetic linkage* and *molecular biology* strategies have identified possible gene defects on a number of chromosomes that could predispose people to develop schizophrenia. In fact, various studies have identified 9 different chromosomes that show these defects. What are three possible reasons for these varied findings?

   a. _____

   _____

   b. _____

   _____

   c. _____

   _____

PsychWatch: Postpartum Psychosis: The Case of Andrea Yates, 436

1. Like Andrea Yates, 1 to 2 in _____ mothers who have recently given birth experience postpartum psychosis, although only a small fraction of those who suffer this disorder actually harm their children.

2. Name some symptoms of postpartum psychosis.

_____

_____

3. *Reflect on the case of Andrea Yates. In addition to the blame assigned to Yates, her husband, her doctors, and her insurers have all come in for criticism by some for their handling of her postpartum psychosis before she drowned her five children. Who or what do you think most deserves the criticism and for what reasons?*

2. Biochemical Abnormalities, 437

*The first of the two distinct biological views of the development of schizophrenia centers on the **dopamine hypothesis**. It states that in schizophrenia, neurons that use the neurotransmitter dopamine fire too often and thus transmit too many messages, leading to symptoms of the disorder. Researchers formulated this hypothesis after observing some interesting effects of antipsychotic medications known as **phenothiazines**.*

Researchers identified the phenothiazines in the 1950s and used them
to treat schizophrenia—Why they were effective was not known

↓

Clinicians noticed that patients with schizophrenia using phenothiazines had
the same kind of muscle tremors as patients with Parkinson's disease

↓

Clues that Linked Schizophrenia to Dopamine Activity

Researchers knew that Parkinson's patients have low levels of dopamine, which causes their tremors

It was also known that L-dopa, a precursor of dopamine, was helpful in treating Parkinson's because it raised dopamine levels

As a Result, Two Hypotheses Were Formed

If antipsychotic drugs generate symptoms of Parkinson's while alleviating schizophrenia, then the drugs must reduce dopamine activity

If increasing dopamine activity too much creates symptoms of schizophrenia in Parkinson's patients, then schizophrenia must be related to excessive dopamine activity.

1. Amphetamines induce or exacerbate psychotic symptoms (called "amphetamine psychosis") because they _____ dopamine activity in the brain.

2. Antipsychotic drugs are dopamine _____, which means that they bind to dopamine receptors (especially *D-2 receptors*), prevent dopamine from binding to those receptor sites, and thus prevent dopaminergic neurons from _____.

3. People with schizophrenia might have a _____ than usual number of dopamine (especially D-2) receptors, which would lead to dopamine overactivity in the brains of those individuals.

4. The dopamine hypothesis has been challenged by the discovery that a new group of drugs, called _____ antipsychotics, are even more effective than the traditional drugs. These drugs, however, bind to D-2 receptors *and* to receptor sites for _____ and other neurotransmitters.

5. A second challenge to the dopamine hypothesis is that it appears to contribute to the _____ symptoms of schizophrenia, but not to the _____ symptoms of schizophrenia.

3. Abnormal Brain Structure, 439

The second distinct biological view of the cause of schizophrenia relates to abnormal brain structure. It has been strengthened by research in the last decade that has linked schizophrenia, particularly cases dominated by negative symptoms, with specific structural abnormalities in the brain.

1. Researchers have found that many people with schizophrenia have enlarged _____.

2. List characteristics of people with schizophrenia who have this brain abnormality.

_____

_____

3. Other significant abnormalities found in people with schizophrenia are reduced or heightened _____ _____ in their brains, smaller _____ and _____ lobes, and smaller amounts of cortical gray matter.

4. Viral Problems, 439

1. Complete the list of factors that have been linked to the brain abnormalities found in people with schizophrenia.

    a. genetic factors

    b. poor

    c. development

    d. complications

    e. reactions

    f. toxins

2. According to the viral theory of schizophrenia, symptoms come about as a result of a virus entering the brain during the _____ period and remain latent until puberty or young adulthood, when it is activated by _____ changes or another viral infection.

3. Summarize the evidence for the viral theory of schizophrenia related to:

    a. season of birth

    _____

    _____

    b. fingerprints

    _____

    _____

    c. viral exposure and antibodies

    _____

    _____

B. Psychological Views, 440

In this subsection, each of the leading psychological theories of schizophrenia is addressed in its own part.

1. The Psychodynamic Explanation, 440

1. Complete these statements regarding Freud's theory of the development of schizophrenia.

    a. Regression, the first part of the two-part process, is when a person regresses to a pre-ego state of primary _____, resulting in symptoms such as neologisms, loose associations, and delusions of grandeur.

    b. During the second part of the process, the person attempts to regain ego control and establish contact with _____; symptoms representing an unconscious attempt to substitute for a lost sense of reality arise, such as _____ _____.

2. Although unsupported by empirical evidence, Fromm-Reichmann's theory suggests that so-called
    _____ (schizophrenia-causing) mothers have certain personality characteristics that
    "set the stage" for the development of schizophrenia in their children.

3. Below, list some of the characteristics of these mothers.

    _____

    _____

2. The Behavioral View, 441

1. Fill in the missing information in this diagram depicting the behavioral view of schizophrenia that
    emphasizes the key role of operant conditioning.

Unusual circumstances, or socially inadequate individuals, prevent a person from being reinforced for paying attention to social cues in his or her environment.	→ As a result, the person stops attending to normal social cues and instead focuses on other, often irrelevant cues, such as _____ _____	→ As the person attends more and more to the irrelevant cues, his or her responses become increasingly more bizarre. Such responses in turn elicit: _____ _____ _____

3. The Cognitive View, 441

Study the diagram below, which depicts the cognitive explanations of schizophrenia.

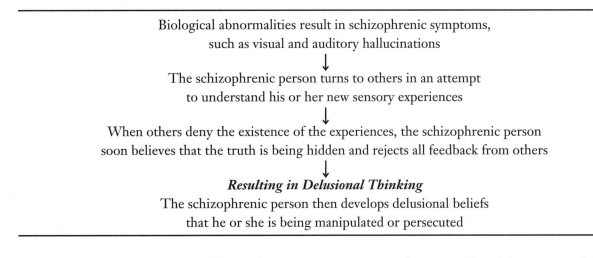

Biological abnormalities result in schizophrenic symptoms,
such as visual and auditory hallucinations
↓
The schizophrenic person turns to others in an attempt
to understand his or her new sensory experiences
↓
When others deny the existence of the experiences, the schizophrenic person
soon believes that the truth is being hidden and rejects all feedback from others
↓
Resulting in Delusional Thinking
The schizophrenic person then develops delusional beliefs
that he or she is being manipulated or persecuted

1. Although people with schizophrenia do experience sensory and perceptual problems, research has
    failed to support the idea that the misinterpretation of these problems _____ the syn-
    drome of schizophrenia.

C. Sociocultural Views, 441

1. Multicultural Factors, 441

1. Prevalence rates of schizophrenia seem to differ among different racial and ethnic groups. For exam-
    ple, the rate of schizophrenia among African Americans is significantly _____ than the rate of
    schizophrenia among white Americans.

2.   Identify three possible reasons for the difference in prevalence noted in question 1.

    a. _____

    _____

    b. _____

    _____

    c. _____

    _____

3.   According to a major study conducted by the World Health Organization, patients with schizophrenia living in developing countries have _____ recovery rates than patients with schizophrenia living in Western and developed countries.

4.   Identify two explanations that have been put forward for the disparity in recovery rates noted in item 3.

    a. _____

    b. _____

2. Social Labeling, 443

1.   Sociocultural theorists believe that the _____ itself causes many of the features of schizophrenia.

2.   Once the label is assigned, it becomes a "_____ _____ prophecy," that leads to schizophrenic symptoms.

You may find it useful to go back and study the coverage related to the Rosenhan (1973) study in Chapter 3, which is discussed again in this subsection.

3. Family Dysfunctioning, 444

*The **double-bind hypothesis** suggests that children respond to their parents' mutually contradictory messages by developing schizophrenic symptoms. Read this case study relating to this hypothesis, then complete the exercise following it.*

Case Study

Pamela is the 10-year-old daughter of divorced parents who are constantly in conflict with each other, particularly concerning visitation issues. Here is an example of a typical interaction between Pamela and her parents:

    Mother: (sarcastically) Pamela, you know it is very important that you go to your father's this weekend, because it was part of our agreement.

    Pamela: Do you want me to stay with you this weekend? I could call him . . .

    Mother: No, I want you to go. I'll be fine here by myself. (crosses arms, facial expression of anger)

    Pamela: Well . . . okay. Are you sure?

    Mother: Yes, of course I'm sure. (Mother hugs Pamela and begins to cry)

    Pamela then goes to her room and sits on her bed. She feels confused and paralyzed. Should she go to her father's house and risk hurting her mother? However, her mother said she wanted her to go. Pamela knows that if she doesn't go, her father will be angry with her.

1. Restate (a) the mother's primary communication and (b) her metacommunication.

   a. _____

   b. _____

2. What does research indicate about the validity of the double-bind hypothesis?

   _____

3. The study of families of schizophrenic people have yielded three trends that support some aspects of the family systems view. One is that parents of schizophrenic people display more conflict. List the other two.

   a. _____

   b. _____

4. Researchers have found that people recovering from schizophrenia are four times more likely to relapse if they live in a family characterized by *high expressed emotion* compared with those who live in families with low expressed emotion. Describe features of the former types of family below.

   _____

   _____

   _____

4. R. D. Laing's View, 445

1. R. D. Laing's theory asserts that we find meaning in our lives by finding our true selves, which is difficult because society requires us to develop "false selves" to meet the demands and expectations of others. Complete the following questions regarding Laing's conceptualization of schizophrenia.

   a. Because they cannot meet the needs of their families and society, some people withdraw into an inner search for strength and purpose.

   b. According to Laing, what would happen if these people were left to themselves?

   _____

   c. However, society responds by telling these people they are _____.

   d. Ultimately, these individuals assume the role of patient and submit to treatments that actually produce more symptoms.

III. Call for Change: DSM-5, 445–446

1. Identify two major changes affecting the classification of schizophrenia and other psychotic disorders that have been proposed by the DSM-5 task force. Briefly state the reason the task force has recommended each change. How do you believe each change, if adopted, would affect the treatment and diagnosis of schizophrenia and other psychotic disorders?

   a. _____

   _____

   _____

b. _____

_____

_____

IV. Putting it Together: Psychological and Sociocultural Models Lag Behind, 446

1. Briefly describe the current state of research into the biological, psychological, and sociocultural influences on schizophrenia. Which area of research has been more successful so far? What conclusion does your textbook draw from this as it looks to the future?

_____

_____

_____

MULTIPLE CHOICE

1. Approximately _____ percent of people worldwide suffer from schizophrenia.
   a. 1
   b. 5
   c. 10
   d. 25

2. Harry believes that Martians have infiltrated the CIA. This is an example of a(n)
   a. loose association.
   b. delusion.
   c. hallucination.
   d. neologism.

3. The area of the brain that is most involved in language production is
   a. Broca's area.
   b. Wernicke's area.
   c. the left temporal lobe.
   d. inactive during auditory hallucinations.

4. Premorbid functioning refers to a schizophrenic person's functioning
   a. just prior to death.
   b. during early childhood.
   c. prior to recovery from the disorder.
   d. prior to the appearance of the disorder.

5. The most common form of hallucination experienced by people with schizophrenia is
   a. visual.
   b. somatic.
   c. olfactory.
   d. auditory.

6. Donald is plagued by delusions and hallucinations. His schizophrenia is most likely related to
   a. serotonin.
   b. dopamine.
   c. acetylcholine.
   d. norepinephrine.

7. According to the _____ perspective, schizophrenia is a result of extreme regression and attempts by the ego to reassert control.
   a. cognitive
   b. existential
   c. behavioral
   d. psychodynamic

8. According to the double-bind hypothesis, a person who is repeatedly exposed to internally contradicting messages may develop schizophrenia if he or she adopts a strategy of
   a. ignoring the primary communication.
   b. responding only to congruent communications.
   c. asking for clarification about the communication.
   d. alternating attention to the primary communication and to the metacommunication.

15 TREATMENTS FOR SCHIZOPHRENIA AND OTHER SEVERE MENTAL DISORDERS

I.   Institutional Care in the Past, 450–452

1. Philippe Pinel's practice of _____ treatment spread to the United States, resulting in the creation of large _____ _____ rather than asylums to care for mentally disturbed individuals.

2. Required by U.S. law, _____ hospitals were established so that institutional care would be available to both poor and rich people.

3. The state hospital system developed numerous problems; list three.

    a. State _____ was too low.

    b. There was a decline in the _____ of care.

    c. _____

4. Complete these statements about the 100-year decline in the quality of mental health care that began in the mid-nineteenth century.

    a. Priorities of public mental health institutions changed dramatically, from _____ care to custodial care or order-keeping.

    b. During this time, hospitals increasingly relied upon _____, isolation, and _____ to treat disruptive patients.

    c. "Advanced" forms of intervention included medical approaches such as _____.

5. Describe characteristics of *social breakdown syndrome,* a result of institutionalization.

    _____

    _____

    _____

II. Institutional Care Takes a Turn for the Better, 452–455

During the 1950s, milieu therapy (based on humanistic principles) and token economy programs (based on behavioral principles) gained prominence as methods of treatment in institutions for mentally ill people. Exercises in this subsection cover the two approaches separately.

A. Milieu Therapy, 452

1. In the **milieu therapy** approach, a climate that builds self-respect, responsibility, and activity is provided to patients within the psychiatric setting. Below, list two specific aspects of the lives of patients who are treated with milieu therapy.

    a. _____

    _____

    b. _____

    _____

2. Research indicates that patients with chronic schizophrenia in milieu programs improve at higher rates than do such patients in _____ care programs, and the approach has proven to be an effective adjunct to other hospital treatments.

B. **The Token Economy, 452**

1. **Token economy programs** apply the systematic application of _____ conditioning techniques.

2. In this exercise you will put yourself in the place of the therapist assigned to design a token economy program for Claude L., a 42-year-old man with schizophrenia. Use your knowledge of the deficits and excesses of behavior that people with the disorder exhibit to complete a list of target behaviors that could be rewarded, set the daily reward in numbers of "TEs" (token exchanges), and complete the list of reinforcements that Claude could purchase with his tokens.

City Hospital Department of Psychiatry

Treatment plan for: Claude L.
Therapist:
Treatment program: Token economy

Self-Care/Hygiene Tasks

1. showering daily (TE = 1 per day) _____

2. _____

3. _____

Social/Behavioral Skills

1. showing physical self-control with others/not fighting (TE = 2 per day) _____

2. _____

3. _____

Ward Responsibilities

1. setting table in dining room (TE = 5) _____

2. _____

3. _____

Reinforcements

1. candy bars and soda (TE = 2) _____

2. going on an escorted trip to the zoo or the museum (TE = 100) _____

3. _____

4. _____

---

3. By the end of the structured token economy implemented by Paul and Lentz (1977), _____ percent of the patients had been released, mostly to sheltered-care facilities. In comparison, only 71 percent of the patients treated in _____ therapy and 45 percent of patients receiving _____ care had been released.

4. Lack of an appropriate _____ group in many studies of token economies limits the validity of these studies, and renders their results questionable.

5. Again putting yourself in the place of a therapist at City Hospital, suppose that one of your colleagues proposes a token economy that requires patients to earn tokens to buy pillows, meals, and

any "outdoor" time. Write a statement on the ethical and legal problems this program would give the hospital.

_____

_____

_____

6. Another therapist at City Hospital has been treating a woman with schizophrenia who insisted on talking to her "evil twin" every day in the mirror. After six months in your colleague's token economy program, the woman stops this behavior.

    a. Critique your colleague's subsequent claim that the program had "worked."

    _____

    _____

    b. How might your colleague rebut your critique?

    _____

    _____

III. Antipsychotic Drugs, 455–458

1. Complete these statements that delineate the history of **antipsychotic medications.**

    a. The group of antihistamine drugs called _____ were administered by the surgeon Henri Laborit to calm patients undergoing surgery.

    b. Because of their calming effects, researchers speculated that this group of drugs could be used to treat _____ disorders.

    c. After being tested in laboratory and clinical settings, chlorpromazine was marketed as the first antipsychotic drug under the trade name _____.

    d. Since the discovery of this drug, other "conventional" antipsychotics have been developed and are known collectively as _____ drugs.

Go back to Chapter 14 and review how the antipsychotic drugs are believed to relieve symptoms of schizophrenia.

A. How Effective Are Antipsychotic Drugs?, 456

1. Antipsychotic drugs seem to relieve symptoms of schizophrenia in at least _____ percent of patients using these medications, and represent the most effective form of intervention for the disorder.

2. In a study demonstrating the risk of relapse among patients with schizophrenia who discontinued antipsychotic drug therapy too soon, researchers found that _____ percent of patients whose medications were changed to a placebo after five years relapsed, whereas only _____ percent of those who continued receiving medications relapsed.

3. List symptoms that (a) are reduced and (b) are less affected by the phenothiazines and related antipsychotic drugs.

    a. _____

    b. _____

B.   The Unwanted Effects of Conventional Antipsychotic Drugs, 457

1.   _____ effects are movement abnormalities produced by antipsychotic medications.

2.   Complete the following table that summarizes important features of some unwanted effects of antipsychotic medications described in the textbook.

Parkinsonian and Related Symptoms

Prevalence

Symptoms

Treatment   prescribe anti-Parkinsonian drugs along with antipsychotic drugs, or reduce antipsychotic drugs

Neuroleptic Malignant Syndrome

Prevalence

Symptoms

Treatment

Tardive Dyskinesia

Prevalence   at least 10 percent of patients will eventually develop to some degree

Symptoms

Treatment

3.   Tardive dyskinesia is called a late-appearing movement disorder because symptoms do not appear until the patient has been on the medication for at least _____ _____.

4.   Imagine that you are training a group of psychiatric residents on appropriate antipsychotic prescription procedures. What three points will you emphasize?

a.   If the patient does not respond to neuroleptic drugs, you should:

_____

b.   When you begin a neuroleptic drug regimen for a patient, you should prescribe the _____ dosage possible.

c.   After the patient reestablishes nonpsychotic functioning you should:

_____

C. Newer Antipsychotic Drugs, 458

Because some patients with schizophrenia do not respond to, or cannot tolerate the effects of, traditional neuroleptic drugs, new antipsychotic drugs have been developed to treat them. These drugs, which include clozapine (Clozaril) and risperidone (Risperdal), have been found to be more effective than conventional drugs.

1. In addition to being more effective drugs, atypical antipsychotic medications have several other advantages over traditional neuroleptic drugs. Complete the list of advantages.

    a. The atypical antipsychotics are much more effective in treating those who experience the _____ symptoms of schizophrenia.

    b. These drugs cause few _____ symptoms.

    c. They do not appear as likely to cause _____.

2. A major concern with clozapine is that it can lead to _____ , a potentially fatal drop in white blood cells, in 1 percent of its users.

PsychWatch: First Dibs on Atypical Antipsychotic Drugs, 459

1. Reread the box on page 459 of your textbook. Describe several prescription patterns that indicate that African Americans may be receiving less effective biological care than white Americans in many cases of schizophrenia. Suggest some reasons for this racial disparity.

    _____

    _____

    _____

    _____

    _____

IV. Psychotherapy, 460–465

Although some clinicians have treated schizophrenic people with psychotherapy alone (emphasizing a trusting and understanding relationship), the majority of practitioners today recognize that medication is a crucial component of the treatment process. Cognitive-behavioral therapy, family therapy, and social therapy can be very helpful to patients, especially after medication has relieved symptoms such as delusional thoughts and incoherence that are barriers to therapeutic interventions.

A. Cognitive-Behavioral Therapy, 460

1. What are the major goals of cognitive-behavioral therapy treatment for schizophrenia?

    _____

    _____

    _____

2. Identify the five main cognitive-behavioral techniques described in your textbook to achieve the goals discussed in question 1.

    a. _____

    b. _____

    c. _____

    d. _____

    e. _____

3.   The new wave of cognitive-behavioral therapists, including those who are practitioners of acceptance and commitment therapy, seek to help clients become detached and comfortable _____ of their hallucinations. They want the clients to be _____ of and _____ their hallucinations, and thus learn to move forward with their lives.

4.   What has research shown about the effectiveness of this form of cognitive-behavioral therapy?

_____

MediaSpeak: Can You Live with the Voices in Your Head?, 462

1.   Read the article about Angelo and the support group, Hearing Voices Network, he attends. Reflect on the ways in which the coping strategies espoused by H.V. N. and other groups like it are similar to the techniques and goals of the cognitive-behavioral treatment of schizophrenia. What do you think about the link between the two strategies? Are there ways in which the strategies are different?

_____

_____

B.   Family Therapy, 462

1.   Recovering patients with schizophrenia are greatly affected by the behavior and attitudes of _____ at home, since over _____ percent of these individuals live with their parents, siblings, spouses, or children.

2.   People with schizophrenia whose relatives have high levels of _____ _____ (i.e., high levels of criticism, emotional overinvolvement, and hostility) often have much higher relapse rates compared with those whose relatives do not.

3.   Psychoeducation provides guidance, advice, support, and education about schizophrenia to families of people with the disorder.

    a.   Psychoeducation also helps family members become _____ in their expectations, more _____ of deviant behavior, less guilt-ridden and confused, and more willing to try new patterns of interaction and communication.

    b.   Psychoeducation also helps the person with schizophrenia to:

_____

_____

C.   Social Therapy, 464

1.   Clinicians who use social therapy in the treatment of schizophrenia focus on the development of problem-solving, decision-making, and social skills in their patients. List two other "practical" interventions in this form of therapy.

_____

V.   The Community Approach, 465–470

1.   Write a brief definition of each of the following terms.

    a. Community Mental Health Act of 1963

_____

_____

b. Deinstitutionalization

_____

_____

c. "Revolving door" syndrome

_____

_____

A. What Are the Features of Effective Community Care?, 466

In order to address the needs of people with schizophrenia, the community care approach provides a range of services that are designed to maximize the potential of these individuals to live and function in the community.

1. Complete this summary table by describing the central characteristics of each component of the community care approach.

Component	Characteristics
Coordinated services	community mental health centers provide medication, therapy, and emergency care; they also coordinate services of other agencies, especially for MICAs
Short-term hospitalization	
Partial hospitalization	
Supervised residencies	
Occupational training and Support	

B. How Has Community Treatment Failed?, 468

1. One inadequacy in community treatment for people with schizophrenia is poor coordination of services, including minimal _____ between agencies and no overall strategy for the provision of services.

2. Describe the work of the **case manager.**

_____

_____

_____

_____

In addition to the shortage of needed community programs, there is an increasing trend in community mental health services away from their stated goals. Those goals are to (1) assist patients suffering from acute mental illness, (2) circumvent hospitalization before it becomes absolutely necessary, and (3) provide services to patients who have just been released from the hospital.

3. Describe the economic factors that led to this shortage of services provided by community mental health services, particularly for people with severe disorders.

_____

_____

4. A large proportion of people with schizophrenia do not receive necessary services from the community and cannot afford private treatment. These individuals are forced to live in situations that can exacerbate their problems. Write a short paragraph describing the plight of these individuals who are forced to live in rooming houses or on the street. Be sure to consider the impact that the deinstitutionalization movement has had on these people.

_____

_____

_____

_____

5. As many as one of every _____ homeless people has a severe mental disorder such as schizophrenia.

C.   The Promise of Community Treatment, 470

1. Despite the serious problems of the community approach, there are several recently developed programs and groups that are committed to providing adequate services to people with schizophrenia. Describe the purpose and/or services offered by the national interest group the National Alliance on Mental Illness.

_____

_____

_____

_____

MediaSpeak: "Alternative" Mental Health Care, 471

1. According to Harry K. Wexler, ___ to ___ percent of U.S. prisoners are mentally ill.
2. Compare mentally ill offenders to other prisoners in terms of recidivism rates, cost to jail, and likelihood of suicide.

_____

_____

_____

3. Explain mental health treatment courts, and describe the success of such programs.

_____

_____

VI. Putting It Together: An Important Lesson, 472

1. Provide two pieces of evidence in support of the textbook author's statement that "no matter how compelling the evidence for biological causation [of schizophrenia] may be, a strictly biological approach to the treatment of psychological disorders is a mistake more often than not."

    a. _____

    _____

    b. _____

    _____

MULTIPLE CHOICE

1. What French physician is credited for beginning the movement toward more humane and moral treatment of mental patients?
   a. Henri Laborit
   b. Philippe Pinel
   c. Pierre Deniker
   d. Maxwell Jones

2. The creation of a therapeutic community was a feature of
   a. moral therapy.
   b. milieu therapy.
   c. a token economy.
   d. sociocultural therapy.

3. Which of the following are antipsychotic medications?
   a. tricyclics
   b. phenothiazines
   c. benzodiazepines
   d. MAO inhibitors

4. Which of the following is least likely to be relieved by a conventional antipsychotic drug?
   a. delusions
   b. flat affect
   c. hallucinations
   d. bizarre behavior

5. The potentially fatal reaction to conventional antipsychotic drugs that involves muscle rigidity, fever, improper ANS functioning, and altered consciousness is known as
   a. neuroleptic malignant syndrome.
   b. tardive dyskinesia.
   c. Parkinson's disease.
   d. schizophrenia.

6. All other things being equal, which of the following patients appears most likely to develop tardive dyskinesia from taking a neuroleptic?
   a. a male
   b. a female
   c. an older person
   d. a younger person

7. Which of the following is most likely to reduce the negative symptoms of schizophrenia?
   a. Haldol
   b. Clozapine
   c. psychotherapy
   d. the phenothiazines

8. Which of the following is not a symptom of schizophrenia?
   a. flat affect
   b. loss of volition
   c. tardive dyskinesia
   d. formal thought disorders

9. Tony spends his days at a center with other individuals with mental disorders. Staff at the center provide supervision as well as some therapy and occupational training. Tony goes home each night. This is an example of a(n):
   a. aftercare program.
   b. day hospital.
   c. semihospital.
   d. half-way house.

10. The trend in treatment for people with schizophrenia and other severe mental disorders since the 1960s has been toward
    a. more inpatient psychotherapy.
    b. short-term hospitalization and community-based services.
    c. a decrease in the hospital's use of medication to manage severe mental disorders.
    d. using only individual psychotherapy with patients prior to release from the hospital.

16 PERSONALITY DISORDERS

REVIEW EXERCISES

The following exercises cover Chapter 16 introductory material on pages 475–479.

1. Complete these exercises about the concepts that form the basis of this chapter.

   a. **Personality** refers to the _____ and enduring patterns of inner experience and _____ _____ displayed by each individual.

   b. Most of us maintain an adaptive flexibility in our changing environment by learning from experiences and experimenting with different responses in our efforts to cope.

   c. Those with a **personality disorder** are frequently unable to do this. Give the definition of a personality disorder from the textbook.

   _____

   _____

   _____

2. Personality disorders are classified in DSM-IV-TR as Axis _____ disorders because they usually do not have periods of clear _____ and do not vary greatly in intensity over time.

3. Personality disorders often coexist with Axis _____ disorders (a relationship that is called).

I. "Odd" Personality Disorders, 479–484

Each of the 10 personality disorders identified by DSM-IV-TR is covered in its own part. Below is a partial representation of Figure 16–1 on page 477—a grid showing the various features of the 10 disorders. Read about the characteristics of each disorder (which comes at the beginning of the coverage of each), then go to this grid and check the features that you think fit it. Finally, compare your choices against the original grid on page 477 to see if you caught the central points.

"Odd" Personality Disorders	Paranoid	Schizoid	Schizotypal
Relationship problems			
Suspicious/distrustful			
Hostile			
Blames others			
Deceitful			
Controlling/manipulative			
Jealous			
Sensitive			
Aloof/isolated			
Self-absorbed			
Self-critical			

	Paranoid	Schizoid	Schizotypal
Impulsive/reckless			
Grandiose/egocentric			
Emotionally unstable			
Overly emotional			
Depressed/helpless			
Anxious/tense			
Cognitive/perceptual eccentricities			
Attention deficiencies			
Psychotic-like episodes			

A. **Paranoid Personality Disorder, 479**

1. Complete this list of features of the **paranoid personality disorder.**

   a. distrustful and suspicious of others' _____, and read "hidden" meaning and hostile intention into the actions of others

   b. quick to challenge the_____ and trustworthiness of others

   c. critical of others' _____ and faults, but unable to recognize their own

   _____

   d. blame and regularly hold _____ against others for things that go wrong

2. Between 0.5 and 3 percent of adults, and apparently more _____ than the other gender, have paranoid personality disorder.

Psychodynamic theorists propose several ways a paranoid personality disorder can emerge from parental mistreatment, hostility, and absence of consistent nurturing. Study this diagram showing potential "outcomes" for people who experience this sort of parental environment, and who later develop a paranoid personality disorder.

Parental mistreatment, hostility, and absence of consistent nurturance leads to children who:

↓   ↓

come to view all environments as hostile and dangerous, resulting in a basic distrust of others   project feelings of hostility and rage onto others, leading to feelings of persecution

↘   ↙

Paranoid Personality Disorder

3. A possible_____ factor in paranoid personality disorder was shown by one study of Australian twin pairs that found a high concordance of excessive suspiciousness.

4. One reason that clinicians find it difficult to treat people with paranoid personality disorder is that unless they are in crisis, few of these individuals think they need therapy. What is another reason?

_____

_____

5. Describe the goals of cognitive and behavioral therapies for paranoid personality disorder, which are often combined.

_____

_____

_____

6. Generally, _____ therapy has been relatively ineffective in the treatment of paranoid personality disorder.

7. The psychodynamic therapists, who are known as self-therapists, try to help clients suffering from paranoid personality disorder reestablish _____-_____ (a unified personality), which the therapists believe has been lost.

B. Schizoid Personality Disorder, 481

1. People with paranoid personality disorder avoid social contact because they distrust others. Why do people with **schizoid personality disorder** avoid others?

_____

2. In addition to having very little interest in relationships, a restricted range of _____ expression is displayed by people with schizoid personality disorder.

3. Psychodynamic and object relations theorists hypothesize that, like other personality disorders, schizoid personality disorder develops as a result of inadequate parenting. Complete these questions about these explanations.

   a. According to these theorists, what characteristics do the parents of people with schizoid personality disorder tend to have?

   _____

   b. Unlike those with paranoid personality disorder, who react with distrust and hostility, those with schizoid personality disorder suffer an inability to _____ or _____ love.

4. Cognitive theorists believe that people with schizoid personality disorder suffer from certain deficits that account for their lack of responsiveness. List them.

_____

_____

5. Behavioral therapists, who often integrate their treatment with cognitive techniques, attempt to help their schizoid clients develop better _____ skills.

6. Group therapy has helped some schizoid patients by providing a contained, safe setting for social contact. Describe one of its potential limitations.

_____

C. Schizotypal Personality Disorder, 482

1. People with **schizotypal personality disorder** experience extreme discomfort in close _____, cognitive or perceptual _____, and behavioral eccentricities.

2. List two types of peculiar thought exhibited by some people with schizotypal personality disorder.

_____

_____

3. Describe some of the eccentric behaviors of people with schizotypal personality disorder.

   _____

   _____

4. Complete these questions relating to studies suggesting that schizophrenia and schizotypal personality disorders have similar roots.

   a. In a study of family relationships as a causal factor, schizotypal personality disorder—like schizophrenia—was linked to family _____ and psychological disorders in parents.

   b. Studies utilizing backward masking tests indicate that defects in _____ and memory processes might contribute to schizotypal personality disorder, just as these defects are related to schizophrenia.

   c. Research on biological factors found that schizotypal patients appear to have higher levels of dopamine activity, as do schizophrenic people. What other biological abnormalities have been found in both groups of patients?

   _____

5. Regardless of the clinician's theoretical orientation, what are usually the central goals in the treatment of schizotypal personality disorder?

   _____

   _____

6. Complete the questions relating to the kinds of interventions offered by different types of treatment approaches to schizotypal personality disorder.

   a. On the cognitive end of cognitive-behavioral therapy, therapists teach clients to evaluate their unusual perceptions or thoughts according to objective evidence and to ignore _____ thoughts.

   b. On the behavioral end of cognitive-behavioral therapy, therapists focuses on reeducative methods such as:

   _____

   c. _____ doses of antipsychotic drugs seems to work best for some patients.

II. "Dramatic" Personality Disorders, 484–501

Here is a grid for testing your understanding of the features of "dramatic" disorders. Compare your selections with those in Figure 16–1 on textbook page 477.

"Dramatic" Personality Disorders				
	Antisocial	**Borderline**	**Histrionic**	**Narcissistic**
Relationship problems				
Suspicious/distrustful				
Hostile				
Blames others				
Deceitful				

	Antisocial	Borderline	Histrionic	Narcissistic
Controlling/manipulative				
Jealous				
Sensitive				
Aloof/isolated				
Self-absorbed				
Self-critical				
Impulsive/reckless				
Grandiose/egocentric				
Emotionally unstable				
Overly emotional				
Depressed/helpless				
Anxious/tense				
Cognitive/perceptual eccentricities				
Attention deficiencies				
Psychotic-like episodes				

A. Antisocial Personality Disorder, 485

1. What are two other terms used for people with **antisocial personality disorder?**

   _____

2. The primary feature of antisocial personality disorder is a pervasive pattern of _____ for and violation of the _____ of others, which is reflected in the disorder's strong association with criminal behavior.

3. What are some of the antisocial behaviors typically seen before age 15 in people who will later be diagnosed with antisocial personality disorder?

   _____

   _____

4. Add to this list of adjectives that describe the characteristics of a person with antisocial personality disorder.

   _____ Deceitful _____   _____

   _____ Irresponsible _____   _____

   _____   _____

   _____   _____

5. Up to 3.5 percent of people in the United States meet the criteria for antisocial personality disorder; men are _____ times more/less likely to be diagnosed than women.

6. Individuals with antisocial personality disorder have higher rates of alcoholism and substance-related disorders than the general population. Complete the following table related to three possible links between substance use and antisocial personality disorder described in your text.

Possibility #1	Possibility #2	Possibility #3
Early _____ and substance abuse triggers the development of _____ .	Antisocial personality disorder leaves a person more _____ to develop _____ _____ problems.	Both antisocial personality disorder AND substance abuse are caused by a third factor such as the need to _____ .

Study this diagram that depicts the psychodynamic explanation of antisocial personality disorder.

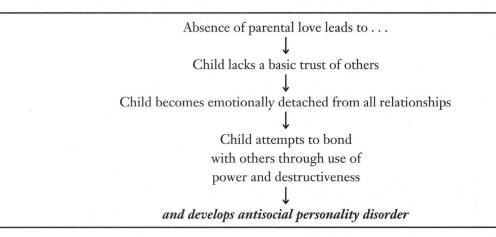

Absence of parental love leads to . . .

↓

Child lacks a basic trust of others

↓

Child becomes emotionally detached from all relationships

↓

Child attempts to bond
with others through use of
power and destructiveness

↓

and develops antisocial personality disorder

7. Complete the following statements relating to different explanations of antisocial personality disorder.

   a. Supporting the psychodynamic view, studies indicate that people with the disorder are more likely to have experienced stressful childhood events, such as poverty and family violence, parental conflicts, or divorce.

   b. Behavioral views hold that people with the disorder might acquire their symptoms through _____ the behaviors of parents and others, and/or that parents may unwittingly reinforce antisocial behaviors.

   c. Cognitive theorists believe that people with the disorder trivialize the _____ of others and have difficulty seeing other _____.

8. Researchers have found that people with antisocial personality disorder feel less _____ than others, which could explain why they fail to learn from _____ experiences and seem to "tune out" the emotional _____ of others.

9. Laboratory studies have shown that people with antisocial personality disorder respond to expectations of a stressful event with low levels of physiological _____, indicating that these individuals may be more able to ignore _____ or emotional situations.

10. Laboratory studies have also shown that antisocial people display both lower than usual _____ activity, which is associated with impulsivity and aggression, and defiant functioning

in their brains' _____ _____ , which are involved in planning, strategizing, and personal relations.

11. Complete the following statements regarding treatment of people with antisocial personality disorder.

    a. No treatment intervention for antisocial personality disorder seems to be _____.

    b. Most people with the disorder do not voluntarily seek treatment, and most of those who do receive it (either voluntarily or not) terminate treatment prematurely. What is the major difficulty in treating these individuals? _____

    _____

    c. Cognitive-behavioral therapists attempt to get people with antisocial personality disorder to consider _____ issues and the _____ of others.

    d. Structured environment approaches emphasize _____ toward others.

B. Borderline Personality Disorder, 489

DSM-IV-TR defines borderline personality disorder is a pervasive pattern of instability in interpersonal relationships, self-image, and mood, as well as marked impulsivity. Read the following case study related to borderline personality disorder which will be followed by an exercise.

Case Study

Belinda T. is a 27-year-old woman who decided to seek therapy from Dr. Platt, an established and highly regarded clinician. During the initial interview, Belinda told Dr. Platt the following: "Things have been getting worse and worse for me. Even when it seems like I'm having a good day, suddenly something goes wrong and I get depressed, or so mad that I see red. [1] A few nights ago I smashed every glass plate in the house and kicked my dog so hard that I had to take him to the vet. [2] The next day I felt so horrible that I drank until I passed out. I get to feeling really awful and alone, like I'm a big nothing inside. Sometimes I cut my arms and stomach with a razor. [3] When I feel the pain and see the blood, I get a rush . . . almost like I feel more "real." [4] This therapy is my last chance; if it doesn't work, I may as well just give up and die."

  Dr. Platt agreed to work with Belinda in therapy and made a provisional diagnosis of borderline personality disorder. After her first therapy session, Belinda told her friends that Dr. Platt was "the most wonderful person in the world," and that she had never met anyone with such understanding and compassion. She said that she was certain Dr. Platt could help her. But just five sessions later, Belinda confronted Dr. Platt by saying, "You are an unfeeling, incompetent bitch! You are the one who needs a shrink." [5] Dr. Platt responded by asking, "I wonder if some of your anger is about my being on vacation last week?" Belinda confirmed Dr. Platt's hypothesis by angrily claiming that Dr. Platt had deserted her and no longer cared about her. [6] Sobbing, Belinda rolled up her sleeve and revealed several new cuts on her arm. "Look at what you made me do! Please don't leave me alone again; I can't stand it. The next time you cancel a session, I might kill myself." [7]

1. Each of the numbered statements in this sample case relates to a particular characteristic of people who suffer from **borderline personality disorder.** Match each statement with the characteristics (a–g) that follow.

   [1]   [2]   [3]   [4]   [5]   [6]   [7]

Characteristics:

a. Anger is expressed in aggressive, violent behavior outward.

b. Fearing desertion, manipulative behaviors such as suicidal threats are used to maintain relationships.

c. Anger is expressed and directed inward through self-destructive and self-mutilating behaviors.

d. Vacillation occurs between overidealizing and devaluing others in relationships.

e. Dramatic, often sudden, shifts in mood are common.

f. Rage and extreme disappointment are felt when expectations, particularly about others "being there" at all times in a relationship, are not met.

g. Self-destructive and self-mutilating behavior can serve to relieve chronic feelings of boredom and emptiness and to validate "personhood."

2. Complete the following statements regarding the prevalence and course of borderline personality disorder.

a. About 75 percent of the estimated 1–2.5 percent of the general population with borderline personality disorder are _____.

b. The symptoms of the disorder most commonly seem to peak during _____ adulthood and decrease with age.

3. Psychodynamic research has focused on the excessive fear of _____ that people with borderline personality disorder have, which has led to a hypothesis that parents' lack of acceptance causes a loss in self-esteem, dependency, and difficulty in coping with _____.

4. In addition to family instability, conflict, and parental loss, early trauma such as physical, _____, and _____ abuse is prevalent in the backgrounds of people diagnosed with borderline personality disorder.

5. Biological factors that have been implicated in borderline personality disorder include an overly reactive _____, an underactive _____, low _____ activity (linked to aggression against self and others), abnormalities in the _____ gene, and other genetic factors.

6. According to the *biosocial theory* of borderline personality disorder, the disorder results from a combination of _____ forces, such as abnormal neurotransmitter reactions and difficulty controlling emotions, and _____ forces, such as environments in which a child's emotions are misinterpreted by parents, or punished, ignored, and trivialized.

7. Sociocultural theorists hypothesize that the increasing prevalence of borderline personality disorder is related to a rapidly changing culture and breakdown of the _____ unit.

8. What are some reasons that some therapists refuse to see clients with borderline personality disorder?

_____

_____

_____

_____

_____

9. Complete these statements about treatment for borderline personality disorder.

   a. Contemporary psychodynamic therapy focuses on _____ disturbance, poor sense of _____, and pervasive _____ and emptiness.

   b. Describe the features of dialectical behavior therapy (DBT), the integrative treatment approach that is now considered in many circles to be the treatment of choice for borderline personality disorder.

   _____

   _____

   _____

   c. The use of drugs (such as antidepressants or antipsychotics) in therapy is controversial in part because of the elevated risk of _____ _____ by patients with borderline personality disorder.

C. Histrionic Personality Disorder, 496

1. Complete the following list of features of persons diagnosed with **histrionic personality disorder.**

   a. They are described as "_____ charged" and have exaggerated, rapid mood swings.

   b. Always "_____," these people are grandiose and theatrical in their language and gestures.

   c. They are _____, self-centered, and _____ in their extreme need for attention.

   d. They exaggerate physical _____ and weaknesses, as well as the intensity of their relationships with others.

   e. They may behave in a sexually _____ manner as a way to get attention from and seduce others.

2. What have recent studies indicated about the prevalence rates of histrionic personality disorder among men versus women?

   _____

3. Psychodynamic theorists believe that histrionic people defend against deep fears of _____ by being overly emotional and inventing crises so that other people will act _____ toward them.

4. Many cognitive explanations focus on the deficient functionings of those with histrionic personality disorder, such as their "lack of substance," extreme _____, and assumption that they are helpless.

5. Sociocultural theorists point to society's _____ and expectations that encouraged childishness in women, resulting in histrionic behaviors that may be viewed as a caricature of _____ as our culture once defined it.

6. List two challenges faced by therapists who treat patients with histrionic personality disorder.

   a. _____

   _____

   b. _____

   _____

7. What is a central goal in the treatment of histrionic personality disorder?

    _____

D. **Narcissistic Personality Disorder, 499**

    1. **Narcissistic personality disorder** is characterized by excessive grandiosity, need for admiration, and lack of empathy. Read the lettered statements below made by a man with this disorder, then describe the characteristic of the disorder that is being displayed in the spaces for letters a–c following the statements.

        Statements:

        a. I think it's quite obvious that I saved the company's ass with my work on that project. I set a standard for the industry. The work could be described as nothing less than brilliant.

        b. Almost nobody is savvy enough to understand how my mind works. Maybe Bill Gates and Ted Turner . . . no, I doubt if even they could understand me.

        c. All the time my co-worker Lance spent lying around the hospital really added to the amount of work I was given, and it wasn't fair! I know he had a heart attack, but I have my own problems.

        a. grandiose sense of self-importance, exaggeration of achievements, arrogance

        b. _____

        c. _____

    2. Of the roughly 1 percent of the adult population with narcissistic personality disorder, up to 75 percent are _____.

    3. Psychodynamic theorists propose that cold and rejecting parents cause children to feel rejected and unworthy, and that some of these children grow up to defend against these feelings by telling themselves they are _____ and desirable.

    4. Behavioral and cognitive theorists give a very different explanation of narcissistic personality disorder, suggesting that people diagnosed with this disorder were treated too _____ early in life.

    5. Sociocultural theorists propose that individual cases of narcissistic personality disorder result from societal breakdowns during "_____ of narcissism."

    6. Narcissistic people might enter therapy with a sense of entitlement that may be manifest in manipulating the therapist to support their sense of _____.

III. "Anxious" Personality Disorders, 501–508

Following is a grid for testing your understanding of the features of "anxious" personality disorders—the last of the three groups. Remember to check the features that you think apply to each disorder, then compare your selections with those in Figure 16–1 on textbook page 477.

"Anxious" Personality Disorders

	Avoidant	Dependent	Obsessive-Compulsive
Relationship problems			
Suspicious/distrustful			
Hostile			
Blames others			
Deceitful			
Controlling/manipulative			
Jealous			
Sensitive			
Aloof/isolated			
Self-absorbed			
Self-critical			
Impulsive/reckless			
Grandiose/egocentric			
Emotionally unstable			
Overly emotional			
Depressed/helpless			
Anxious/tense			
Cognitive/perceptual eccentricities			
Attention deficiencies			
Psychotic-like episodes			

A. Avoidant Personality Disorder, 501

1. **Avoidant personality disorder** is characterized by social avoidance, persistent feelings of _____, and hypersensitivity to _____ evaluations and rejection.

2. Complete the following questions relating to the relationship between avoidant personality disorder and social anxiety disorder.

   a. Symptoms that are common to both disorders include fear of _____ and low _____.

   b. Some theorists believe that important differences between the two disorders include the fact that people with social anxiety disorder primarily fear social _____, whereas people with avoidant personality disorder mostly fear social _____.

3. Psychodynamic theorists suggest that after being repeatedly _____ or punished by parents during toilet training, children develop a negative self-image, a distrust of others, and a belief that "I am unlovable"—all of which contribute to avoidant personality disorder.

4. The _____ view of avoidant personality disorder suggests that because of past criticisms, those affected expect and fear _____, misinterpret people's reactions, and discount positive feedback.

5. Describe why therapists often find it difficult to keep individuals with avoidant personality disorder in treatment.

   _____

   _____

6. Treatment for avoidant personality disorder is very similar to treatment for people with _____ disorders such as social phobias.

7. Complete this table by giving an example of an intervention for people with avoidant personality disorder from each of the perspectives given.

Perspective	Example of Intervention
Psychodynamic	
Cognitive	
Behavioral	provide social skills training and exposure treatment requiring clients to gradually increase their social contacts
Biological	

B. Dependent Personality Disorder, 504

1. In each of the following areas, give *two* examples of behaviors that might be characteristic of Wilma, a woman with **dependent personality disorder**.

   Relationships:

   a. *Wilma's extreme fear of separation and need to be "taken care of" result in submissive, clinging, and obedient behavior.*

   b. _____

   _____

   Decision making:

   a. _____

   _____

   b. _____

   _____

Emotions/Mood:

a. _____

_____

b. _____

_____

2.   Complete the following statements regarding the various explanations of dependent personality disorder.

  a. In the past, psychodynamic theorists believed that, like depression, dependent personality disorders were a result of a fixation at the _____ stage of psychosexual development.

  b. Other psychodynamic theorists hold that the parents of people with the disorder were overprotective, thus fostering dependent behaviors and heightening the child's feelings of insecurity and anxiety about _____.

  c. _____ theorists believe that parents unintentionally rewarded their child's clinging behavior and punished _____ behavior.

  d. According to cognitive theorists, one maladaptive assumption underlying this disorder held by those who have it is that they are inadequate and helpless to deal with the world. What is the other underlying maladaptive assumption?

  _____

3.   Key concerns for clinicians in the treatment of patients with dependent personality disorder include how to get them to accept _____ for themselves and what to do about the patient's _____ or parent—who is probably playing a role in the maintenance of dependent behaviors.

4.   Psychodynamic therapists must inevitably work through the dependent patient's _____ of dependency needs onto the therapist.

C. Obsessive-Compulsive Personality Disorder, 506

1.   People with obsessive-compulsive personality disorder are preoccupied with order, _____ and _____.

2.   Complete this list by providing the usual result or outcome of each characteristic of obsessive-compulsive personality disorder.

  a. Fixation on organization and details: _____

  _____

  b. High standards for self and others: _____

  _____

  c. Fear of making mistakes: _____

  d. Inflexible morals, ethics, and values: _____

  e. Miserly behavior: _____

3.   While many people diagnosed with obsessive-compulsive (anxiety) disorder also have an obsessive-compulsive personality disorder, no specific link has found empirical support.

4.   According to Freudian theorists, people with obsessive-compulsive personality disorder are described as _____ _____ (characterized by orderly, stubborn, and re-

strained behavior) as a result of their parents being very harsh and punitive toward them during the toilet-training stage.

5. Cognitive theorists believe that illogical thinking processes, such as _____ thinking, maintain the symptoms of people with obsessive-compulsive personality disorder.

6. One difference between obsessive-compulsive *anxiety* disorder and obsessive-compulsive *personality* disorder is how they are treated. Rather than drug or behavioral therapy, which treatments are most effective for the obsessive-compulsive personality disorder?

_____

IV. Multicultural Factors: Research Neglect, 508–509

1. Although there has not been systematic research on the issue, identify two possible explanations that theorists have put forth to explain the fact that 75 percent of people diagnosed with borderline personality disorder are female.

_____

_____

_____

2. Some multicultural theorists believe that borderline personality disorder may be attributable more to social _____ than to _____ factors.

3. A research study has shown a disproportionately high prevalence of borderline personality disorder among Hispanic Americans compared with the rates among white Americans and African Americans. What are the explanations for this result that some multicultural theorists are suggesting?

_____

_____

_____

V. What Problems Are Posed by the DSM-IV-TR Categories?, 509–510

1. Of all the categories in the DSM-IV-TR, personality disorders are among the most difficult to accurately diagnose. Complete the following statements related to three central problems that can lead to misdiagnosis of these disorders.

   a. Many diagnostic criteria cannot be directly _____, so they must rely on the impression of _____ clinicians.

   b. There is considerable _____ of symptoms *within* clusters of personality disorders and even *between* the clusters themselves.

   c. People with very _____ personalities are often given the same diagnosis.

VI. Are There Better Ways to Classify Personality Disorders?, 510–511

1. Today's leading criticism of DSM-IV-TR's approach to personality disorders is that the classification system uses categories rather than _____ of personality, assuming a personality disorder is either entirely present or absent.

2. Briefly describe a dimensional approach to classifying personality pathology.

_____

_____

3. List the five "supertraits," or personality factors, identified by proponents of the "Big Five" theory of personality and personality disorders.

    a. _____

    b. _____

    c. _____

    d. _____

    e. _____

4. How many broad personality factors are identified in Jonathan Shedler and Drew Westen's dimensional model of personality, put forth as an alternative to the "Big Five" model? _____

VII. Call for Change: DSM-5, 512–513

1. Under the new hybrid model for diagnosing personality disorders that has been proposed by the DSM-5 task force, only some of the disorders listed in this chapter would be retained. Identify those categories that would be retained if this recommendation by the task force is adopted in the DSM-5. Also, identify the reason the task force has recommended eliminating the other categories.

    _____

    _____

2. Briefly describe the proposed diagnosis of *personality disorder trait specified (PDTS)*, which the task force has proposed as a new route by which people may receive a diagnosis of personality disorder.

    _____

    _____

3. Why has the new model proposed by the DSM-5 task force caused so much controversy in the clinical community?

    _____

    _____

VIII. Putting It Together: Disorders of Personality—Rediscovered, Then Reconsidered, 513–514

1. Complete this list of questions about personality disorders that researchers and clinicians continue to ask.

    a. How common are the various personality disorders?

    b. _____

    c. _____

    d. _____

    e. _____

MULTIPLE CHOICE

1. An inflexible pattern of inner experience and outward behavior that deviates markedly from the expectations of one's culture is called a
   a. neurosis.
   b. fugue state.
   c. personality trait.
   d. personality disorder.

2. In a study of role playing, subjects with paranoid personality disorder generally responded to ambiguous behavior with
   a. anger.
   b. confusion.
   c. withdrawal.
   d. confrontation.

3. A lack of interest in sexual behavior is likely to be a feature of the
   a. schizoid personality disorder.
   b. paranoid personality disorder.
   c. antisocial personality disorder.
   d. dependent personality disorder.

4. The symptom of bodily illusions displayed by many schizotypal patients involves
   a. loose associations.
   b. sensing an external force or presence.
   c. the belief that unrelated events pertain to them.
   d. conversing in a vague manner and making inappropriately elaborate statements.

5. What childhood patterns place a person at risk for developing antisocial personality disorder as an adult?
   a. autism
   b. serious misbehavior (conduct disorder)
   c. childhood depression
   d. generalized anxiety disorder

6. Which characteristic is not typical of borderline personality disorder?
   a. major mood changes
   b. unstable self-image
   c. constant depression
   d. impulsivity

7. People who are diagnosable with histrionic personality disorder are somewhat unusual compared with those with other personality disorders in that they
   a. are unhappy.
   b. tend to seek treatment.
   c. display strange behavior.
   d. behave in a maladaptive way.

8. The avoidant personality disorder is one of the
   a. odd personality disorders.
   b. Axis I personality disorders.
   c. anxious personality disorders.
   d. dramatic personality disorders.

9. Decision making is a particular problem for the person who suffers from
   a. borderline personality disorder.
   b. dependent personality disorder.
   c. narcissistic personality disorder.
   d. obsessive-compulsive personality disorder.

10. Max spends so much time organizing his attack on the problem that he never gets to work on the problem. This is a habitual pattern with him. His behavior is a symptom of
    a. avoidant personality disorder.
    b. antisocial personality disorder.
    c. dependent personality disorder.
    d. obsessive-compulsive personality disorder.

17 DISORDERS OF CHILDHOOD AND ADOLESCENCE

I. Childhood and Adolescence, 518–519

1. Even youths who do not have a diagnosable disorder experience difficulties from time to time.

    a. About _____ of all children worry about things such as school, health, and their safety.

    b. Other common problems among children include _____, nightmares, _____, and restlessness.

    c. Teenagers often feel anxious or confused over _____ and _____ changes, or social and academic _____.

2. About one-_____ of children and adolescents in the United States experience a diagnosable psychological disorder.

3. _____ with psychological disorders outnumber _____, which is interesting because the prevalence of disorders by gender is generally the opposite in adulthood.

4. More than _____ of students report being bullied frequently, and more than _____ percent report having been a victim at least once. Identify some of the feelings associated with being the victim of bullying.

    _____

5. The disturbing trend of bullying via technology such as e-mail, text messages, and social networking sites is known as _____.

II. Childhood Anxiety Disorders, 519–521

1. Identify three major factors that contribute to childhood and adolescent anxiety.

    a. _____

    b. _____

    c. _____

2. Like adults, children can suffer from specific phobias, _____ anxiety disorder, and _____ anxiety disorder.

3. Although childhood anxiety disorders can be explained in the same way as adult anxiety disorders, anxiety disorders in children can also develop as a result of some unique features of childhood. To each unique feature listed, give an example of something that might contribute to the development of an anxiety disorder.

    a. *Compared with adults, children have few experiences with the world.*

    _____

    _____

    b. *Today's society exposes children to many frightening images and messages.*

    _____

    _____

c. *Children are highly dependent on their parents for emotional support and guidance, and may be greatly affected by parental inadequacies.*

_____

_____

4. Why do generalized anxiety disorder and social anxiety disorder rarely appear in earnest until children are at least 7 years old?

_____

_____

A. Separation Anxiety Disorder, 520

1. Children who suffer from **separation anxiety disorder** experience _____ anxiety whenever they are separated from _____ or a parent.

2. In some cases, a childhood separation anxiety disorder can further take the form of a school _____ , or a school refusal.

B. Treatments for Childhood Anxiety Disorders, 521

1. In addition to treatment techniques that mirror adult therapies for anxiety disorders but are tailored to a child's unique life experience, some therapists use play therapy and hypnotherapy when treating children who are suffering anxiety disorders. Briefly describe the two techniques and why they are effective for children.

    a. Play therapy

    _____

    _____

    b. Hypnotherapy

    _____

    _____

III. Childhood Mood Problems, 522–525

A. Major Depressive Disorder, 522

1. Around _____ percent of children currently experience major depressive disorder. What is a major reason for the disparity between this rate and the rate of depression among adults?

    _____

    _____

2. Depression in younger children can be caused by negative _____ _____, major changes, _____, or ongoing _____.

3. Identify two unique features of childhood depression.

    a. _____

    b. _____

4. Before the age of 13, there is no significant difference in rates of depression between boys and girls. However, by age 16, _____ are twice as likely as the other gender to experience depression.

5. What are some possible reasons for the major shift in depression prevalence by gender in the early teenage years?

_____

_____

6. Most research has indicated that cognitive-behavioral therapy, interpersonal approaches, and anti-depressant drugs have all proven effective in the treatment of childhood and adolescent depression. Identify two recent developments that have called this into question, and briefly summarize the controversy that attends both developments.

   a. _____

   b. _____

B. Bipolar Disorder, 524

1. Bipolar disorder had previously been considered an adult-only disorder, but in the past fifteen years a sharply increasing number of children and adolescents have been diagnosed with bipolar disorders. How do most theorists explain this new trend?

_____

_____

2. Why do some theorists disagree with the increased diagnoses of bipolar disorder among children?

_____

_____

3. Around one-_____ of children in treatment for bipolar disorder receive an antipsychotic drug; one-_____ of them receive an antibipolar (mood stabilizing) drug, and many others receive _____ or _____ drugs. Relatively few of these drugs have been tested on and specifically approved for children.

IV. Oppositional Defiant Disorder and Conduct Disorder, 525–530

1. In this table, summarize the characteristics and prevalence rates of the two types of disruptive behavior disorders listed.

Disorder	Characteristics	Prevalence
Oppositional defiant disorder		10 percent of children
Conduct disorder		

2. List the most common behaviors leading to the arrest of juvenile (a) boys and (b) girls.

   a. _____

   b. _____

A. **What Are the Causes of Conduct Disorder?, 527**

    1. Along with drug use and biological, genetic, and socioeconomic factors, family _____ is often a cause in the development of conduct disorders.

    2. Give three examples of parental behaviors that have been associated with the emergence of conduct disorders.

        _____

        _____

B. **How Do Clinicians Treat Conduct Disorder?, 527**

    1. Treatment for conduct disorders is generally more effective with children under the age of _____, because disruptive behavior patterns become more resistant to change as a child grows older.

    2. Family interventions are often effective in the treatment of conduct disorder. List two types of family intervention below.

        a. _____

        b. _____

    3. Institutionalization in _____ _____ centers appears to exacerbate behavior problems among young offenders.

    4. _____ programs that begin in early childhood are also very promising because they focus on increasing training opportunities, _____ facilities, alleviating poverty, _____ care, and improving _____ skills.

    5. Identify and describe two child-focused treatments that have achieved some success in the treatment of conduct disorder in recent years.

        a. _____

        b. _____

    6. Studies suggest that _____drugs may help in reducing aggressive behaviors in children with conduct disorder.

V. **Attention-Deficit/Hyperactivity Disorder, 530–535**

    1. After reading through the case of "Steven" in the text, list five behaviors that exemplify his overactivity and impulsivity.

        _____

        _____

        _____

    2. ADHD often coexists with _____ , or communication problems, poor school performance, and social skills deficits.

    3. Complete these statements about the prevalence of ADHD.

        a. Of the 4 to 9 percent of children with ADHD, as many as _____ percent are boys.

        b. The disorder persists into adulthood for between _____ and _____ percent of affected people.

    4. ADHD is a difficult disorder to assess. List five important assessment tools and techniques that clinicians use to assess ADHD.

        a. _____

b. _____

c. _____

d. _____

e. _____

5.   Many children are diagnosed with ADHD by pediatricians or family physicians. Studies suggest that only _____ of these diagnoses are based on psychological or educational testing.

A.   What Are the Causes of ADHD?, 532

1.   Biological factors, high levels of _____, and _____ dysfunction are all possible causal factors in ADHD, although none has received consistent empirical support.

2.   The symptoms of ADHD, as well as the diagnostic label itself, can exacerbate _____ problems of children with the disorder and can even produce additional _____.

B.   How Is ADHD Treated?, 532

1.   Complete these statements relating to drug treatment for children with ADHD.

   a.   The stimulant drug **methylphenidate (Ritalin)** has a _____ effect on many children with ADHD.

   b.   Methylphenidate increases the ability of children to solve _____ and to control _____ at home and school.

2.   Many children with ADHD are taken off Ritalin. What do studies show is the outcome for many of these children after they are taken off the drug?

   _____

3.   Given that Ritalin can affect the growth of some children, how do doctors prevent such an effect in their patients who take it?

   _____

4.   Behaviorists use operant conditioning treatments that involve teaching parents to systematically _____ appropriate behavior—a method that seems most effective when it is combined with _____ therapy.

C.   Multicultural Factors and ADHD, 534

1.   Identify three possible reasons why American children from racial minority groups are less likely than white American children to receive an ADHD diagnosis and undergo treatment.

   _____

   _____

VI.   Elimination Disorders, 535–538

1.   Elimination disorders are characterized by the repeated urination or defecation in clothes, beds, or on the floor, after an age at which the child should be able to _____ these bodily functions.

2.   Complete these statements regarding **enuresis,** the usually involuntary bed-wetting or wetting of one's clothes.

   a.   Children must be at least _____ years old to receive this diagnosis.

   b.   Prevalence of enuresis _____ with age for both sexes, and no more than _____ percent of 15-year-olds experience it.

c. A _____ event such as hospitalization, the birth of a sibling, or entrance into _____ can precipitate enuresis.

3. Describe the explanations for enuresis by theorists of the (a) psychodynamic, (b) family systems, (c) behavioral, and (d) biological perspectives.

   a. It is a symptom of other conflicts and anxieties.

   b. _____

   c. _____

   d. _____

4. Study the top part of this diagram describing a classical conditioning approach to the treatment of enuresis, then provide the appropriate components that are missing from the bottom part of the diagram.

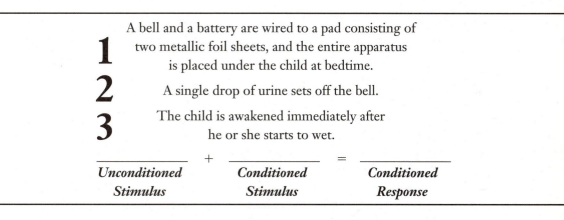

1 A bell and a battery are wired to a pad consisting of two metallic foil sheets, and the entire apparatus is placed under the child at bedtime.

2 A single drop of urine sets off the bell.

3 The child is awakened immediately after he or she starts to wet.

_____ + _____ = _____
Unconditioned   *Conditioned*   *Conditioned*
Stimulus   *Stimulus*   *Response*

5. A less common elimination disorder is **encopresis,** which is repeatedly and involuntarily _____ into one's clothing, usually beginning after the age of _____.

VII. Long-Term Disorders That Begin in Childhood, 538–556

A. Pervasive Devlopmental Disorders, 538

1. Pervasive developmental disorders are often marked by impaired _____, unusual _____ _____, and inappropriate responses to _____ in the environment.

2. Identify the four pervasive developmental disorders.

   a. _____

   b. _____

   c. _____

   d. _____

1. Autistic Disorder, 539

1. The symptoms of **autistic disorder** typically appear before the age of _____ and include extreme unresponsiveness to others, poor _____ skills, and _____ behavior.

2. Complete these statements that relate to the prevalence and course of autism.

   a. Approximately _____ percent of autistic children are boys.

   b. _____ out of ten autistic children remain severely impaired into adulthood.

3. Autistic children can display many behaviors that indicate a profound unresponsiveness to, and lack of interest in, other people (e.g., failure to make eye contact with parents). List three other examples of these behaviors.

    _____

    _____

    _____

    _____

4. About half of autistic children fail to speak or develop language skills. Those who do develop some level of verbal skills show many peculiarities in their communication patterns. Complete this description of these patterns.

    a. In _____, the child repeats exact words and phrases spoken by others without comprehension.

    b. An example of _____ _____would be an autistic child saying, "You want to watch TV now" when he or she wants to watch television.

Read this case study and complete the exercise that follows.

Case Study

Jodie is a 10-year-old autistic girl. Her parents are constructing a deck on the back of their house, and Jodie is having great difficulty dealing with this change, even though her parents are careful to keep everything in the house the same. Further, they are puzzled by the fact that Jodie does not seem to hear the extremely noisy electric saw but will turn her head if one of the workers drops a nail. Most distressing is the fact that when Jodie is agitated, she will bang her head on the wall repeatedly, a behavior that prompted her parents to keep a protective helmet in the closet. Jodie's parents have noticed other unusual, but less frightening behaviors in their child. For example, Jodie insists on picking up "dust bunnies" from underneath furniture and keeping them in her pocket at all times. She will take plates out of the kitchen cupboard, sit on the floor, and spin them around for hours on end. Jodie also seems fascinated by twirling her fingers near her face, an activity that seems to have a calming effect when she is upset.

---

5. As illustrated by this case, autistic children display very unusual responses to their environments. Describe each feature of autism listed in the table, then match the feature with the appropriate example in the sample case about Jodie.

Feature	Examples of Behavior Seen in the Case Study
Repetitive and rigid behavior	
Unusual motor movements	
Disturbed and paradoxical perceptual reactions	

2. Asperger's Disorder, 541

1. People with Asperger's disorder, or Asperger's syndrome, tend to experience many of the same impairments as people with autistic disorder. Identify four characteristics shared by most people with either Asperger's disorder or autism.

   a. _____

   b. _____

   c. _____

   d. _____

2. Unlike autistic individuals, people with Asperger's often have normal _____, _____, and _____ skills.

3. Some researchers have distinguished three subtypes of Asperger's sufferers, and called them rule boys, logic boys, and emotion boys. Briefly describe each subtype.

   a. rule boys _____

   _____

   b. logic boys _____

   _____

   c. emotion boys _____

   _____

3. What Are the Causes of Pervasive Developmental Disorders?, 541

Currently many clinicians and researchers believe that other pervasive developmental disorders are caused by many of the same factors as autism.

Although the idea that family and environment play a causal role in autism has lost most of its popularity (because of lack of empirical support, and because of the blame this view places on parents), these factors continue to influence the clinical field.

1. Complete these statements related to sociocultural views of autism.

   a. Leo Kanner argued that certain personality characteristics of "refrigerator parents," such as being very _____, yet obsessive and _____, contributed to autism.

   b. Some theorists believe that _____ and _____ stress contribute to autism; this view has not been supported by research.

*One psychological theory of autism holds that, compared to normal children, autistic children have not developed a **theory of mind** that would allow them to engage in make-believe play, develop relationships, and use language in ways that appreciate others' perspectives.*

2. Apply this theory to explain the following behavior of a child with autism: Eight-year-old Timothy asks for ice cream, then has a tantrum when his mother brings him some. He wanted strawberry ice cream, not the chocolate ice cream his mother gave him.

   _____

   _____

3. For the first two of the listed biological factors implicated in autistic disorder, a research finding that supports it is given. Provide another.

    a. *Genetic factors:*

       The prevalence of autism among siblings of autistic children is much higher than in the general population.

       _____

    b. *Prenatal difficulties or birth complications:*

       Having rubella while pregnant increases a mother's chances of giving birth to an autistic child.

       _____

    c. *Name some specific biological abnormalities found in many individuals with autism:*

       _____

4. How Do Clinicians and Educators Treat Pervasive Developmental Disorders?, 544

1. What are the goals of behavioral interventions for autistic children?

    _____

    _____

    _____

    _____

2. _____ techniques attempt to get autistic children to imitate appropriate behaviors of others, and _____ conditioning strategies reinforce adaptive behaviors in the autistic child.

3. A recent long-term controlled study examined the effectiveness of a behavioral intervention program with autistic children. Nineteen autistic children received intensive behavioral interventions from ages 3 to 7, whereas a control group of autistic children did not receive these interventions. How did these groups compare at the end of the study?

    _____

    _____

    _____

4. The *Learning Experiences . . . An Alternative Program (LEAP)* for preschoolers with autism integrates autistic children and normal children in a classroom setting to teach social and communication skills to the autistic children. Briefly describe how the autistic children have fared under this program, and how the normal children have fared.

    _____

    _____

    _____

5. Under a federal law, autism is one of 10 disorders for which school districts must provide a free education from birth to age _____.

6. In _____ _____ integration therapy programs, children with Asperger's disorder are taught to be more flexible with regard to rules, problem solving, and behavioral choices.

7. _____ training helps the 50 percent of children with autism who do not speak to develop other forms of language; these interventions include teaching sign language, _____ communication, and **augmentative communication systems.**

8. Some treatment programs for autistic children use _____ - _____ interactions to improve their communication skills. In these programs, _____ reinforcers, rather than trivial ones, are identified and used to inspire better communication.

9. Thinking back to the case study of Jodie, how might Jodie's parents be included in a treatment program?

   _____

   _____

10. Programs such as _____ homes and sheltered _____ help people with autism live and work in the community.

B. Mental Retardation (Intellectual Disability), 547

1. A DSM-IV-TR diagnosis of **mental retardation** is warranted if a person develops the following symptoms before the age of 18.

   a. A person manifests subaverage general _____ functioning (an IQ of _____ or below), and

   b. displays concurrent deficits or impairments in present adaptive behavior—that is to say, he or she cannot meet set standards in at least two of these skill areas:

      _____

      _____

1. Assessing Intelligence, 547

1. Complete this list of statements that relate to concerns about the validity of intelligence tests.

   a. Correlations between IQ scores and _____ performance is around .50, which is a less-than-perfect relationship.

   b. IQ tests seem to be socioculturally _____, as evidenced by the fact that middle- to upper-socioeconomic-level households have an advantage because they are regularly exposed to the same kinds of tasks that the tests measure.

   c. IQ tests do not measure "street sense," which requires intellectual ability.

2. Assessing Adaptive Functioning, 548

1. Various scales have been developed to measure adaptive behavior. Because these scales are not always accurate, clinicians must _____ and judge the functioning level of each individual, and take into account the person's _____ and community standards.

3. What Are the Features of Mental Retardation?, 550

1. The most important, consistent difference between retarded and nonretarded people is that retarded people _____ more slowly; the other differences relate to attention, _____ memory, _____ and language.

2. In the following table, give the DSM-IV-TR and the American Association of Mental Retardation (AAMR) terms for levels of mental retardation based on IQ range. The AAMR identifications are based on the level of support needed.

IQ	DSM-IV-TR	AAMR (Level of Support Required)
50–70	mild	intermittent
35–49		
20–34		
below 20		

3. As many as _____ percent of all people with mental retardation are **mildly retarded,** or "_____ retarded."

4. Mild mental retardation is usually first detected when the child enters _____ ; intellectual performance seems to _____ as the child ages and progresses through school.

5. Give two examples of (a) sociocultural/psychological factors and (b) biological factors that are linked to mild mental retardation. *(Note that sociocultural/psychological factors seem to play the primary causal role in mild mental retardation.)*

   a. _____

   b. _____

6. Complete this summary table by giving the percentages and characteristics of each listed group of individuals with mental retardation (MR).

Disorder	Prevalence	Characteristics
Moderate retardation (IQ 35–49)	10 percent of the population of persons with MR	
Severe retardation (IQ 20–34)		
Profound retardation (IQ under 20)		

4. What Are the Causes of Mental Retardation?, 551

1. The primary causes of moderate to profound retardation are _____.

2. Complete the statements about **Down syndrome,** the most common chromosomal disorder that leads to mental retardation.

   a. Fewer than one in every _____ children are born with Down syndrome.

   b. Among children born to women over the age of _____, the incidence rises considerably.

3. The physical characteristics of people with Down syndrome include a small head, _____ face, slanted eyes, high cheekbones, and, in some cases, a protruding _____.

4. One of the three types of chromosomal abnormalities that may cause Down syndrome is named *trisomy 21*. (a) Describe trisomy 21, then (b) list and describe another type of chromosomal abnormality linked to Down syndrome.

   a. _____

   b. _____

5. The IQ of most people with Down syndrome ranges from _____ to _____.

6. The _____ process seems to occur more rapidly in people with Down syndrome; many show signs of _____ as they approach age 40.

7. Metabolic disorders that result in retardation are typically caused by the pairing of two defective _____ genes, one from each parent.

8. Infants with *phenylketonuria (PKU)* can develop normal _____, as long as they are started on a low-phenylalanine diet before 3 months of age.

9. *Tay-Sachs disease* is a metabolic disorder found primarily in people of Eastern _____ _____ ancestry and is characterized by progressive _____ deterioration, loss of visual and _____ function, and finally death.

10. Complete this table by describing prenatal and birth-related causes of retardation.

Problem	Cause
Cretinism	
	mother abuses alcohol during pregnancy
Birth-related causes	a. b.

11. Serious head injuries, as a result of an accident or abuse, can result in mental retardation. List other accident- or injury-related causes of mental retardation in children.

   _____

   _____

5. Interventions for People with Mental Retardation, 553

1. Until recent decades, people with mental retardation were usually cared for in _____ schools, which tended to be overcrowded and neglectful.

2. Denmark and Sweden initiated _____ programs that provided people with mental retardation flexible routines, opportunities to make their own decisions, social and _____ opportunities, and economic freedom.

3. Define each type of educational program and strategy for children with mental retardation.

    Special education:

    _____

    _____

    Mainstreaming, or *Inclusion:*

    _____

    _____

    Operant conditioning:

    _____

    _____

4. Because about _____ percent of people with mental retardation also experience psychological disorders, individual, group, and drug therapies may be provided to them.

    *On pages 555 and 556 of the textbook, read about **dating skills programs** and **sheltered workshops** that provide individuals with mental retardation opportunities to enhance their personal, social, and occupational skills.*

VIII. Call for Change: DSM-5, 556–557

1. In its 2011 draft, the DSM-5 task force recommended eliminating the overall grouping "Disorders Usually First Diagnosed in Infancy, Childhood, or Adolescence," and redistributing the disorders discussed in this chapter among other groupings, several of them new. Identify which disorders from this chapter would be listed under the following proposed groupings if this recommendation is adopted in the DSM-5.

    a. Neurodevelopmental disorders: _____

    _____

    b. Disruptive, impulse control, and conduct disorders: _____

    _____

    c. Elimination disorders: _____

    _____

    d. Anxiety disorders: _____

    _____

2. Identify several new categories proposed by the DSM-5 task force that would include disorders discussed in this chapter. _____

    _____

3. Explain what will happen to the classification and diagnosis of the following disorders if the DSM-5 task force's proposed changes are adopted.

    a. Mental retardation (intellectual disability): _____

_____

    b. Asperger's disorder: _____

_____

IX. Putting It Together: Clinicians Discover Childhood and Adolescence, 557

1.   Mental health professionals acknowledge that the **family perspective** is particularly useful in terms of explaining and treating psychological problems among youth. Explain why this is the case.

_____

_____

_____

_____

_____

2.   However, there are some dangers in relying exclusively on the family perspective. List two of these risks or dangers.

_____

_____

_____

MULTIPLE CHOICE

1. Nadia frequently becomes nauseous when she is faced with being away from her mother. Consequently, Nadia often stays home from school and refuses to go to other children's houses to play. Nadia's mother describes her as needy and clingy. Nadia might be diagnosed with

    a. separation anxiety disorder.
    b. depression.
    c. oppositional defiant disorder.
    d. autism.

2. The development of juvenile delinquency appears to be closely tied to problems in
    a. socioeconomic class.
    b. attention deficit disorder.
    c. parent-child relationships.
    d. parental monitoring of child behaviors.

3. The drugs that are sometimes helpful for children with attention-deficit/hyperactivity disorder are
    a. stimulant drugs.
    b. antianxiety drugs.
    c. antipsychotic drugs.
    d. antidepressant drugs.

4. Tara often says "me" when she apparently means "you." She just cannot seem to get this part of speech correct. This error is called
    a. echolalia.
    b. neologism.
    c. nominal aphasia.
    d. pronominal reversal.

5. The diagnosis of profound mental retardation is given when the IQ score is
    a. 50–70.
    b. 35–49.
    c. 20–34.
    d. below 20.

6. Down syndrome is caused by
    a. the presence of a third, free-floating twenty-first chromosome.
    b. the presence of a third twenty-first chromosome attached to another chromosome.
    c. a mixture of cells with 2 or 3 twenty-first chromosomes.
    d. any of the above may cause Down syndrome.

7. Melissa's baby was born looking a bit dwarflike. Early testing revealed a thyroid gland deficiency. The diagnosis of the baby's condition is likely to be
    a. cretinism.
    b. Tay-Sachs disease.
    c. fragile X syndrome.
    d. phenylketonuria (PKU).

8. Which of the following focuses on helping people who are mentally retarded learn job skills?
    a. special education
    b. mainstreaming
    c. state schools
    d. sheltered workshops

9. Troy is a nine-year-old who is in therapy because he is terrified of going to school. His therapist has encouraged him to draw pictures and to write a funny story. This is an example of
    a. group therapy.
    b. play therapy.
    c. hypnotherapy.
    d. family therapy.

10. The *Treatments for Adolescents with Depression Study (TADS)* found which treatment method, typically believed to be effective in treating depression in adolescents, to be barely more helpful than placebo therapy?
    a. antidepressant prescription
    b. electroconvulsive therapy
    c. cognitive-behavioral therapy
    d. group therapy

18 DISORDERS OF AGING AND COGNITION

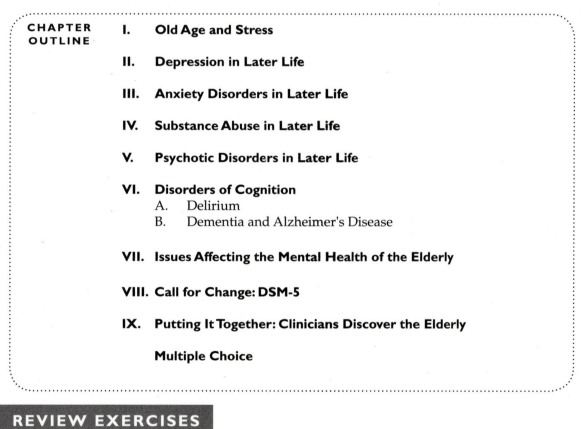

REVIEW EXERCISES

I.   Old Age and Stress, 562–563

1. "Old age" is arbitrarily defined as life after the age of _____ .

2. List three stressful changes that are more likely to occur as people age.

_____

_____

_____

3. Studies have shown that although as many as _____ percent of older individuals could benefit from psychological services, fewer than _____ percent actually receive these services.

4. A small percentage of clinicians specialize in _____, psychology dedicated to the mental health of the elderly.

II. Depression in Later Life, 564–565

1. Complete these statements regarding the prevalence of depression in older adults.

   a. Older people who have suffered the loss of a _____ (or some similar trauma) and who have serious _____ illnesses have the highest rate of depression.

   b. As many as _____ percent of older adults experience depression.

2. List three medical problems that appear to be exacerbated by depression in older adults.

   _____

   _____

3. Risk of suicide increases steadily as people age. The elderly in the United States have a suicide rate of _____ per 100,000 persons, compared with the overall national rate of 11.5 per 100,000 persons.

4. More than _____ percent of elderly patients are helped with combinations of cognitive-behavioral therapy, interpersonal therapy, and antidepressant medications. Why must special precautions be used with prescribing medications to the elderly? _____

   _____

III. Anxiety Disorders in Later Life, 566

1. _____ anxiety disorder is especially common in older individuals but might be underreported because physical symptoms of anxiety such as _____ _____ _____ and sweating could be attributed to a medical condition.

2. Elizabeth is 82 years old and has been diagnosed with generalized anxiety disorder. What may have caused her disorder? How might she be treated?

   a. possible causes: _____

   b. possible treatment: _____

IV. Substance Abuse in Later Life, 566–567

1. The prevalence of substance abuse problems seems to decline among those who are age _____ and over; however, rates are significantly higher among older patients who are _____.

2. Early-onset problem drinkers are aging abusers who typically have had alcohol-related problems since their 20s or 30s. At about what age do late-onset alcohol abusers typically start drinking? Why do they typically start drinking?

   _____

   _____

3. The often unintentional misuse of _____ drugs is a leading substance problem among the elderly.

4. Research suggests that _____ drugs are being given to nearly 30 percent of the nursing home population in the United States in order to sedate patients, despite the fact that many of the people receiving the drugs do not display symptoms that would indicate a need for them.

V. Psychotic Disorders in Later Life, 567–569

1. Symptoms of schizophrenia often _____ in later life, and new cases are extremely rare.

2. Delusional disorder is characterized by _____

   _____ .

VI. Disorders of Cognition, 569–581

A. Delirium, 569

1. Delirium is a clouding of _____ that is characterized by confusion, as well as attention and concentration difficulties.

2. List some of the causes of delirium.

   _____

   _____

B. Dementia and Alzheimer's Disease, 570

1. List the symptoms of dementia.

   _____

   _____

   _____

2. The prevalence of dementia increases with age, affecting only about 1 to 2 percent of those age 65, but as much as _____ percent of those over age 85.

3. Although some causes of dementia, such as _____ disorders, are reversible, most cases of dementia are caused by irreversible problems such as _____ disease.

4. Around _____ percent of all cases of dementia are a result of **Alzheimer's disease** (making this the most common form of dementia).

5. This exercise asks you to describe key features associated with the early and later stages of Alzheimer's disease. Features of the middle stages are provided for you.

	Features of Alzheimer's Disease
Early stages	
Middle stages	Difficulty completing complicated tasks, memory difficulties worsen, decreasing awareness of limitations, general physical health remains intact
Later stages	

6. Structural changes in the brain occur in all people as they grow older. Some of these changes seem to be excessive in people with Alzheimer's disease, however. Complete the statements below related to these structural changes. *People with Alzheimer's disease have . . .*

   a. an unusually high number of _____ _____, which are twisted strands of protein found _____ cells of the hippocampus and other brain areas.

b. excessive formation of _____ _____, which are deposits of beta-amyloid proteins that form in the spaces _____ cells in the hippocampus and which can lead to the breakdown and death of these cells.

7. In some individuals, Alzheimer's disease could be caused by genetic factors. Specifically, some people may have inherited a mutated (or abnormal) gene, which is responsible for the production of several _____.

8. Complete this diagram that depicts the two memory systems described in the text.

_____ *Memory*

Collects new information that is then transferred or consolidated into:

↓

_____ *Memory*

The repository of all information stored over the years.

9. The most important brain areas associated with short-term memory are the _____ _____, whereas the _____ lobes and the diencephalon are very important to long-term memory.

10. Biological researchers have discovered that certain chemicals (such as acetylcholine, _____, RNA, and _____) "tell" key brain cells to produce _____, which are crucial to the formation of memories.

11. What could happen if the activity of these chemicals is disrupted in some way?

_____

_____

_____

12. Complete the following statements describing four possible genetic causes of Alzheimer's disease.

a. Abnormal activity of _____ protein and _____ protein may cause plaques and tangles in the hippocampus.

b. Abnormal activity of the neurotransmitters _____ and _____ may be involved.

c. Environmental toxins such as _____ or _____ may be involved.

d. An _____ _____ might trigger the immune system to react against the body's own tissues.

13. The symptoms of **vascular dementia** (also known as _____ dementia) may be caused by a stroke that results in loss of _____ flow and subsequent damage to specific areas of the brain.

14. Below, write in the name of the particular disease that can result in dementia next to the descriptions provided.

_____ a progressive, neurological disorder characterized by motor symptoms (e.g., tremors, rigidity), as well as dementia in some cases

_____ a disorder very similar to Alzheimer's disease (but more rare) that impairs functioning of the frontal and temporal lobes

_____ a disorder marked by memory, mood, personality, and movement problems that is caused by genetic factors

_____ a disorder that leads to dementia and is caused by a slow-acting virus

15. Dementia may be caused by other physical disorders. List three of these below.

_____

_____

16. Brain researcher Lisa Mosconi's long-term PET scan studies found that those who develop mild dementia and Alzheimer's disease displayed lower _____ activity on initial PET scans, before developing symptoms, than those who did not later develop symptoms. Overall, the PET scans predicted mild dementia with an accuracy rate of _____ percent, and Alzheimer's disease with an accuracy rate of _____ percent.

17. Describe the action and effects of _tacrine_ (trade name, Cognex), _donepezil_ (Aricept), rivastigmine (Exelon), _galantamine_ (Reminyl), and _memantine_ (Nameda), which are used to _treat_ (not cure) Alzheimer's disease.

Action:

_____

_____

Effects:

_____

_____

18. Other medications that seem to reduce the risk of Alzheimer's disease include the hormone _____ and the nonsteroid anti-inflammatory drugs _____ and _____.

19. Behavioral therapists teach family members how and when to apply _____ in order to change problematic patient behaviors such as _____ at night or incontinence.

20. Research suggests that cognitive activity can help _____ or _____ mild cognitive impairment or Alzheimer's disease.

21. Clinicians are becoming increasingly aware of the need to provide services to caregivers of individuals with amnestic disorders and dementia, who frequently report feeling angry, depressed, and overwhelmed by their responsibilities. Complete the list below of services provided to caregivers.

   a. Programs that educate families about their loved one's disease

   b. _____

   c. _____

22. Explain how assisted living facilities might be designed to meet needs of patients with dementia.

_____

VII. Issues Affecting the Mental Health of the Elderly, 582–584

1. In recent years, clinicians have focused on several central concerns regarding the provision of mental health care to elderly individuals. Give specific examples of why each of the two issues listed below can be problematic or distressing.

a. *Elderly individuals representing ethnic minority groups may be discriminated against or face unique barriers in mental health settings.*

_____

_____

_____

_____

b. *Many older persons require long-term care.*

_____

_____

_____

_____

2.   Increasingly, clinicians are advising young adults to take a health maintenance, or _____ , approach to their aging process, because physical and psychological health promotes a more positive adaption to life changes and stressful events as people age.

VIII. Call for Change: DSM5, 584–585

1.   The DSM-5 task force has recommended a number of significant changes to the classification of the disorders of cognition discussed in this chapter. For example, it recommended that all such disorders be grouped under the term "Neurocognitive Disorders." Why?

_____

_____

2.   Why did the DSM-5 task force recommend replacing the term "dementia" with "major neurocognitive disorder," a change which, if adopted, would significantly affect many of the disorders discussed in this chapter?

_____

_____

3.   Why has the DSM-5 task force proposed the addition of the new distinct category "mild neurocognitive disorder"?

_____

_____

IX. Putting It Together: Clinicians Discover the Elderly, 586

1.   How has clinicians' approach to treating the elderly changed in recent years?_____

_____

_____

MULTIPLE CHOICE

1. One of the most common mental health problems of older adults is
   a. Pick's disease.
   b. depression.
   c. schizophrenia.
   d. substance abuse.

2. Who of the following is at the highest risk for abusing alcohol?
   a. Alex, male, age 25
   b. Brenda, female, age 25
   c. Charles, male, age 65
   d. Mildred, female, age 65

3. Mr. Mathews is 85 years old. He is in the emergency room because he is confused. He cannot seem to concentrate and is not apparently aware of his immediate surroundings. He cannot think straight. This happened over the last several hours. He is displaying
   a. delirium.
   b. dementia.
   c. depression.
   d. an anxiety attack.

4. Symptoms of the middle stage of Alzheimer's disease include
   a. denial of symptoms.
   b. anger about symptoms.
   c. indifference to symptoms.
   d. anxiety or depression about symptoms.

5. On autopsy a brain is seen to have an extraordinary number of neurofibrillary tangles and senile plaques. What did the person most likely have?
   a. presenile delirium
   b. Alzheimer's disease
   c. multiple-infarct dementia
   d. Creutzfeldt-Jakob

6. Adeline was diagnosed with Alzheimer's type-dementia and no longer recognizes members of her family. This illustrates a failure in
   a. short-term memory.
   b. working memory.
   c. declarative memory.
   d. procedural memory.

7. Chronic alcoholism can lead to Korsakoff's syndrome, which is characterized by the loss of
   a. memory for factual knowledge.
   b. memory for general knowledge.
   c. intelligence.
   d. procedural memories.

8. Ajay has experienced increasing memory problems, personality changes, and mood difficulties. Additionally, he experiences facial tics and spasms. Ajay might have
   a. Pick's disease.
   b. Creutzfeldt-Jakob disease.
   c. Huntington's disease.
   d. Parkinson's disease.

CHAPTER

19 LAW, SOCIETY, AND THE MENTAL HEALTH PROFESSION

REVIEW EXERCISES

I. Law and Mental Health, 590–609

1. When clinicians and researchers act within the legal system, the relationship is termed
_____ _____ _____; when legislative and judicial systems act upon the clinical field, the relationship is called _____ _____ _____.

2. What are some activities of forensic psychologists? _____

_____

A. Psychology in Law: How Do Clinicians Influence the Criminal Justice System?, 590

United States courts hand out punishment on the assumption that individuals are responsible for their crimes and are capable of defending themselves in court.

1. If either part of the assumption described in the statement above cannot be made, then our courts may not find these individuals _____ for their actions, nor will they _____ them in the usual manner.

2. There are two potential outcomes for people who are accused of a crime and who are deemed mentally unstable. Both involve **criminal commitment** in which the person is sent to a mental institution for treatment. Complete these statements regarding the two types of this kind of commitment.

   a. When individuals are deemed "mentally unstable at the time of their _____," the court finds them **not guilty by reason of** _____.

   b. These individuals are committed for treatment until they improve enough to be _____.

   c. When a person is deemed "mentally unstable at the time of their _____," it is because they are not capable of understanding court procedures or participating in their own defense.

   d. These individuals are committed for treatment until they are judged_____ to stand trial.

I. Criminal Commitment and Insanity During Commission of a Crime, 591

1. Defendants with clinically diagnosed mental disorders do not necessarily meet the court's criteria for "insanity" because "insanity" is a _____ term, not a clinical one, that is set by _____ rather than clinicians.

2. In the John Hinckley case, the _____ had to prove that the defendant was **sane** (which it failed to do). Currently, in federal and most state courts, it is the burden of the _____ to prove that the defendant is **insane.**

3. Our tradition of a jury being able to acquit a defendant based on "insanity" goes back to nineteenth-century England. Several important changes in the definition of "insanity" have occurred since then. Complete the following table, which summarizes the tests of the insanity defense that have contributed to the current legal definition of "insanity."

Test	M'Naghten Test
Change in criteria	in addition to mental disorder, defendant must have been unable to know right from wrong at the time of the crime
Criticisms or problems	

Test	Irresistible Impulse Test
Change in criteria	in addition to mental disorder, defendant must have been unable to know right from wrong at the time of the crime
Criticisms or problems	

Test	**Durham Test**
Change in criteria	
Criticisms or problems	definition was too broad; it could include virtually any problem listed in DSM-I and relied on contradictory opinions of clinicians

Test	**American Law Institute (ALI) Guidelines**
Change in criteria	
Criticisms or problems	in light of verdict in case of President Reagan's would-be assassin, guidelines were seen as too lenient

4. In 1983, the American Psychiatric Association recommended that legal definitions of insanity retain only the "right from wrong" criterion, essentially a return to the _____ test; this test is used in all federal courts and about 50 percent of state courts.

5. The other half of the state courts still use the broader ALI guidelines, except for Idaho, Kansas, Montana, and Utah. What have those four states done?

6. About two-thirds of defendants who are acquitted by reason of insanity qualify for a diagnosis of schizophrenia. Describe some other characteristics of the typical person acquitted by reason of insanity.

One interesting criticism of the insanity defense lies in the seeming incompatibility between the assumptions, goals, and philosophy of the legal system and those of the behavioral sciences. Read the material in the section titled "What Concerns Are Raised by the Insanity Defense?, then think very carefully about this concern. Do you agree with it?

7. Other critics suggest that contradictory clinical testimony during trials points to a lack of professional consensus about mental health. What is one of the recent efforts to correct this impression that might be cited to counter this argument?

8. The widespread fear that the insanity defense systematically allows dangerous criminals to escape would seem to be belied by the fact that less than one in _____ defendants in the United States is actually found not guilty by reason of insanity.

9. Complete these statements regarding criticisms of the insanity plea.

   a. Until recently, a defendant who successfully pled insanity received what amounted to a _____ prison sentence because _____ were reluctant to assert that the offender was unlikely to commit another crime.

   b. As a result of effective _____ treatment in institutions, the bias against extended institutionalization, and the emphasis on patients' _____, criminal defendants are being released sooner from mental hospitals of late.

   c. A 1992 Supreme Court ruling found the only basis for determining the release of offenders from mental hospitals is whether they are still _____, not whether they might be

_____.

*When defendants use the insanity plea, juries can find the defendant not guilty, acquit on the grounds of insanity, or find the defendant guilty. In 14 states, juries have another option—a verdict of **guilty but mentally ill.** By rendering this verdict, juries are essentially saying, "We believe that you had a mental illness at the time of the crime, but we do not feel that this illness was sufficiently related to or responsible for the crime."*

10.   Complete these statements relating to the "guilty but mentally ill" verdict.

   a.   The verdict allows juries to _____ a defendant, while trying to ensure that the person gets necessary mental health services.

   b.   Research findings indicate that this verdict option has not reduced the number of not-guilty-by-reason-of-insanity verdicts.

   c.   Critics say that prisoners already have a right to mental health services, and that in truth, the verdict is no different than a _____ verdict.

11.   Another defense is sometimes called *guilty with diminished capacity.* Note that unlike "guilty but mentally ill," it is not a verdict that juries may render, but a defense plea. Complete these statements regarding this defense.

   a.   A defense attorney using this plea argues that the defendant is guilty, but that his or her mental _____ is an extenuating circumstance that should be considered to determine what crime the defendant was guilty of committing.

   b.   Further, the defense attorney using this plea argues that the dysfunction prevented the defendant from _____ to commit a particular crime, and that the defendant should therefore be convicted only of a lesser crime.

12.   Complete these statements relating to "sex offender" statutes.

   a.   Sex offender statutes traditionally presume that people who _____ commit certain sex crimes are mentally ill, and are thus labeled *mentally disordered sex offenders.*

   b.   Give an important *difference* between the way the legal system views mentally disordered sex offenders and those found not guilty by reason of insanity.

   _____

   _____

   c.   Give an important *similarity* between the way the legal system deals with mentally disordered sex offenders and those found not guilty by reason of insanity.

   _____

   _____

2.   Criminal Commitment and Incompetence to Stand Trial, 597

1.   *Dusky v. United States* (1960) held that in order for a defendant to be found **mentally competent** to stand trial, he or she must demonstrate the following:

   a.   an understanding of the _____ he or she is facing, and

   b.   sufficient ability to _____ with his or her attorney in preparing and conducting an adequate _____.

2. To ensure due process, the judge may recommend a_____ _____ for any defendant whose competence is questioned.

3. If a court rules that a defendant is not competent to stand trial at the present time, what happens to the defendant?

_____

When a defendant is criminally committed, it is usually because he or she was deemed mentally incompetent, rather than found "not guilty by reason of insanity."

4. What is the greatest inherent risk of competence provisions?

_____

_____

The risk described above was addressed by the U.S. Supreme Court in Jackson v. Indiana *(1972), when it ruled that an incompetent defendant cannot be committed as a "criminal" for an indefinite length of time. Specifically, what did the court rule? (Complete the following statement.)*

5. After a reasonable length of time, the defendant should be found _____ and tried, set free, or transferred to a mental health facility under _____ commitment procedures.

B. **Law in Psychology: How Do the Legislative and Judicial Systems Influence Mental Health Care?, 598**

1. **Civil commitment** is a legal procedure whereby certain people can be _____ to undergo mental health treatment.

2. Psychologically disturbed people from racial minority groups are _____ likely than disturbed white Americans to be sent to prison, as opposed to mental health facilities.

3. In the United States, when white and nonwhite defendants are evaluated for their competence to stand trial, nonwhite defendants are _____ likely to be found incompetent to stand trial.

I. **Civil Commitment, 598**

1. Generally, individuals can be involuntarily committed if they are considered to be both in _____ of treatment and _____ to themselves or to others.

2. Complete the statements concerning the two principles upon which the state's authority to commit disturbed individuals rests.

   a. The principle of *parens patriae* allows the state to make decisions that promote the individual's best interest and protects him or her from _____.

   b. *Police power* enables the state to protect _____ from harm that may be inflicted by a person who is violent or otherwise dangerous.

3. Apply the Supreme Court's decisions related to civil commitment to the following situations. In each situation, describe the process the parents will have to follow in having their child committed.

   a. *A mother and father become increasingly concerned about the bizarre behavior of their daughter, who is a high school sophomore. Concerned that she might pose a danger to others, they seek to have her involuntarily committed.*

   _____

   _____

b. *The situation is the same as in item a, except that the daughter is a 24-year-old woman, living on her own.*

_____

_____

4. In *Addington v. Texas* (1979), the Supreme Court stated that in order for a person to be committed, a _____ standard of _____ must be met; specifically, the court ruled that there must be "_____" and "_____" proof that the person is mentally ill and has met the state's criteria for involuntary commitment.

5. In what instance might an emergency commitment (without due process) occur?

_____

_____

6. What is a "2 PCs" certification?

_____

_____

7. Although about _____ percent of people with mental disorders are not violent, research findings indicate a _____ relationship between severe mental disorders and violent behavior.

8. Research suggests that mental health professionals are not very good at accurately predicting dangerousness in their patients. Complete these statements regarding this research.

   a. These professionals tend to _____ the likelihood that a patient will eventually engage in violent behavior (a long-term prediction).

   b. However, the short-term predictions of _____ violence are more accurate than their long-term predictions.

9. One criticism of civil commitment is that the legal definitions of "mental illness" and "dangerousness" are so vague that they could be applied to people simply deemed undesirable in some way. What is another criticism?

_____

_____

_____

Since the Robinson v. California *decision in 1962, civil commitment rates have declined. In part, this has been the result of the application of more specific criteria to commitment decisions. Read through the section "Trends in Civil Commitment" on textbook page 602 and consider the following question: Do you think that the narrowing of civil commitment criteria ultimately benefits society or not?*

2. Protecting Patients' Rights, 603

1. In *Wyatt v. Stickney* (1972) a federal court decision ordered Alabama to provide "adequate treatment" to all persons who had been involuntarily committed. In the ruling, specific services that Alabama was compelled to provide were spelled out. They included more therapists and better living conditions. List three more.

_____

_____

_____

2. Complete the statements regarding two U.S. Supreme Court rulings on the right to treatment for those in mental health institutions.

   a. *O'Conner v. Donaldson* (1975) established that the institutions must engage in periodic reviews of patients' cases, and that the state cannot confine a non-_____ person who is capable of living successfully in the community.

   b. In *Youngberg v. Romeo* (1982), the court again broadened the rights of mental patients by ruling that the involuntarily committed have a right to "reasonably _____ confinement conditions" and "reasonable care and safety."

3. In order to ensure that mental health patients maintained their rights, Congress passed the _____ and _____ for Mentally Ill Individuals Act in 1986, which gave patients' rights advocates the power to _____ and legally pursue possible cases of patient abuse and neglect.

4. Briefly state why mental health advocates across the country are suing federal and state agencies to fulfill promises of the community mental health movement.

   _____

   _____

5. Most of the **right to refuse treatment** rulings have involved _____ treatments such as psychosurgery that are viewed as more intrusive, aversive, and _____ than psychotherapy.

6. Many states have recognized a patient's right to refuse _____, although the extent to which states allow such refusals varies greatly.

7. Patients in some states have the right to refuse psychotropic drugs, but their refusal may be denied if it is deemed incompetent, _____, or irrational.

8. In another court ruling regarding rights of patients, *Dixon v. Weinberger* (1975) found that individuals with psychological disorders have a right to treatment in the least _____ facility available; the right to community treatment was later confirmed in *Olmstead v. L.C. et al.* (1999).

9. Consider what you have read so far in this chapter, then respond to the following statement: Mental health professionals—not the courts—are the only ones who should make decisions regarding the care and treatment of their patients.

   _____

   _____

   _____

   _____

   _____

C. In What Other Ways Do the Clinical and Legal Fields Interact?, 605

All four subsections of this section—malpractice suits, professional boundaries, jury selection, and psychological research of legal topics—will be covered in this part of the workbook.

1. What does the tongue-in-cheek term "litigaphobia" mean?

   _____

   _____

2.   Lawsuits are filed against clinicians for many alleged acts of negligence or wrongdoing, including sexual activity with a client, improper termination of treatment, and negligence regarding a client who commits suicide. List three events that can precipitate claims against clinicians.

_____

_____

_____

3.   Briefly describe evidence reported by Brodsky and Poythress (1990), as well as a more recent study of psychiatrists in northern England, indicating that fear of litigation has affected clinicians' judgments about their patients:

_____

_____

_____

4.   In recent years, the legislative and judicial systems have given greater authority to psychologists— oftentimes authority that was once reserved for psychiatrists. Briefly describe an example of psychologists' increasing responsibilities in terms of patient care.

_____

_____

_____

5.   Clinicians known as "jury _____" advise lawyers on jury selection and strategies on winning over jurors during trials.

6.   Eyewitness testimony can be flawed due to a variety of factors. Describe the potential problems associated with each of the following.

a.   eyewitness memory: _____

_____

b.   suggestive questioning: _____

_____

c.   eyewitness confidence: _____

_____

7.   Describe a potential problem of the process used for criminal profiling.

_____

_____

_____

PsychWatch: Serial Murderers: Madness or Badness?, 608

Reread this box on page 608 of your textbook. Identify some traits that are shared by the majority of serial killers, and suggest some factors that may partly explain what drives them to kill.

_____

_____

II. What Ethical Principles Guide Mental Health Professionals?, 609–611

Mental health professionals regulate practices within their own profession by developing and enforcing ethical guidelines. The American Psychological Association (APA) has developed extensive guidelines that promote the ethical practice of psychologists and call for psychologists to guard against "factors that might lead to misuse of their influence."

1.   Imagine that you are a member of an ethics board that fields questions posed by psychologists. Write responses based on APA ethical guidelines to the following questions.

> I have been ordered to testify in a legal case involving a client that I evaluated 1 year ago. What are the ethical guidelines I should attend to?

a. _____

_____

> I completed treatment with a client 2 months ago, and now I would like to ask her out for a date. Is this okay?

b. _____

_____

> I was asked to appear on a talk show to help couples negotiate areas of conflict. Am I allowed to do that?

c. _____

_____

> I am interested in what the APA says about ethical guidelines for the publication of research. What can you tell me?

d. _____

_____

2.   **Confidentiality** in therapy means that clinicians are obligated to refrain from disclosing information about their clients to other people. However, there are certain circumstances under which confidentiality may be compromised. List two of them.

_____

_____

3.   In *Tarasoff v. Regents of the University of California* (1976), the California Supreme Court declared that "the protective [client-therapist] privilege ends where the _____ _____ begins."

4.   Psychologists' ethical guidelines mandate that therapists have a(n) _____ to _____ their clients and others from harm, even if it means disclosing _____ information that was obtained during a client's therapy sessions.

5.   California courts have extended *Tarasoff* to include the duty to protect people who are close to a(n) _____ victim.

III. Mental Health, Business, and Economics, 611–612

The two subsections of this section—"Bringing Mental Health Services to the Workplace" and "The Economics of Mental Health"—will be covered together in the workbook.

1. Psychological disorders are thought to be among the _____ leading work-related disorders and injuries in the United States.

2. Businesses often pay for programs such as employee _____ programs and stress-reduction and _____ seminars conducted in occupational settings that are designed to help prevent and remedy psychological disorders in the workplace.

3. Psychological problems, particularly _____ abuse and other _____ problems, significantly increase the rates of absenteeism, work-related accidents, and worker terminations.

4. Although government funding allocated to people with mental disorders has increased, the money seems to be spent on income support and housing subsidies for those individuals rather than directly on _____ _____ _____, such as mental health medications.

5. The growing economic role of private insurance companies has had a significant effect on the way clinicians go about their work. Complete the following statements regarding ways in which that interaction has occurred.

   a. Many insurance companies have developed _____ care systems in which the insurance company often determines which therapists clients may use, as well as the _____ and the _____ of sessions.

   b. **Peer review systems** have been instituted in which a panel of clinicians who work for the insurers may review a therapist's report of a client's treatment and recommend that _____ _____ either be continued or terminated.

   c. Many therapists and clients dislike managed care and peer reviews. List one of their criticisms.

      _____

      _____

IV. Technology and Mental Health, 612–615

A. New Triggers and Vehicles for Psychopathology, 613

1. Identify the impact that your textbook suggests emerging technological trends may have on the following abnormal behaviors and disorders:

   a. impulse control disorders: _____

      _____

   b. pedophilia and other paraphilias: _____

      _____

   c. antisocial behavior and conduct disorder: _____

      _____

      d. problems with attention: _____

_____

2.   What are some positive and some negative effects that social networking can have on people with psychological dysfunctioning?

      a. positive _____

_____

      b. negative _____

_____

B. New Forms of Psychopathology, 614

1.   At least _____ percent of all people display the pattern of Internet addiction, which has led to some calls for it to be a category in the DSM.

C. Cybertherapy

1.   Cybertherapy is a treatment option that is rapidly growing as Internet usage becomes more and more prevalent. Identify four forms this type of treatmeant can take.

      a. _____

      b. _____

      c. _____

      d. _____

2.   What are some significant limitations inherent in all forms of online treatment for psychological dysfunctioning?

_____

V. The Person Within the Profession, 615–617

The main purpose of this final section of the textbook is to get you to think about how society views mental health care professionals. Keep in mind that the work clinicians do is influenced by their own personal strengths and weaknesses. As you will read in the textbook, many of them have themselves sought treatment for the same problems they are treating in others. This is why it is important to consider the words of the textbook relating to the human context in which the study and practice of psychology exists: "Mental health researchers and clinicians are human beings, within a society of human beings, working to serve human beings."

VI. Putting It Together: Operating Within a Larger System, 617

1.   This chapter makes clear the fact that when individuals seek help for psychological problems, they are entering a system that is influenced by many forces, only one of which is the actual treatment provider. Based on what you have read, discuss aspects or components of this system that you believe (a) contribute to and (b) detract from the quality of services provided to consumers.

      a. _____

_____

_____

_____

_____

b. _____
_____
_____
_____
_____

MULTIPLE CHOICE

1. Mario has been accused of a killing. Just as the court date arrives, he starts displaying the symptoms of schizophrenia. In a couple of days he is essentially not functional anymore. What is likely to happen in court?
   a. He is likely to be tried for the crime.
   b. He is likely to be committed indefinitely.
   c. He is likely to get off because he is not competent.
   d. He is likely to be committed until he is competent to stand trial.

2. John Hinckley was found not guilty of shooting President Ronald Reagan in 1981. The basis for the finding was that:
   a. he had a mental disorder.
   b. no crime was committed.
   c. he was mentally unstable at the time of the crime.
   d. he was mentally unstable at the time of the trial and unable to defend himself.

3. According to the 1955 criteria of the American Law Institute, a person is judged not criminally responsible if he or she has functioned
   a. under a mental disease or mental defect.
   b. under a compulsion or an irresistible impulse to act.
   c. without the knowledge of the nature of the act he or she was doing or that what he or she was doing was wrong.
   d. without appreciation for the wrongfulness of his or her conduct, or lacking the ability to conform his or her conduct to the requirements of law, as a result of mental disease or defect.

4. What percentage of defendants *who use the insanity plea* are actually found not guilty?
   a. 1 percent
   b. 14 percent
   c. 26 percent
   d. 33 percent

5. In *Jackson v. Indiana,* the U.S. Supreme Court ruled that when a person is judged not competent to stand trial
   a. prison confinement is an option.
   b. indefinite commitment is not legal.
   c. a person must be released from custody.
   d. a person may be committed indefinitely under criminal status.

6. One of the justifications for civil commitment is that a person
   a. needs treatment.
   b. has been found guilty but mentally ill.
   c. has been found not competent to stand trial.
   d. has been found not guilty by reason of insanity.

7. What is the function of the two-physician certificate ("2 PC") commitment procedure?
   a. It is used for the commitment of a child.
   b. It is only used in cases of criminal commitment.
   c. It allows family members to order civil commitment.
   d. It allows quick commitment in an emergency situation.

8. In the case of *Robinson v. California,* the U.S. Supreme Court ruled that
   a. involuntarily committed people had a right to treatment or release.
   b. committing drug addicts to treatment facilities may violate the Constitution.
   c. sending drug addicts to prison for being addicts may violate the Constitution.
   d. when a person is ruled legally not competent, he or she gives up all constitutional rights.

9. What form of therapy are patients most likely to be granted the right to refuse?
   a. ECT
   b. medications

c. psychosurgery

d. psychotherapy

10. New Mexico and Louisiana are currently the only states to give psychologists the privilege to

   a. prescribe drugs.

   b. do psychoanalysis.

c. admit patients to hospitals.

d. perform ECT and other forms of biological treatments of mental disorders.

Answers to most short-answer questions are provided. For questions with longer answers, the textbook source for the question is noted. Where answers will vary, no answer is given.

CHAPTER 1   ABNORMAL PSYCHOLOGY: PAST AND PRESENT

REVIEW EXERCISES

I. and II. What Is Psychological Abnormality? What Is Treatment?

1b. distress
1c. deviance
1d. dysfunction
2. p. 5
3. abnormal; normal
4a. sufferer
4b. healer
4c. emotional; behavior
5. many possible answers

PsychWatch: Marching to a Different Drummer: Eccentrics

1. freely; pleasure
2. fewer

III. How Was Abnormality Viewed and Treated in the Past?

1. many possible answers

PsychWatch: Modern Pressures: Modern Problems

1. "terrorism terror"
2. "crime phobia"
3. "cyberfear"

A. Ancient Views and Treatments

1. external
2a. trephination; p. 9
2b. exorcism; p. 9

B. Greek and Roman Views and Treatments

1. p. 10
2a. brain
2b. humors

C. Europe in the Middle Ages: Demonology Returns

1. After the fall of Rome, the power of the clergy grew and with it a rejection of scientific beliefs.
2. mass madness
3a. tarantism; p. 10
3b. lycanthropy
4. p. 10

D. The Renaissance and the Rise of Asylums

1. Weyer
2. p. 11
3. pp. 11–12

E. The Nineteenth Century: Reform and Moral Treatment

1. La Bicetre (Paris); Philippe Pinel
2. p. 12
3. Tuke
4. moral
5. p. 12
6. pp. 12–13
7a. staff
7b. humanity/dignity
7c. prejudice

F. The Early Twentieth Century: The Somatogenic and Psychogenic Perspective

1a. and 1b. pp. 13–14
2. psychological
3. hysterical
4. physical symptoms, such as paralysis that do not have a physical cause
5. hypnosis; psychological
6. Josef Breuer
7. psychoanalysis; unconscious
8. insight; outpatient

IV. Current Trends

A. How Are People with Severe Disturbances Cared For?
1.   deinstitutionalization
2.   Outpatient
3.   p. 16

B. How Are People with Less Severe Disturbances Treated?
1.   p. 17
2.   6
3.   anxiety; marital; school

C. A Growing Emphasis on Preventing Disorders and Promoting Health
1.   prevention
2.   pp. 18–19

D. Multicultural Psychology
1.   p. 19

E. The Growing Influence of Insurance Coverage
1.   managed care
2.   p. 20

F. What Are Today's Leading Theories and Professions?
1a. psychoanalytic; unconscious
1b. biological; psychotropic
2a. psychiatrists; 3 to 4
2b. internship
2c. psychiatric social workers

V. Putting It Together: A Work in Progress
1.   pp. 21–22

MULTIPLE CHOICE
1.   b
2.   c
3.   d
4.   b
5.   d
6.   b
7.   b
8.   b
9.   c
10. d

CHAPTER 2   RESEARCH IN ABNORMAL PSYCHOLOGY

REVIEW EXERCISES

I. What Do Clinical Researchers Do?
1.   nomothetic understanding
2.   p. 26
3.   a change in one variable causes a change in another
4.   p. 27

II. The Case Study
1.   pp. 27–29

A. How Are Case Studies Helpful?
1a. behavior; theory
1b. assumptions
1c. techniques
1d. p. 29

B. What Are the Limitations of Case Studies?
1.–6.   p. 30

III. The Correlational Method
1.   p. 30
2.   Is procrastination related to, or associated with, test anxiety?
Do procrastinators also experience significant test anxiety?
3.   pp. 30–31

A. Describing a Correlation
1.   see pp. 31–33
2.   strength
3.   correlation coefficient
4. $-.82$; $.61$; $-.58$; $.50$; $-.01$

MediaSpeak: On Facebook, Scholars Link Up with Data
1.   There is controversy regarding whether Facebook users have given permission to be part of psychological research.

B. When Can Correlations Be Trusted?
1.   chance
2.   p. 34

C. What Are the Merits of the Correlational Method?
1. external; generalized
2. internal; relationship
3a. Being satisfied in the marriage leads couples to communicate better.
3b. People who communicate better have more satisfying marital relationships.

D. Special Forms of Correlational Research
1. *Incidence:* the number of *new* cases of a disorder that emerge during a given period of time (e.g., new diagnoses from 1995–2000) *Prevalence:* the *total* number of cases of a disorder in a population during a given period of time (e.g., all cases from 1995–2000)
2. p. 35
3. order; causes; causation

IV. The Experimental Method
1a. independent
1b. dependent
2. temperature of milk (warm or cold); type of shampoo; amount of hair loss; posttreatment depression level
3. p. 36
4. p. 36

A.–C. The Control Group, Random Assignment, and Blind Design
1. exposure to the independent variable
2. p. 38
3. help; subject bias
4. p. 38
5a.–5c. pp. 38–39
6a.–6c. many possible answers
7. many possible answers (check the redesign of the study with your instructor)
8. pp. 37–38

V. Alternative Experimental Designs

A. Quasi-Experimental Designs
1. randomly; experimental; control
2. p. 39
3. p. 39

B. Natural Experiment
1. independent; observes
2a.–2c. p. 40
3. repeated; generalizations

C. Analogue Experiment
1. independent; ethical
2. p. 40
3. control
4a. and 4b. p. 40
5. pp. 40–41

D. Single-Subject Experiment
1. p. 41
2. manipulations
3. p. 41
4. controls
5. p. 41
6. **B**-Expectation: head-banging should decrease in frequency.
   A-Step Taken: Nathan is no longer rewarded with fruit juice.
   B-Step Taken: fruit juice is reintroduced as a reward to Nathan for not banging his head.
   B-Expectation: head-banging should decrease in frequency.
7. the reinforcement program (the independent variable) was the cause of the improvement in Nathan's behavior.
8. Single-subject experiments expose the participant to an independent variable.

PsychWatch: Humans Have Rights, Too
1a. new drug studies
1b. placebo studies
1c. symptom-exacerbation studies
1d. medication-withdrawal studies
2. symptom-exacerbation

VI. Putting It Together: The Use of Multiple Research Methods
1a.–1e. pp. 43–44

MULTIPLE CHOICE

1. b	6. d
2. c	7. b
3. d	8. d
4. b	9. c
5. a	10. d
	11. b

CHAPTER 3   MODELS OF ABNORMALITY

REVIEW EXERCISES

I. The Biological Model

A. Biological Explanations
   1. brain
   2. Neurons; glia
   3a. nerve endings
   3b. neurotransmitters
   3c. dendrites
   3d. receptors
   3e. axon
   3f. synapse
   4. depression
   5. endocrine; hormones
   6. cortisol
   7. Genes
   8. p. 50
   9. thrive; adapt
   10. p. 51
   11. viruses
   12. viral; anxiety; psychotic

B. Biological Treatments
   1. all answers on p. 51
   2a. depression
   2b. 65 to 140; seizure
   2c. 7 to 9
   3. frontal lobes
   4. not responded

C. Assessing the Biological Model
   1a. interplay
   1b. p. 53

II. The Psychodynamic Model
   1a. conflicts
   1b. relationships; traumatic
   1c. deterministic

A. How Did Freud Explain Normal and
    Abnormal Functioning?
   1. The Id
   1. pleasure; gratification
   2. sexual; Libido

   2. The Ego
   1. p. 54
   2. c; e; a; b; f; all definitions are in Table 3-1,
       p. 54

   3. The Superego
   1. parents'
   2. conscience

   4. Developmental Stages
   1. fixated
   2. 0–18 months; anal, 18 months–3 years;
       phallic, 3–5 years; latency, 5–12 years; geni-
       tal, 12 years–adult
   3. p. 55

B. How Do Other Psychodynamic Explanations Differ
    from Freud's?
   1. p. 55
   2. p. 55
   3. p. 55

C. Psychodynamic Therapies
   1. p. 55
   2. pp. 55–56
   3a. free association
   3b. therapist
   4. repression
   5. manifest; latent
   6. a reliving of past repressed feelings
   7. "Working through"

8. dynamic focus

9. relational psychoanalytic

D. Assessing the Psychodynamic Model

    1. biological; systematically

    2. unconscious

III. The Behavioral Model

    1. pp. 58–59

    2. laboratories; conditioning

    3. p. 59

A. How Do Behaviorists Explain Abnormal Functioning?

1a. and 1b. p. 59

    2. pp. 59–60

    3. US: car honking and tires screeching

       CS: Foo Fighters song

    4. pp. 59–60

B. Behavioral Therapies

    1. relaxation skills; fear hierarchy; relaxation; relax in the presence of all items on the fear hierarchy

C. Assessing the Behavioral Model

1b. and 1c. p. 61

    2. self-efficacy

    3. cognitive–behavioral

IV. The Cognitive Model

A. How Do Cognitive Theorists Explain Abnormal Functioning?

    1. pp. 62–63

    2. pp. 62–63

B. Cognitive Therapies

1a. negative; interpretations

1b. challenge

C. Assessing the Cognitive Model

    1. p. 64

    2. acceptance; commitment

    3. mindfulness-based; acceptance

V. The Humanistic–Existential Model

    1. self-awareness, values, meaning, and choice

    2. self-actualize

    3. existential; p. 65

    4. client-centered

    5. actions

A. Rogers's Humanistic Theory and Therapy

1a. dysfunction

1b. regard

1c. positive regard; self-regard

2a., 2b., and 2c. p. 66

    3. approaches; psychiatrists

B. Gestalt Theory and Therapy

    1. Perls

    2. acceptance; frustrating

    3. p. 67

C. Spiritual Views and Interventions

    1. p. 67

    2. lonely; depressed; anxious

D. Existential Theories and Therapy

    1. freedom of choice; responsibility; frustration; alienation; depression; boredom

    2. p. 68

PsychWatch: Cybertherapy: Surfing for Help

    1. opportunity to link geographically disparate people with similar issues; free exchange of advice and support

    2. unknown people at other end; untested advice; potential for insult

    3. p. 69

    4. p. 69

E. Assessing the Humanistic-Existential Model

1a. and 1b. p. 70

    2. p. 70

VI. The Sociocultural Model: The Family-Social and Multicultural Perspectives

1a. norms

1b. roles

1c. cultural; family

1d. view

A. How Do Sociocultural Theorists Explain Abnormal Functioning?

    I. Social Labels and Roles

    1. p. 71

2.   p. 71; schizophrenia; 7 to 52; staff; powerless, invisible, and bored

2. Social Connections and Supports
1.   p. 71
2.   p. 71

3. Family Structure and Communication
1.   p. 72
2.   enmeshed; disengagement
3.   p. 72

B. Family-Social Treatments

1. Group Therapy
1.   pp. 72–73
2.   individual
3.   clinician
4.   500,000; 3 million; 3; 4

2. Family Therapy
1.   p. 74
2.   power; relationships
3.   conjoint

3. Couple Therapy
1a. and 1b.   p. 75
2.   half

4. Community Treatment
1.   p. 75
2a.   Primary
2b.   identify; treat
2c.   long-term
3.   pp. 75–76

C. How Do Multicultural Theorists Explain Abnormal Functioning?
1.   values; beliefs; histories
2.   pp. 76–77
3   multicultural
4   p. 76
5   p. 77

D. Multicultural Treatments
1b.   less often
1c.   p. 77

2.   culture-sensitive; gender-sensitive
3a.   special cultural instruction of therapists in graduate training programs
3b.   awareness by therapist of client's cultural values
3c.   awareness by therapist of stress, prejudice, and stereotypes client is exposed to due to minority status
3d.   awareness by therapist of hardships faced by children of immigrants
3e.   therapists help clients recognize the impact of both their own culture and the dominant culture
3f.   therapists help clients identify and express suppressed anger and pain
3g.   therapists help clients achieve a bicultural balance
3h.   therapists help clients raise their self-esteem

E. Assessing the Sociocultural Model
1a. and 1b.   p. 78

VII. Putting It Together: Integration of the Models
1.   biopsychosocial
2.   psychological; predisposition; stress

MULTIPLE CHOICE
1.   c
2.   c
3.   a
4.   b
5.   a
6.   a
7.   c
8.   a
9.   b
10.   d
11.   b
12.   c
13.   b

CHAPTER 4   CLINICAL ASSESSMENT, DIAGNOSIS, AND TREATMENT

REVIEW EXERCISES

I.   Clinical Assessment
1b.   to determine how a person might be helped
1c.   to evaluate treatment progress
2.   theoretical

A.   Characteristics of Assessment Tools
1.   p. 84
2a.   consistency
2b.   p. 84
2c.   agree; scored and interpreted
3.   accuracy
4a.   Face; trustworthy
4b.   predictive validity
4c.   measures (or scores) gathered from other assessment techniques

B.   Clinical Interviews
1.   pp. 85–86
2.   cognitive; biological; behavioral; psychodynamic; humanistic; sociocultural
3a. and 3b.   p. 86; many possible answers
4.   structured; schedules
5.   p. 86
6b.   accurate
6c.   interviewer biases—relying too much on first impressions; giving too much weight to unfavorable information; gender and race biases
6d.   p. 87

C.   Clinical Tests
  I.   Projective Tests
  1.   personality; task
  2.   p. 88; many possible answers
  3.   psychological
  4a. and 4b.   p. 88
  5.   What led up to it?; thinking and feeling; What is the outcome?
  6.   sentence; Person
  7a. and 7c.   p. 90

Table 4-1: Multicultural Hot Spots in Assessment and Diagnosis
    p. 91; many possible answers

  2.   Personality Inventories
  1.   Multiphasic Personality Inventory
  2.   c; g; i; f; e; b; a; h; j; d
  3.   120; 70
  4.   p. 92
  5b.   objective scoring
  5c.   standardization
  5d.   greater test–retest reliability
  6.   cultural

  3.   Response Inventories
  1.   p. 92

  4.   Psychophysiological Tests
  1.   physical; psychological
  2.   p. 93
  3a. and 3b.   p. 93

  5.   Neurological and Neuropsychological Tests
  1.   head injury, brain tumors, brain malfunctions, alcoholism, infections
  2a., 2b., 2c., and 2d.   p. 94
  3.   perception; memory; coordination
  4.   p. 96
  5.   battery

PsychWatch: The Truth, the Whole Truth, and Nothing but the Truth
  1.   8

  6.   Intelligence Tests
  1.   p. 96
  2.   intelligence quotient; IQ
  3.   p. 96

D.   Clinical Observations
1a. and 1b.   pp. 96–97
2a., 2b., and 2c.   pp. 97–98
3.   behavior is often specific to a particular situation, so observations in one situation cannot always be applied to other situations.
4.   p. 98

MediaSpeak: Tests, eBay, and the Public Good
  1.   p. 97

II. Diagnosis: Does the Client's Syndrome Match a Known Disorder?

A. Classification Systems
  1. clinical picture; disorder
  2a. International Classification of Diseases, the classification system used by the World Health Organization
  2b. Diagnostic and Statistical Manual of Mental Disorders, the classification system developed by the American Psychiatric Association

B. DSM-IV-TR
  1. 400
  2. pp. 99–100
  3. a, j, f;
     g, k; longstanding, frequently overlooked problems;
     e, l; general medical conditions (current);
     i, b; psychosocial and environmental problems;
     Global Assessment of Functioning (GAF) Scale, a general overall rating of the person's functioning

PsychWatch Culture-Bound Abnormality
  1. p. 101

C. Is DSM-IV-TR an Effective Classification System?
  1. p. 102
  2. p. 102
  3. predictive
  4a. qualitatively
  4b. discrete

D. Call for Change: DSM-5
  1a.–1h. p. 104

E. Can Diagnosis and Labeling Cause Harm?
  1. p. 105
  2. p. 105–106

III. Treatment: How Might the Client Be Helped?

A. Treatment Decisions
  1a. nature; causes
  1b. broad
  1c. orientation
  1d. research

B. The Effectiveness of Treatment
  1. p. 107
  2. 75
  3. uniformity myth
  4. p. 109
  5. drug therapy; behavioral therapies

PsychWatch: Dark Sites
  1. 500
  2. p. 108

IV. Putting It Together: Assessment and Diagnosis at a Crossroads
  1. p. 110

MULTIPLE CHOICE
  1. d
  2. a
  3. c
  4. c
  5. a
  6. c
  7. b
  8. a
  9. b
  10. a

CHAPTER 5   ANXIETY DISORDER

REVIEW EXERCISES

I. Generalized Anxiety Disorder
  1. free-floating
  2. 6 months
  3a., 3b., 3c., and 3d. pp. 114–115
  4. childhood; adolescence; two

A. The Sociocultural Perspective: Societal and Multicultural Factors
  1. dangerous
  2. p. 116
  3. *nervios*

Table 5-2: Eye on Culture: Anxiety Disorders
1. higher
2. obsessive-compulsive disorder
3. specific phobias

B. **The Psychodynamic Perspective**
1a., 1b., and 1c.   p. 116
2. pp. 116–117
3a. normal subjects often forget/repress aspects of threatening events; people with GAD react defensively when asked to discuss upsetting experiences
3b. more anxiety among people who were excessively punished/threatened as children; extreme parental overprotectiveness leads to anxiety in children
4. p. 117
5a. and 5b.   p. 117

C. **The Humanistic Perspective**
1. they do not receive unconditional positive regard from others, develop conditions of worth, and experience great anxiety; pp. 117–118
2. client-centered
3. p. 118

D. **The Cognitive Perspective**
1. maladaptive assumptions
2a. 4
2b. 2
2c. 1
2d. 5
2e. 3
3. metacognitive theory; intolerance of uncertainty theory; avoidance theory, pp. 120–121
4b. and 4c.   more appropriate assumptions are suggested; clients are helped with changing maladaptive assumptions
5. mindfulness-based

E. **The Biological Perspective**
1a. and 1b.   pp. 122–123
3a. too few GABA receptors
3b. GABA receptors do not capture GABA efficiently
4a. GABA

4b. causal; GABA reception
5 prefrontal cortex; anterior cingulate cortex; amygdala
6. barbiturate; drowsiness, physical dependence
7. GABA; stops; GABA's ability to bind to the receptor sites is enhanced, thereby reducing arousal
8b. physically dependent
8c. enhance
9a. antidepressant
9b. antipsychotic
10. physical; psychological
11. electromyograph; muscles
12. reducing
13. physical

II. **Phobias**
1. unreasonable; object; activity; situation
2a. persistent
2b. avoid

A. **Specific Phobias**
1. pp. 126–127, 132

1. **What Causes Specific Phobias?**

a. *Behavioral Explanations: How Are Fears Learned?*
1. classical
2. car accident; cars; car travel; fear, panic
3. p. 128
4. stimulus generalization
5. p. 128

b. *How Have Behavioral Explanations Fared in Research?*
1. p. 128
2a. and 2b.   p. 129
3. even though specific phobias can be acquired through classical conditioning and modeling, they might not be ordinarily acquired this way

c. *A Behavioral-Evolutionary Explanation*
1. preparedness
2. evolutionary predisposition: certain tendencies to fear have evolved over generations (transmitted genetically)

2.   **How Are Specific Phobias Treated?**
1.   behavior
2.   exposure; exposed
3a., 3b., 3c.   pp. 130–131
4.   exposed; harmless
5.   relaxation; gradual
6.   therapist; client
7.   in vivo; covert
8.   virtual reality

B.   Social Phobia (Social Anxiety Disorder)
1.   higher
2.   50; more
3.   narrow; broad

1.   What Causes Social Phobias?
1.   cognitive
2a.   unreasonably high social standards; belief they must perform perfectly in social situations
2b.   view themselves as unattractive social beings
2c.   view themselves as socially unskilled
2d.   see themselves as in constant danger of behaving poorly in social situations
2e.   expect inevitable terrible consequences for their socially inept behavior
2f.   believe they have no control over feelings of anxiety during social situations
3.   avoidance; safety; p. 133
4.   they overestimate how poorly social event went; they overestimate anticipated negative results; keep event alive and increase fears about future events
5.   no research to indicate why some have these thoughts and feelings while others do not

1.   Treatments for Social Phobias
1.   lack of social skills

a.   How Can Social Fears Be Reduced?
1.   antidepressant
2.   exposure
3.   p. 134
4.   rational-emotive

b.   How Can Social Skills Be Improved?
1.   model; role-play; feedback and reinforcement

III.   **Panic Disorder**
1.   10
2.   p. 135
3.   reason; unpredictably
4a.   having another attack
4b.   meaning of the attack
4c.   behavior around a possible future attack
5.   p. 136

A.   The Biological Perspective
1.   benzodiazepine
2.   locus ceruleus
3.   amygdala; ventromedial nucleus of the hypothalamus; central gray matter; locus ceruleus
4.   p. 138
6.   80
7.   agoraphobia

PsychWatch: Panic: Everyone Is Vulnerable
1.   Many possible answers

B.   The Cognitive Perspective
1.   p. 139
2.   p. 139
3.   p. 139
4.   misinterpret
5a. and 5b.   p. 140
6.   80
7.   it is at least equally effective

IV.   **Obsessive-Compulsive Disorder**
1a.   unreasonable
1b.   distress
1c.   time-consuming

A.   What Are the Features of Obsessions and Compulsions?
1.   foreign
2.   anxiety increases and the obsessions come back more strongly than ever
3.   d
4.   e
5.   a
6.   c
7.   b
8.   pp. 141–142

9. both
10. The fear that they will act out their obsessions; it is usually not warranted.

MediaSpeak: Dining Out: The Obsessive-Compulsive Experience

1. Many possible answers

B. **The Psychodynamic Perspective**
1. p. 143
2. control

C. **The Behavioral Perspective**
1. p. 144
2. obsessive; compulsive
3b.–3d.   pp. 144–145
4. 55; 85
5. p. 145

D. **The Cognitive Perspective**
1. p. 145
2. they blame themselves for having them, and expect terrible things to happen
3. because neutralizing relieves anxiety, it is reinforcing and is likely to be used again and again
4a. depressed
4b. conduct; morality
4c. harm; responsibility
4d. control
5. p. 146

6. p. 146

E. **The Biological Perspective**
1a. antidepressant; serotonin; low serotonin
1b. sensory; actions
1c. sexual, violent
1d. actively
2. Anafranil, Prozac, or Luvox; serotonin

V. **Call for Change: DSM-5**
1a.–1d.   p. 148

VI. **Putting It Together: Diathesis-Stress in Action**
1. p. 149

MULTIPLE CHOICE

1. a
2. b
3. a
4. a
5. a
6. d
7. c
8. b
9. d
10. d
11. a
12 d
13. a

CHAPTER 6   STRESS DISORDERS

REVIEW EXERCISES

I. **Chapter Introduction and Stress and Arousal: The Fight-or-Flight Response**
1a. stressor; an event or situation that creates a demand to change
1b. stress response; an individual's particular reaction to those demands
2a. hypothalamus
2b. autonomic nervous system; central nervous system
2c. sympathetic; parasympathetic
2d. pituitary; adrenal; corticosteroids
3a. and 3b.   p. 156

II. **The Psychological Stress Disorders: Acute and Posttraumatic Stress Disorders**
1. 4; months or years; 29; 30
2b. p. 157
2c. p. 157
2d. p. 157

A. **What Triggers a Psychological Stress Disorder?**
1. Combat and Stress Disorders
1b. shell shock
1c. combat fatigue
2. 29; 10
3. 20

2. Disasters and Stress Disorders
1. pp. 159–160
2. pp. 159–160

3. Victimization and Stress Disorders
1. p. 160
2a. 29; 32; 29
2b. acquaintances; relatives
2c. acute stress disorder
3. p. 160
4a. and 4b. many possible answers
5a. – 5d. p. 162

B. Why Do People Develop a Psychological Stress Disorder?
1a., 1b., 1c., 1d., 1e, and 1f. pp. 162–165
2. Hispanic Americans may tend to view traumatic events as inevitable and unalterable. Hispanic-American cultural emphasis on social relationships and support may place them at a disadvantage when they are deprived of important support systems.

C. How Do Clinicians Treat the Psychological Stress Disorders?
1a., 1b., and 1c. p. 165

1. Treatment for Combat Veterans
1a.–1c. pp. 165–166
2. p. 166
3. insight; impact
4. Rap
5. pp. 166–167

2. Psychological Debriefing
1. psychological; critical incident
2. sessions are intended to prevent or reduce stress reactions
3. p. 168

3. Does Psychological Debriefing Work?
1. p. 169

III. The Physical Stress Disorders: Psychophysiological Disorders
A. Traditional Psychophysiological Disorders
1. pp. 170–172

I. Biological Factors
1b. the development of ulcers or asthma, respectively
1c. increased blood pressure, leading to hypertension and heart disease

2. Psychological Factors
1. attitudes
2. repressive
3. A; coronary heart
4a. and 4b. p. 174
5a. and 5b. p. 174
6. hostility/anger/time urgency

3. Sociocultural Factors: The Multicultural Perspective
1b. and 1c. pp. 174–176
2. racial; nonracial

B. New Psychophysiological Disorders
I. Are Physical Illnesses Related to Stress?
1. Holmes; Rahe; Social Adjustment
2. life change units
3. pp. 178–179

2. Psychoneuroimmunology
1. Antigens
2. blood cells
3a. multiply
3b. seek out and destroy body cells infected by viruses
3c. antibodies; destruction
4. susceptibility
5. spouse; Alzheimer's
6a. norepinephrine
6b. increase; inhibitory
7. corticosteroids
8. cytokines; inflammation
9. p. 181
10. p. 181
11. helpless; anger
12. lonely

C. Psychological Treatments for Physical Disorders
1. Behavioral; prevent
2. pp. 182–184

IV. **Call for Change: DSM-5**

1a. acute distress disorder

1b. posttraumatic stress disorder

1c. adjustment disorder

1d. posttraumatic stress disorder in preschool children

2. The grouping would clarify that anxiety is simply one of several symptoms of these disorders. The grouping better emphasizes traumatic event as key feature in these disorders.

3a. conversion disorder

3b. hypochondriasis

V. **Putting It Together: Expanding the Boundaries of Abnormal Psychology**

1. pp. 185–186; many possible answers

MULTIPLE CHOICE

1. b

2. c

3. d

4. b

5. b

6. b

7. c

8. c

9. b

10. c

11. a

CHAPTER 7   SOMATOFORM AND DISSOCIATIVE DISORDERS

REVIEW EXERCISES

I. **Somatoform Disorders**

A. **What Are Hysterical Somatoform Disorders?**

1. pp. 190–193

2a. and 2b. pp. 193–194

3. malingering

4. intentionally

5a. and 5b. p. 194

6. Munchausen

B. **What Are Preoccupation Somatoform Disorders?**

1. overreact; symptoms

2. hypochondriasis

3. dysmorphophobia; defects

4. pp. 195–196

5. p. 196

6. 30

C. **What Causes Somatoform Disorders?**

1. anxiety

2. uterus; ungratified

1. **The Psychodynamic View**

1a. conversion; emotional

1b. phallic

1c. anxiety

1d. p. 198

2a. and 2b. p. 198

2. **The Behavioral View**

1. rewards

2. many possible answers

3. p. 199

3. **The Cognitive View**

1. communicate; fear

2. p. 199

4. **The Multicultural View**

1. inappropriate; common

2. highest; more

3. p. 200

5. **A Possible Role for Biology**

1. placebos

2. pp. 200–201

D. **How Are Somatoform Disorders Treated?**

1. anxiety; obsessive–compulsive; exposure; response

2. reinforcement; confrontation; p. 202

3. more—conversion and pain disorders; less—somatization disorders

4. p. 201

II. Dissociative Disorders

1. past; future

2. dissociative identity disorder; depersonalization disorder; pp. 202–203

A. Dissociative Amnesia

1. traumatic; physical

2a.–2d. p. 204

3. encyclopedic; personal or autobiographical

4. wartime; disasters

5. p. 205

B. Dissociative Fugue

1. identities; location

2. p. 205

3a. and 3b. pp. 206–207

4a. suddenly

4b. recurrence

4c. changes

C. Dissociative Identity Disorder (Multiple Personality Disorder)

1. two; host

2. sudden; stressful

3a. adolescence; adulthood

3b. 5; abuse

3c. three

4. p. 208

5. 15; 8

6. *The Three Faces of Eve*

7. p. 209

8a. suggest

8b. hypnosis

8c. reinforce

9. p. 210

D. How Do Theorists Explain Dissociative Disorders?

I. The Psychodynamic View

1. repression

2. single

3. continuous; traumatic

4. pretending; safely

5. case histories

2. The Behavioral View

1a. operant conditioning

1b. anxiety

1c. reinforces

2. p. 211

3. p. 211

3. State-Dependent Learning

1. pp. 211–212

2. arousal

3. narrow; exclusively

4. Self-Hypnosis

1. suggestibility

2a. p. 212

2b. p. 212

3. subjects; suggestible

4. pp. 212–213

E. How Are Dissociative Disorders Treated?

I. How Do Therapists Help People with Dissociative Amnesia and Fugue?

1. search

2. hypotherapy

3. barbiturate

2. How Do Therapists Help Individuals with Dissociative Identity Disorder?

1. pp. 214–215

F. Depersonalization Disorder

1. experience; mental functioning; unreal

2a. and 2b. p. 216

3. many possible answers

4. symptoms of depersonalization disorder are recurrent and persistent

5. panic disorder

III. Call for Change: DSM-5

1. p. 217

2. It would be listed under the new grouping "Obsessive-Compulsive and Related Disorders."

3. It would be eliminated and merged into the category of dissociative amnesia.

IV. Putting It Together: Disorders Rediscovered

1. p. 220

MULTIPLE CHOICE

1. c	8. c
2. c	9. b
3. d	10. d
4. a	11. d
5. b	12. b
6. b	13. a
7. a	14. d

CHAPTER 8   MOOD DISORDERS

REVIEW EXERCISES

I. Unipolar Depression

A. How Common Is Unipolar Depression?
1b. 19
1c. increased
1d. women
1f. 85; 40
2. 26

B. What Are the Symptoms of Depression?
pp. 225–227

MediaSpeak: The Crying Game: Male vs. Female Tears
1. p. 226
2. Many possible answers

C. Diagnosing Unipolar Depression
1. 5; 2
2. seasonal; postpartum; recurrent; catatonic; melancholic
3a. disabling
3b. two years
3c. double depression

II. What Causes Unipolar Depression?
1. stressful
2a. and 2b. p. 228

PsychWatch: Sadness at the Happiest of Times
1. a year; 10; 30
2. p. 229
3. shame, fear of judgment, belief that new motherhood should be joyous

A. The Biological View
  1. Genetic Factors
  1a. Family pedigree

1b. 46; 20
1c. Biological; biological

  2. Biochemical Factors
  1. lowered serotonin and/or norepinephrine activity; they increase either serotonin or norepinephrine activity
  2. p. 232
  3a. cortisol; the stress hormone
  3b. melatonin, the "Dracula" hormone
  4. p. 232

  3. Brain Anatomy and Brain Circuits
  1a. prefrontal cortex
  1b. hippocampus
  1c. amygdala
  1d. Brodmann Area 25
  2. prefrontal cortex
  3. neurogenesis
  4. amygdala
  5. p. 233

  4. Immune System
  1. white blood; lymphocytes; C-reactive protein
  2a.–2d. p. 234

B. Psychological Views
  1. Psychodynamic View
  1a. and 1b. those whose parents did not meet needs during the oral stage; those whose parents gratified oral stage needs excessively
  2. symbolic, or imagined, loss
  3. dependence; self-reliance
  4a. anaclitic

4b.   father

5.   affectionless; protection

6a.   Research findings on the relationship between childhood loss and depression are inconsistent.

2.   The Behavioral View

1a.   p. 236

1b.   p. 236

2.   social; depressive

3.   Cognitive Views

a.   Negative Thinking

1a. and 1b.   p. 237; answers will vary

2.   negative

3.   experiences; future

4a.   negative conclusions based on little evidence; p. 237

4b.   minimizing importance of positive experiences/magnifying importance of negative experiences; p. 237

5.   inadequacies; hopelessness

6.   p. 238

b.   Learned Helplessness

1a. and 1b.   p. 239

2a.   periodic

2c.   p. 239

3.   p. 239

4a. and 4b.   pp. 239–240

5.   f; c; b; e

6.   internal; global; stable

7.   hopelessness

8a. and 8b.   pp. 240–241

C.   The Sociocultural View

1.   pp. 241–244

1.   The Family-Social Perspective

1.   p. 241

2.   three; more

3.   one-third

2.   The Multicultural Perspective

1.   twice

2a – 2f.   pp. 242–243

3.   physical; cognitive

4a.   the likelihood that an individual will experience recurrent episodes of a disorder

4b.   p. 243

III.   Bipolar Disorders

A.   What Are the Symptoms of Mania?

1.   inappropriate

2.   pp. 244–245

B.   Diagnosing Bipolar Disorders

1.   high; irritable; three

2.   hypomanic

3a. and 3b.   pp. 245–246

4a.   socioeconomic

4b.   15; 44

5.   cyclothymic

C.   What Causes Bipolar Disorders?

1.   p. 249

2.   serotonin

3.   serotonin; norepinephrine; norepinephrine

4a.   sodium

4c.   potassium

5.   mania; depression

6.   basal ganglia; cerebellum; dorsal raphe nucleus; striatum; amygdala; prefrontal cortex

7.   genetic makeup

8a.   generations

8c.   color blindness, red hair, medical syndromes

IV.   Call for Change: DSM-5

1a.–1e.   pp. 252–253

V.   Putting It Together: Making Sense of All That Is Known

1.   p. 253

2.   biological

MULTIPLE CHOICE

1.   c
2.   b
3.   b
4.   c
5.   d
6.   b
7.   d
8.   a
9.   a
10.   d
11.   c

CHAPTER 9   TREATMENT FOR MOOD DISORDERS

REVIEW EXERCISES

I. Treatments for Unipolar Depression

A. Psychological Approaches

   1. Psychodynamic Therapy

   1.   p. 259

   2a. and 2b.   pp. 259–260

   2. Behavioral Therapy

   1.   p. 261

   2.   combine; mild

   3. Cognitive Therapy

   1.   pp. 262–263

   2.   50; 60

   3.   cognitive-behavioral

   4.   discard; acceptance and commitment therapy; accept

B. Sociocultural Approaches

   1.   cognitive-behavioral

   2.   less

   3.   p. 265

   4.   50; 60

   5.   p. 266

   6.   50

   7.   p. 266

C. Biological Approaches

   1. Electroconvulsive Therapy

   1a.   bilateral; unilateral

   1b.   seizure

   1c.   6; 12; weeks

   2a.   metrazol

   2b.   Insulin coma

   2c.   Cerletti

   3a. and 3b.   p. 269

   4.   p. 269

   5.   severe depression with delusions

   2. Antidepressant Drugs

   a. MAO Inhibitors

   1b.   monoamine oxidase

   1c.   p. 269

   1d.   p. 269

   2.   pp. 269–270

   b. Tricyclics

   1.   imipramine

   2.   60; 65; 10

   3a.   relapse

   3b.   5 months; continuation

   3c.   3; maintenance

   4a.–4c.   pp. 270–271

   5a. and 5b.   p. 271

   c. Second-Generation Antidepressants

   1.   serotonin reuptake inhibitors

   2.   p. 272

PsychWatch: First Dibs on Antidepressant Drugs?

   1.   half

   2.   p. 272

   3. Brain Stimulation,

   a. Vagus Nerve Stimulation

   1.   electroconvulsive therapy

   2.   p. 273

   3.   p. 274

   b. Transcranial Magnetic Stimulation

   1.   prefrontal cortex

   2.   p. 274

   c. Deep Brain Stimulation

   1.   Area 25

   2.   p. 274

D. How Do the Treatments for Unipolar Depression Compare?

   1.   cognitive; cognitive-behavioral; biological

   2a.   elimination of symptoms in 50–60% of subjects

   2b.   29% of subjects improved

   2c.   p. 275

   2d.   Cognitive; cognitive-behavioral; drug

   3.   30; maintenance

   4.   couple

   5.   Behavioral

   6.   psychodynamic

   7.   psychotherapy; drug

   8a.   quickly

   8b.   medications; ECT

   8c.   50; 80

II. Treatments for Bipolar Disorders

A. Lithium and Other Mood Stabilizers
1. blood; urine
2. pp. 279–280
3. 60
4. 28; prophylactic
5a. phosphoinositides
6. substituting

B. Adjunctive Psychotherapy
1. psychotherapy; drug; individual; group; family
2. p. 281
3. p. 281
4. hospitalization; job retention

III. Putting It Together: With Success Come New Questions

1. p. 282

MULTIPLE CHOICE

1. c
2. d
3. d
4. c
5. b
6. a
7. c
8. b
9. a
10. c

CHAPTER 10   SUICIDE

REVIEW EXERCISES

1. 36,000; 600,000; parasuicides
2a. frowned on
2b. coroners cannot always separate suicides from unintentional or accidental deaths

I. What Is Suicide?

1. intentional; conscious
2. p. 288; b; d; c; a
3. pp. 288–289
4. pain from self-injury offers temporary relief from emotional suffering; behavior offers a distraction from problems; behavior helps individual deal with feelings of emptiness, boredom, and identity confusion
5. studies show self-injury predicts later attempts at suicide, p. 289

A. How Is Suicide Studied?
1b. therapy
1c. suicide notes
1d. p. 289

B. Patterns and Statistics
1. pp. 289 and 291
2. Religious
3. 1:3; 4:1
4. p. 291

5a. divorced people
5b. married or cohabitating people
6. twice; African
7. poverty, alcohol use, modeling, availability of guns

II. What Triggers a Suicide?

A. Stressful Events and Situations
1. p. 292
2. pp. 292–293

B. Mood and Thought Changes
1. anxiety, tension, frustration, anger, shame
2. pp. 293 and 295

PsychWatch: Can Music Inspire Suicide?
1. many possible answers, p. 294

C. Alcohol and Other Drug Use
1. 70
2. fear; aggression; judgments

D. Mental Disorders
1. mood disorders, substance-related disorders, schizophrenia
2. p. 296
3b. p. 296
4. demoralization

E.   Modeling: The Contagion of Suicide
   1.   family members and friends; celebrities, highly publicized cases, co-workers/colleagues
   2.   many possible answers

III.   What Are the Underlying Causes of Suicide?
A.   The Psychodynamic View
   1.   depression; redirected
   2.   negative; anger; hatred
   3.   Thanatos; others; themselves
   4.   p. 298

B.   Durkheim's Sociocultural View
   1.   p. 299

C.   The Biological View
   1.   4; 0
   2.   pp. 300–301
   3.   aggressive; impulsive
   4.   serotonin

IV.   Is Suicide Linked to Age?
A.   Children
   1a.   boys
   1b.   false
   2.   p. 302
   3.   p. 302

B.   Adolescents
   1.   third
   2.   p. 305
   3.   impulsive
   4a. and 4b.   p. 303
   5.   p. 303
   6.   uncertain
   7b.   anomic
   7c. and 7d.   pp. 304–305
   8.   p. 305

A Closer Look: The Black Box Controversy: Do Antidepressants Cause Suicide?
   1.   p. 304

C.   The Elderly
   1.   19; 12
   2.   pp. 305–307
   3a. and 3b.   p. 307

V.   Treatment and Suicide
A.   What Treatments Are Used After Suicide Attempts?
   1.   psychotherapy
   2a.   help them achieve a nonsuicidal state of mind
   2b.   help them to develop better ways of handling stress
   3.   16; 30
   4a – 4d.   p. 309

B.   What Is Suicide Prevention?
   1.   suicide prevention programs, suicide hotlines
   2.   p. 310
   3.   understanding and clarifying the problem, b; assessing suicide potential, a; assessing and mobilizing the caller's resources, e; formulating a plan, c
   4.   p. 310

C.   Do Suicide Prevention Programs Work?
   1.   white men; African American; female
   2.   8,000
   3.   visible; available
   4.   public education

VI.   Putting It Together: Psychological and Biological Insights Lag Behind
   1.   sociocultural
   2.   treatment; education

MULTIPLE CHOICE
   1.   c
   2.   a
   3.   b
   4.   a
   5.   c
   6.   c
   7.   b
   8.   b
   9.   d

CHAPTER 11   EATING DISORDERS

REVIEW EXERCISES

I. Anorexia Nervosa
- 1a.   85
- 1b.   overweight
- 1c.   distorted
- 1d.   menstruation
- 2.   restricting
- 3a.   90; 95
- 3b.   14; 18
- 3c.   0.5–3.5
- 3d.   stressful
- 3e.   2; 6; starvation

A. and B. The Clinical Picture and Medical Problems
- 1.   pp. 319–320

II. Bulimia Nervosa
- 1.   binge-purge
- 2.   p. 320
- 3a.   nonpurging type
- 3b.   purging type
- 4.   normal
- 5.   binge-eating

A. Binges
- 1.   pp. 321–322

B. Compensatory Behaviors
- 1a. and 1b.   p. 323

C. Bulimia Nervosa vs. Anorexia Nervosa
- 1a.–1e.   pp. 323–324
- 2.   bulimia nervosa; anorexia nervosa

III. What Causes Eating Disorders?
- 1.   multidimensional risk

A. Psychodynamic Factors: Ego Deficiencies
- 1.   psychodynamic
- 2.   p. 324
- 3a.   people with eating disorders perceive internal cues inaccurately
- 3b.   people with eating disorders rely excessively on the opinions and wishes of others

B. Cognitive Factors
- 1.   core pathology
- 2a. and 2b. pp. 326–327

C. Mood Disorders
- 1.   p. 327

D. Biological Factors
- 1a.   6
- 1b.   23; 9
- 2.   serotonin
- 3.   lateral; ventromedial
- 4.   weight set point
- 5.   LH; restore; producing; lowering
- 6.   VMH; remove; reducing; increasing

E. Societal Pressures
- 1.   p. 330
- 2.   pp. 330–331
- 3.   more

F. Family Environment
- 1.   thinness; dieting
- 2.   affectionate, loyal
- 3.   Case

G. Multicultural Factors: Racial and Ethnic Differences
- 1.   pp. 332–334
- 2.   p. 334

H. Multicultural Factors: Gender Differences
- 1.   5; 10
- 2a. and 2b.   p. 334
- 3a. and 3b.   pp. 334–335
- 4.   reverse anorexia nervosa; muscle dysmorphobia

IV. How Are Eating Disorders Treated?
A. Treatments for Anorexia Nervosa
- 1.   pp. 335–338
- Posttreatment Positive Outcomes
- 2a.   90
- 2b.   Menstruation
- Posttreatment Negative Outcomes
- 2a.   25
- 2b.   50

3.   lines drawn through; a lot of; short; older person; did

B.   Treatments for Bulimia Nervosa
1.   b, e;
a, d; effective in as many as 75 percent of bulimia cases;
c, f; h;
g; as many as 40 percent of patients reduce binging and purging
2a.   40; 20
2b.   75
2c.   stress
2d.   2

V.   **Call for Change: DSM-5**
1a.–1c.   p. 343

VI.   **Putting It Together: A Standard for Integrating Perspectives**
1.   pp. 343–344
2.   p. 344

MULTIPLE CHOICE
1.   c
2.   c
3.   c
4.   c
5.   c
6.   c
7.   d
8.   b
9.   b
10.   b
11.   a

CHAPTER 12   SUBSTANCE-RELATED DISORDERS

REVIEW EXERCISES

1.   e
2.   b
3.   f
4.   d
5.   a
6.   c
7.   11
8.   Indians; Asian

I.   **Depressants**
A.   Alcohol
1.   5; 5
2.   two
3.   blood
4.   less; dehydrogenase
5.   metabolized; sobering-up
6.   time and metabolism

1.   Alcohol Abuse and Dependence
1.   seniors; elementary
2.   two
3.   p. 353
4a.   tolerance
4b.   p. 353
4c.   delirium tremens; hallucinations

2.   What Is the Personal and Social Impact of Alcoholism?
1.   p. 354
2.   p. 354
3.   thiamine; confusion, memory loss, confabulation
4.   p. 355

B.   Sedative-Hypnotic Drugs
1.   calming; sleep

1.   Barbiturates
1.   receptors; GABA
2a.   slow or inhibit
2b.   respiration; lower
3.   p. 355
4.   lethal; tolerance

2.   Benzodiazepines
1a.   Xanax, Valium, Ativan
1b.   drowsiness; overdose

C.   Opioids
1a.   heroin
1b.   narcotics
1c.   opium
1d.   methadone
1e.   morphine

2.   mainlined; bloodstream

3a.   rush, p. 357

3b.   high, p. 357

4.   endorphins; pain; reduce

1.   Heroin Abuse and Dependence

1a.   anxiety; sweating

1c.   third; eighth

2.   What Are the Dangers of Heroin Abuse?

1.   respiratory

2.   p. 358

II.   Stimulants

A.   Cocaine

1.   natural; coca

2.   smoked

3.   p. 359

4.   dopamine, norepinephrine, serotonin

5.   p. 359

6.   p. 359

7a.   free-basing

7b.   crack

B.   Amphetamines

1.   manufactured

2.   p. 361

3.   pill/capsule; crank

4b.   letdown

4c.   dopamine; norepinephrine; serotonin

5.   pp. 361–362

6.   6

7.   equally

8.   neurotoxicity

C.   Caffeine

1.   p. 362

2.   dopamine, serotonin, norepinephrine

3.   (left column) I, I, I
     (right column) D, I, I

4.   p. 363

III.   Hallucinogens, Cannabis, and Combinations of Substances

A.   Hallucinogens

1.   trips

2.   lysergic acid; Ecstasy

3.   ergot alkaloids

4.   p. 364

5.   synesthesia

6.   6

7a.   powerful

7b.   Recurrent; flashbacks

B.   Cannabis

1.   hemp; THC

2.   hashish; marijuana

3b.   Time; sizes

3c.   p. 366

4.   2; 6

5.   today, marijuana is at least 4 times more powerful than what was available in the 1970s

6.   p. 367

C.   Combinations of Substances

1.   p. 369

2b.   they all depress the central nervous system

2c.   antagonistic

2d.   p. 369

3.   polysubstance

IV.   What Causes Substance-Related Disorders?

A.   Sociocultural Views

1a.   alcoholism; unemployment

1b.   socioeconomic

1d.   limits

B.   Psychodynamic Views

1.   nurtured

2.   dependent, antisocial, impulsive, novelty-seeking, depressive

3.   p. 371

C.   Cognitive-Behavioral Views

1a.   pp. 371–372

1b.   p. 372

D.   Biological Views

1.   Genetic Predisposition

1.   p. 373

2.   Biochemical Factors

1.   GABA; endorphins; dopamine; possibly anandamide, a neurotransmitter that operates like THC

2. reward; pleasure; dopamine

3. reward-deficiency

4. p. 374

V. How Are Substance-Related Disorders Treated?

A. Psychodynamic Therapies

1. conflicts; effective

B. Behavioral Therapies

1. a

2. b

3. c

4. motivated

C. Cognitive-Behavioral Therapies

1a. p. 378

1b. p. 378

1c. limits; rate

1d. younger, not physically dependent

2. p. 378; planning ahead

D. Biological Treatments

1. systematic; withdrawal

2. p. 378

3. psychotherapy

4. block; change

5a. Antabuse

5b. opiods; withdrawal

6. pp. 379–380

7. partial; full

E. Sociocultural Therapies

1. p. 380

2a. and 2b. p. 381

3. p. 381

4. p. 380

5. p. 382

VI. Call for Change: DSM-5

1. pp. 382–383

VII. Putting It Together: New Wrinkles to a Familiar Story

1. pp. 383–384

MULTIPLE CHOICE

1. b

2. d

3. b

4. c

5. a

6. d

7. b

8. b

9. b

10. b

CHAPTER 13   SEXUAL DISORDERS AND GENDER IDENTITY DISORDER

REVIEW EXERCISES

I. Sexual Dysfunctions

1. p. 388

2. Desire phase: pp. 388–392; Excitement phase: pp. 392–395; Orgasm phase: pp. 395–399

A. Disorders of Desire

1a.–1c. p. 389; PsychWatch, p. 391

2. high; low; either high or low

3. serotonin; dopamine

4. cocaine, marijuana, amphetamines, heroin

5. pp. 390 and 392

B. Disorders of Excitement

1. Female Sexual Arousal Disorder

1. orgasmic

2. Male Erectile Disorder

1. vascular

2. p. 393

3a. nocturnal penile tumescence

3b. REM sleep

3c. physical

4. job; financial

5b. p. 395

C. Disorders of Orgasm

    I. Rapid, or Premature, Ejaculation

    1. inexperienced; arousal

    2. p. 396

    3a. p. 396

    3b. p. 396

    3c. p. 396

    2. Male Orgasmic Disorder

    1a. p. 397

    1b. p. 397

    3. Female Orgasmic Disorder

    1. assertive; masturbating

    2. psychoanalytic; pathological; clitoris

    3a. diabetes, multiple sclerosis

    3b. changes in skin sensitivity and structure of the clitoris and vaginal walls

    3c. women taking certain serotonin-enhancing antidepresent drugs may have problems with arousal and orgasm

    4. p. 398

    5. sexuality

    6. p. 398

    7. p. 398

    8. sexual molestation or rape

D. Disorders of Sexual Pain

    1a. muscles; contract

    1b. learned; painful

    2. p. 399

    3. p. 399

    4. p. 399

    5a.–5d. p. 399

    6. hypoactive sexual desire

II. Treatments for Sexual Dysfunctions

A. What Are the General Features of Sex Therapy?

    1a.–1i. pp. 401–402

B. What Techniques Are Applied to Particular Dysfunctions?

    1. p. 402

    2a. sensate; caresses

    2b. Viagra; one

    2c. vacuum erection; blood

    3. p. 403

    4. pause; arousal

    5. self-exploration; awareness

    6b. during caressing by partners

    6c. during intercourse

    7. normal; education

    8a. vaginal; voluntary

    8b. dilators; penetration

    9. p. 405

C. What Are the Current Trends in Sex Therapy?

    1a. live together

    1b. depression

    1c. marital discord; handicapped

    1d. homosexual; addictions

III. Paraphilias

    1a. nonhuman; nonconsenting; humiliation

    1b. 6

    2. the large market for paraphillic pornography

    3. pp. 407–415

    4. p. 415

IV. Gender Identity Disorder

    1. gender identity disorder

    2. 2

    3. p. 416

    4. transvestic fetishism

    5. do not become adults with the disorder

    6a. hypothalamus; half

    6b. female

    6c. sexual

    7a. hormone

    7b. partial removal; clitoris; vagina

    7c. mastectomy; phalloplasty

    8. many possible answers

    9a. p. 417

    9b. p. 417

    9c. pp. 417–418

V. Call for Change: DSM-5

    1a.–1f. pp. 420–421

MediaSpeak: A Different Kind of Judgment

    Many possible answers

VI. Putting It Together: A Private Topic Draws Public Attention

    1. p. 421

MULTIPLE CHOICE

1.	d
2.	d
3.	a
4.	b
5.	c
6.	b
7.	a
8.	a
9.	c
10.	c

CHAPTER 14   SCHIZOPHRENIA

REVIEW EXERCISES

1a.   fragmentation
1b.   thoughts; emotion
1c.   reality
2.   one
3a.   poverty
3b.   fall from a higher to a lower socioeconomic
      level
4.   p. 426

I.   The Clinical Picture of Schizophrenia
1.   p. 427

A.   What Are the Symptoms of Schizophrenia?
   I.   Positive Symptoms
   1.   fact
   2.   b; a; d; c; p. 429

PsychWatch: Mentally Ill Chemical Abusers
   1.   20; 50
   2.   usually young; usually male; below average
        social functioning; below average school
        achievement; usually poor; frequently "act
        out;" higher than average number of emer-
        gency room visits; higher number of
        encounters with criminal justice system;
        greater distress and poorer treatment out-
        comes than mentally ill people who do not
        abuse substances
   3.   mental illness could come first, with sub-
        stance abuse as self-medication or result of
        impaired judgment; conversely, substance
        abuse may cause or exacerbate mental
        illness
   4a. patients do not report their substance abuse
   4b. facilities are designed and funded to treat
        either substance abuse or mental illness, and

many MICAs are turned away from both
kinds
   5.   10; 20; remain homeless longer, more likely
        to experience very harsh conditions; more
        likely to be jailed, prostitute themselves,
        engage in risky behavior, and be victimized

   b.   Disorganized Thinking and Speech
   3.   thought; speech
   4.   d
   5.   a
   6.   c
   7.   b
   8.   sights; sounds
   9.   syllable; background
   10. pursuit
   11. p. 430
   12. Auditory; commands
   13. external; Broca's
   14. c
   15. e
   16. d
   17. a
   18. f
   19. b
   20. p. 431

   2.   Negative Symptoms
   1a. speech; content
   1b. p. 432
   2.   p. 432
   3.   anhedonia
   4.   apathy; interest; ambivalence
   5.   ideas; fantasies

   3.   Psychomotor Symptoms
   1.   posturing; stupor; excitement; rigidity

B. What Is the Course of Schizophrenia?
1. 25; problems
2. p. 433

C. Diagnosing Schizophrenia
1a. six
1b. work; social
2. c; e; d; b; a; p. 433
3a. and 3b. pp. 433–434
4. p. 434

II. How Do Theorists Explain Schizophrenia?
A. Biological Views
1. Genetic factors
1. p. 434
2. identical; fraternal
3. p. 435
4. p. 435
5a. Environmental; genetic
5b. biological; adoptive
6. p. 437

PsychWatch: Postpartum Psychosis: The Case of Andrea
Yates
1. 1,000
2. p. 436
3. many possible answers

2. Biochemical Abnormalities
1. increase
2. antagonists; firing
3. larger
4. atypical; serotonin
5. positive; negative

3. Abnormal Brain Structure
1. ventricles
2. p. 439
3. blood flow; temporal; frontal

4. Viral Problems
1b. nutrition
1c. fetal
1d. birth
1e. immune
2. prenatal; hormonal
3a. p. 439
3b. p. 439
3c. p. 439

B. Psychological Views
1. The Psychodynamic Explanation
1a. narcissism
1b. reality; auditory hallucinations
2. schizophrenogenic
3. p. 440

2. The Behavioral View
1. p. 441

3. The Cognitive View
1. produces

C. Sociocultural Views
1. Multicultural Factors
1. higher
2a.–2c. p. 442
3. better
4a. and 4b. pp. 442–443

2. Social Labeling
1. diagnosis
2. self-fulfilling

3. Family Dysfunctioning
1. p. 444
2. Its validity has not been supported.
3a. have more trouble communicating with each other
3b. are more critical of and overinvolved with their children
4. p. 444

4. R. D. Laing's View
1b. p. 445
1c. sick

III. Call for Change: DSM-5
1a.–1b. pp. 445–446

IV. Putting It Together: Psychological and Sociocultural Models Lag Behind
1. p. 446

MULTIPLE CHOICE
1. a
2. b
3. a
4. d

5. d 7. d
6. b 8. a

CHAPTER 15   TREATMENTS FOR SCHIZOPHRENIA AND OTHER SEVERE MENTAL DISORDERS

REVIEW EXERCISES

I. Institutional Care in the Past
1. moral; mental hospitals
2. state
3a. funding
3b. quality
3c. p. 451
4a. humanitarian
4b. restraints; punishment
4c. lobotomy
5. p. 452

II. Institutional Care Takes a Turn for the Better
A. Milieu Therapy
1a. and 1b. p. 452
2. custodial

B. The Token Economy
1. operant
2. pp. 453–454
3. 98; milieu; custodial
4. control
5. p. 454
6a. and 6b. pp. 454–455

III. Antipsychotic Drugs
1a. phenothiazines
1b. psychological
1c. Thorazine
1d. neuroleptic

A. How Effective Are Antipsychotic Drugs?
1. 65
2. 75; 33
3a. hallucinations; delusions
3b. flat affect, poverty of speech, loss of volition

B. The Unwanted Effects of Conventional Antipsychotic Drugs
1. Extrapyramidal
2. pp. 457–458

3. one year
4a. stop the drugs
4b. lowest
4c. gradually reduce or stop the drug

C. Newer Antipsychotic Drugs
1a. negative
1b. extrapyramidal
1c. tardive dyskinesia
2. agranulocytosis

PsychWatch: First Dibs on Atypical Antipsychotic Drugs
1. p. 459

IV. Psychotherapy
A. Cognitive-Behavioral Therapy
1. pp. 460–461
2a.–2e. p. 461
3. observers; mindful; accept
4. It is often very helpful to clients with schizophrenia.

MediaSpeak: Can You Live with the Voices in Your Head?
1. pp. 462–463; answers will vary

B. Family Therapy
1. relatives; 50
2. expressed emotion
3a. realistic; tolerant
3b. p. 463

C. Social Therapy
1. p. 464

V. The Community Approach
1a. p. 465
1b. pp. 465–466
1c. p. 466

A. What Are the Features of Effective Community Care?
1. pp. 466–468

B. How Has Community Treatment Failed?
1. communication
2. p. 468
3. pp. 468–469
4. pp. 469–470
5. three

C. The Promise of Community Treatment
1. p. 470

MediaSpeak: "Alternative" Mental Health Care
1. 16; 20
2. higher recidivism rates; higher cost to jail; more likely to commit suicide
3. p. 471

VI. **Putting It Together: An Important Lesson**
1a. and 1b.   p. 472

MULTIPLE CHOICE
1. b
2. b
3. b
4. b
5. a
6. c
7. b
8. c
9. b
10. b

CHAPTER 16   PERSONALITY DISORDERS

REVIEW EXERCISES

1a. unique; outward behavior
1c. p. 475
2. II; improvement
3. I; comorbidity

I. **"Odd" Personality Disorders**
See grid on p. 477

A. Paranoid Personality Disorder
1a. motives
1b. loyalty
1c. weaknesses; mistakes
1d. grudges
2. men
3. genetic
4. p. 481
5. p. 481
6. drug
7. self-cohesion

B. Schizoid Personality Disorder
1. they truly prefer to be alone
2. emotional
3a. unaccepting, abusive
3b. give; receive
4. p. 482
5. social

6. p. 482

C. Schizotypal Personality Disorder
1. relationships; oddities
2. p. 483
3. p. 483
4a. conflicts
4b. attention
4c. enlarged brain ventricles, smaller temporal lobes, and loss of gray matter
5. p. 484
6a. inappropriate
6b. p. 484
6c. Low

II. **"Dramatic" Personality Disorders**
grid p. 477

A. Antisocial Personality Disorder
1. psychopath, sociopath
2. disregard; rights
3. p. 485
4. p. 486
5. four
6. intoxication; antisocial PD; prone; substance abuse; take risks
7b. modeling
7c. needs; points of view
8. anxiety; negative; cues
9. arousal; threatening

10. serotonin; frontal lobes

11a. effective

11b. they lack a conscience and do not want to change, p. 489

11c. moral; needs

11d. responsibility

B. Borderline Personality Disorder

1. e; a; c; g; d; f; b

2a. women

2b. young

3. abandonment; separation

4. sexual; psychological

5. amygdala; prefrontal cortex; serotonin; 5-HTT

6. internal; external

7. family

8. p. 493

9a. relationship; self; loneliness

9b. pp. 494–495

9c. attempted suicide

C. Histrionic Personality Disorder

1a. emotionally

1b. on-stage

1c. vain; demanding

1d. illnesses

1e. provocative

2. they are likely equal

3. loss; protectively

4. suggestibility

5. norms; femininity

6a.–6b p. 499

7. p. 499

D. Narcissistic Personality Disorder

1b. pp. 499–500

1c. pp. 499–500

2. men

3. perfect

4. positively

5. eras

6. superiority

III. "Anxious" Personality Disorders

See grid on p. 477

A. Avoidant Personality Disorder

1. inadequacy; negative

2a. humiliation; confidence

2b. circumstances; relationships

3. ridiculed

4. cognitive; rejection

5. p. 503

6. anxiety

7. pp. 503–504

B. Dependent Personality Disorder

1. pp. 504–505

2a. oral

2b. separation

2c. Behavioral; independent

2d. pp. 505–506

3. responsibility; spouse

4. transference

C. Obsessive-Compulsive Personality Disorder

1. perfection; control

2a.–2e.   p. 507

4. anal regressive

5. dichotomous

6. psychodynamic and cognitive

IV. Multicultural Factors: Research Neglect

1. pp. 508–509

2. inequalities; psychological

3. p. 509

V. What Problems Are Posed by the DSM-IV-TR Categories?

1a. observed; individual

1b. overlap

1c. different

VI. Are There Better Ways to Classify Personality Disorders?

1. dimensions

2. pp. 510–511

3. neuroticism; extroversion; openness to experiences; agreeableness; conscientiousness

4. 12

VII. Call for Change: DSM-5
1. schizotypal; antisocial; borderline; narcissistic; avoidant; obsessive-compulsive; features of other disorders overlap significantly with features of these categories
2. p. 512
3. pp. 512–513

VIII. Putting It Together: Disorders of Personality—Rediscovered, Then Reconsidered
1. pp. 513–514

MULTIPLE CHOICE
1. d
2. a
3. a
4. b
5. b
6. c
7. b
8. c
9. b
10. d

CHAPTER 17   DISORDERS OF CHILDHOOD AND ADOLESCENCE

REVIEW EXERCISES

I. Childhood and Adolescence
1a. half
1b. bed-wetting; temper tantrums
1c. physical; sexual; pressures
2. fifth
3. Boys; girls
4. one-quarter; p. 519
5. cyberbullying

II. Childhood Anxiety Disorders
1a. p. 519
1b. p. 519
1c. p. 519
2. social; generalized
3a. p. 519
3b. p. 519
3c. p. 519
4. pp. 519–510

A. Separation Anxiety Disorder
1. extreme; home
2. phobia

B. Treatments for Childhood Anxiety Disorders
1a. and 1b.   p. 521

III. Childhood Mood Problems
A. Major Depressive Disorder
1. 2; children lack cognitive skills that help produce depression
2. life events; rejection; abuse
3a. children lack interest in toys and games
3b. childhood depression often manifests itself as headache, stomachache, or irritability
4. girls
5. p. 552
6a. and 6b.   pp. 552–554

B. Bipolar Disorder
1. p. 525
2. p. 525
3. half; third; antidepressant; stimulant

IV. Opposition Defiant Disorder and Conduct Disorder
1. pp. 525–526; 10 percent of children (more boys than girls)
2a. and 2b.   p. 527

A. What Are the Causes of Conduct Disorder?
1. conflict
2. p. 527

B. How Do Clinicians Treat Conduct Disorder?
1. 13
2a. and 2b.   pp. 527–528
3. juvenile training
4. Prevention; recreational; health; parenting
5a. problem-solving skills therapy, p. 530
5b. Anger Coping and Coping Power Program, p. 530
6. stimulant

V. Attention-Deficit/Hyperactivity Disorder
1. pp. 530–528
2. learning
3a. 70
3b. 35; 60
4a.–4e. p. 532
5. one-third; one-half

A. What Are the Causes of ADHD?
1. stress; family
2. interpersonal; symptoms

B. How Is ADHD Treated?
1a. quieting
1b. problems; aggression
2. They fare poorly.
3. They have their patients take "drug holidays," where the patients periodically cease taking the drug.
4. reinforce; drug

C. Multicultural Factors and ADHD
1. pp. 534–535

VI. Elimination Disorders
1. control
2a. 5
2b. decreases; 1
2c. stressful; school
3b., 3c., and 3d. p. 536
4. bell; sensation of full bladder; waking up
5. defecating; 4

VII. Long-Term Disorders That Begin in Childhood
A. Pervasive Developmental Disorders
1. social interactions; communications; stimuli
2a.–2d. autistic disorder; Asperger's disorder; Rett's disorder; childhood disintegrative disorder

1. Autistic Disorder
1. 3; communication; repetitive
2a. 80
2b. Nine
3. p. 539
4a. echolalia
4b. pronominal reversal
5. pp. 540–541

2. Asperger's Disorder
1. social deficits; impaired expressiveness; idiosyncratic interest; restricted and repetitive behaviors
2. intellectual; adaptive; language
3a.–3c. p. 541

3. What Are the Causes of Pervasive Developmental Disorders?
1a. intelligent; cold
1b. social; environmental
2. p. 543
3a.–3c. p. 543–544

4. How Do Clinicians and Educators Treat Pervasive Developmental Disorders?
1. p. 544
2. Modeling; operant
3. p. 545
4. autistic children have significantly improved cognition, social engagement, peer interactions, play behaviors, and other behaviors; normal children experience no negative effects
5. 22
6. cognitive social
7. Communication; simultaneous
8. child-initiated; intrinsic
9. pp. 546–547
10. group; workshops

B. Mental Retardation (Intellectual Disability)
1a. intellectual; 70
1b. p. 548

1. Assessing Intelligence
1a. school
1b. biased

2. Assessing Adaptive Functioning
1. observe; background

3. What Are the Features of Mental Retardation?
1. learn; short-term; planning
2. moderate; limited; severe; extensive; profound; pervasive
3. 85; educably
4. school; improve

5a. and 5b.   pp. 550–551

6.   3–4 percent of retarded population; 1–2 percent of retarded population; p. 551

4.   What Are the Causes of Mental Retardation?

1.   biological
2a. 1,000
2b. 35
3.   flat; tongue
4a. person has 3 twenty-first chromosomes instead of 2
4b. translocation or mosaicism; p. 552
5.   35; 55
6.   aging; dementia
7.   recessive
8.   intelligence
9.   European Jewish; mental; motor
10. pp. 552–553
11. p. 553

5.   Interventions for People with Mental Retardation

1.   state
2.   normalization; sexual
3.   pp. 554–555
4.   30

VIII.   Call for Change: DSM-5

1a.–1d.   pp. 556–557
2.   intellectual developmental disorder; autism spectrum disorder; social communication disorder; disruptive mood dysregulation disorder; non-suicidal self-injury
3a. p. 556
3b. pp. 556–557

IV.   Putting It Together: Clinicians Discover Childhood and Adolescence

1.   p. 557
2.   p. 557

MULTIPLE CHOICE

1.   a
2.   d
3.   a
4.   d
5.   d
6.   d
7.   a
8.   d
9.   b
10. c

CHAPTER 18   DISORDERS OF AGING AND COGNITION

REVIEW EXERCISES

I.   Old Age and Stress

1.   65
2.   p. 562
3.   50; 20
4.   geropsychology

II.   Depression in Later Life

1a. spouse; physical
1b. 20
2.   p. 565
3.   16
4.   50; p. 565

III.   Anxiety Disorders in Later Life

1.   Generalized; heart palpitations

2a. p. 566
2b. p. 566

IV.   Substance Abuse in Later Life

1.   60; institutionalized
2.   pp. 566–567
3.   prescription
4.   antipsychotic

V.   Psychotic Disorders in Later Life

1.   lessen
2.   p. 567 and p. 569

VI.   Disorders of Cognition

A.   Delirium

1.   consciousness
2.   p. 569

B. Dementia and Alzheimer's Disease
1. p. 570
2. 50
3. nutritional; Alzheimer's
4. 66
5. p. 571
6a. neurofibrillary tangles; within
6b. senile plaques; between
7. proteins
8. *Short-term*; *Long-term*
9. prefrontal lobes; temporal
10. glutamate; calcium; proteins
11. p. 574
12a. beta-amyloid; tau
12b. acetylcholine; glutamate
12c. zinc; lead
12d. autoimmune response
13. multi-infarct; blood
14. Parkinson's disease; Pick's disease; Huntington's disease; Creutzfeldt-Jakob disease
15. pp. 575–576
16. hippocampus; 71; 83
17. p. 578
18. estrogen; ibuprofen; naprosyn
19. reinforcement; wandering
20. prevent; delay

21a and 21c.   p. 580
22.   p. 581

VII. **Issues Affecting the Mental Health of the Elderly**
1a. p. 582
1b. pp. 582–583
2. wellness

VIII. **Call for Change: DSM-5**
1. p. 585
2. p. 584
3. p. 585

IX. **Putting It Together: Clinicians Discover the Elderly**
1. p. 586

MULTIPLE CHOICE
1. b
2. a
3. a
4. d
5. b
6. c
7. a
8. c

CHAPTER 19   LAW, SOCIETY, AND THE MENTAL HEALTH PROFESSION

REVIEW EXERCISES

I. Law and Mental Health
1. psychology in law; law in psychology
2. p. 590

A   Psychology in Law: How Do Clinicians Influence the Criminal Justice System?
1. guilty; punish
2a. crimes; insanity
2b. released
2c. trial
2d. competent

I. Criminal Commitment and Insanity During Commission of a Crime
1. legal; legislators

2. prosecution; defense
3. pp. 591–592
4. M'Naghten
5. more or less abolished the insanity plea
6. p. 592
7. p. 592
8. 400
9a. longer; clinicians
9b. drug; rights
9c. insane; dangerous
10a. convict
10c. guilty
11a. dysfunctioning
11b. intending
12a. repeatedly
12b. they are considered responsible for their crimes

12c.   they are committed to a mental health facility

2.   **Criminal Commitment and Incompetence to Stand Trial**
1a.   charges
1b.   work; defense
2.   psychological examination
3.   p. 597
4.   p. 598
5.   competent; civil

B.   **Law in Psychology: How Do the Legislative and Judicial Systems Influence Mental Health Care?**
1.   forced
2.   more
3.   more

1.   **Civil Commitment**
1.   need; dangerous
2a.   self harm
2b.   society
3a.   pp. 599–600
3b.   p. 600
4.   minimum; proof; clear; convincing
5.   p. 600
6.   pp. 600–601
7.   90; small
8a.   overestimate
8b.   imminent
9.   p. 602

2.   **Protecting Patients' Rights**
1.   p. 603
2a.   dangerous
2b.   nonrestrictive
3.   Protection; Advocacy; investigate
4.   p. 603
5.   biological; dangerous
6.   ECT
7.   dangerous
8.   restrictive
9.   answers will vary

C.   **In What Other Ways Do the Clinical and Legal Fields Interact?**
1.   fear of being sued for malpractice
2.   p. 605

3.   pp. 605–606
4.   p. 606
5.   specialists
6a.–6c.   p. 607
7.   pp. 608–609

PsychWatch: Serial Murderers: Madness or Badness?
p. 608

II.   **What Ethical Principles Guide Mental Health Professionals?**
1a.–1d.   pp. 609–610
2.   pp. 610–611
3.   public peril
4.   duty; protect; confidential
5.   intended

III.   **Mental Health, Business, and Economics**
1.   ten
2.   assistance; problem-solving
3.   alcohol; substance-related
4.   mental health services
5a.   managed; cost; number
5b.   insurance benefits
5c.   p. 612

IV.   **Technology and Mental Health**

A.   New Triggers and Vehicles for Psychopathology
1a.–1d.   pp. 613–614
2a. and 2b.   p. 614

B.   New Forms of Psychopathology
1.   1

C.   Cybertherapy
1a.   therapy over Skype
1b.   therapy offered by computer programs
1c.   treatment enhanced by video game avatars and virtual reality experiences
1d.   Internet-based support groups
2.   pp. 614–615

VI.   **Putting It Together: Operating Within a Larger System**
1.   many possible answers

MULTIPLE CHOICE

1. d
2. c
3. d
4. c
5. b
6. a
7. d
8. c
9. c
10. a